One Nation Under God?

One Nation Under God?
An Evangelical Critique of Christian America

JOHN D. WILSEY

With a Foreword by Richard Land

☙PICKWICK *Publications* · Eugene, Oregon

ONE NATION UNDER GOD?
An Evangelical Critique of Christian America

Copyright © 2011 John D. Wilsey. All rights reserved. Except for brief quotations in critical publications or reviews, no part of this book may be reproduced in any manner without prior written permission from the publisher. Write: Permissions, Wipf and Stock Publishers, 199 W. 8th Ave., Suite 3, Eugene, OR 97401.

Pickwick Publications
An Imprint of Wipf and Stock Publishers
199 W. 8th Ave., Suite 3
Eugene, OR 97401

www.wipfandstock.com

ISBN 13: 978-1-60899-792-3

Cataloguing-in-Publication data:

Wilsey, John D.

    One nation under God? : an evangelical critique of christian America / John D. Wilsey ; with a foreword by Richard Land.

    xxii + 204 p. ; 23 cm. Includes bibliographical references.

    ISBN 13: 978-1-60899-792-3

    1. Christianity and culture—United States—History. 2. Christianity and politics—United States—History. 3. Evangelicalism—United States—History. I. Title.

BR1642 U5 W55 2011

Manufactured in the U.S.A.

To Mandy, Caroline, and Sally

Contents

Foreword by Richard Land / ix

Preface / xiii

Acknowledgments / xvii

Introduction / xxi

1. The Relationship between Religion and the State, 1630–1789 / 1
2. The Thematic Landscape of the Christian America Thesis, 1977–2007 / 43
3. Christian Contributions to American Notions of Freedom / 95
4. Critiquing the Christian America Thesis / 115
5. Closing Arguments and Areas for Further Study / 172

Bibliography / 191

Foreword

THIS IS AN IMPORTANT book. In *One Nation Under God? An Evangelical Critique of Christian America*, John D. Wilsey has produced a carefully researched, well-documented, persuasively argued, "historical, philosophical, and theological critique" of the popularly argued concept of "America as a Christian nation."

It is an important book because Wilsey's case is so well-argued that in the future anyone seeking to make a serious theological, historical, or philosophical case for a "Christian America" will have to take into account and answer Wilsey's critique. If they avoid doing so it will be difficult for serious scholars of the issue to take them seriously.

Wilsey does an excellent job of surveying the major contributors to the historiography of the issues surrounding God and religion's role in America's founding and subsequent history. He has accomplished this task with a scholar's precision and judicious restraint. I am not aware of a more balanced and comprehensive survey of the history of the debate anywhere.

In *One Nation Under God? An Evangelical Critique of Christian America*, Wilsey documents the numerous historical, religious, and philosophical forces that shaped English-speaking settlement on this continent. In doing so, he paints a far more varied and heterogeneous national family tree than the one assumed or described by advocates of a "Christian America."

Perhaps Wilsey's greatest contribution to the ongoing "Christian America" debate is his persuasive and well-documented presentation of the multiple philosophical and theological sources that culminated in the American Revolution. In the section subtitled "Christian Theology Not the Primary Authority for America's Founding," Wilsey documents the contributions of English Civil War and Commonwealth period political theorists as well as the "Real Whig" tradition which they spawned in the early eighteenth century.

While all of these writers were influenced to varying degrees by a biblical worldview (How could they not have been as inhabitants of seventeenth and eighteenth century England?), they developed, and were influenced by other political and philosophical ideas as well, including the Enlightenment.

As Wilsey concludes, "The ideas that defined the American revolutionary and founding periods were not singularly Christian, but arose from a mixture of 'Protestant and secular sources.'"

Indeed, as one whose doctoral dissertation examined the 17th century English Civil War period, I can attest to the extent to which the political theories born in that era resurfaced and influenced American revolutionary thought. To put it simply, the American Revolution was the product of British citizens revolting against the Crown in the protection of their "unalienable" rights as free-born Englishmen in terms and concepts the English philosopher John Locke would find intimately familiar.

While I share Wilsey's concerns about the concept of America as a Christian nation, I am less comfortable with his blanket critique of American "exceptionalism." As defined by the advocates of a Christian America as God's chosen nation, the equivalent of a second Israel, I concur completely with his critique. America is not the new Israel and Americans are not God's chosen people—the Jews are.

However, I believe there is room for an American "exceptionalism" defined as God having chosen to intervene in American history in unique ways for His purposes, and in His providence has chosen to bless us in manifold ways throughout our history. Blessings, it must be remembered, are by definition, undeserved, and incur obligations. The New Testament reminds us that, "to whom much is given, much is required" (Luke 12:48).

For me, and for many other Americans through the generations, American "exceptionalism" has been a doctrine of obligations, responsibilities, and sacrificial service in the name of individual freedom, not a doctrine of pride and privilege.

I believe fervently that the blessings America has experienced in her history did not happen accidentally or automatically, but providentially. We have been the recipients not of mere fortuitous circumstance, but providential watchcare.

President George W. Bush described this poignantly in his first inaugural address, referring to, "our nation's grand story of courage and its simple dream of dignity. We are not this story's author, who fills time and eternity with His purpose. Yet His purpose is achieved in our duty, and our duty is fulfilled in service to one another."

For me, the president's statement is an affirmation of divine providence, purpose, and blessing; not that America is a Christian nation.

However, such is the power of Wilsey's argument that he has caused me, though a long time student of the era and the issue, to articulate my belief in American "exceptionalism" more carefully and with a more generous acknowledgment of its British, as well as biblical, antecedents.

Well done, John D. Wilsey. This book will challenge and inform all serious readers in compelling ways.

Richard Land, DPhil
Nashville, Tennesee

Preface

To underscore the significance of the issues to be addressed in this work, I wish to quote a statement made by James Madison in a letter he wrote to his friend, William Bradford of Pennsylvania, dated January 24, 1774. Madison was relating to Bradford his great desire to meet with him in religiously free Pennsylvania. He was also lamenting the reality of religious persecution in his home colony of Virginia. Pennsylvania had long been a model of religious freedom in colonial America, and for Madison, its religious climate presented a stark contrast to that of Virginia. In his letter to Bradford, Madison wrote, "I want again to breathe your free Air. I expect it will mend my Constitution and confirm my principles. I have indeed as good an Atmosphere at home as the Climate will allow: but have nothing to brag of as to the State and Liberty of my Country.... That diabolical Hell conceived principle of persecution rages among some and to their eternal Infamy the Clergy can furnish their quota of Imps for such business.... So I [leave you] to pity me and pray for Liberty of Conscience [to revive among us]."[1] Madison, who is often referred to as the Father of the Constitution, valued personal freedom of conscience so dearly. He helped develop the Virginia Statute of Religious Liberty in 1786 and the First Amendment to the U.S. Constitution in 1790, which disestablished religion from the state and guaranteed forever the individual's freedom to exercise her faith.

So, the first chapter of the book asks and answers the question, between the founding of the Massachusetts Bay Colony and the enacting of the U.S. Constitution, how did conceptions of the relationship between religion and the state change? Massachusetts Bay Colony was established in 1630 as a Christian commonwealth. It was one of the first of the British North American colonies that would eventually become a state in the American Union on the basis of the Constitution. But the

---

1. Madison to Bradford, January 24, 1774.

Constitution did not establish a Christian nation, but provided for full religious freedom in the First Amendment. Three movements of thought brought about this shift from 1630 to 1789: the Great Awakening, the English Enlightenment, and radical Whig ideology. These dynamics, over the course of a century and a half, were central in shaping the American attitude toward the role of religion in the state—from that of defining the state's identity to being separate from it altogether.

The second chapter addresses the Christian America thesis (CA) itself as it has been manifested since the publication of *The Light and the Glory* by Peter Marshall and David Manuel in 1977. The publication of this work, combined with the formation of the Moral Majority and the rise of evangelical Christian influence in American political life, encouraged the development of the CA thesis over the past three decades. Fourteen historical, philosophical, and theological themes, appearing predominately in the CA literature since 1977, are surveyed in order to set the stage for the critique. These themes include:

- from an historical perspective:
    1. The Christian faith of the founders;
    2. The Christian character of the sources drawn from by the founders;
    3. The Christian character of colonial documents and early state constitutions;
    4. The Christian character of early colleges;
    5. The powerful Christian influence of the Great Awakening and radical Whig ideology on the revolutionary generation;
- from a philosophical perspective:
    1. The original intent of the founders may be accurately discerned by applying the same evangelical hermeneutical method as used when interpreting Scripture;
    2. The original intent of the Founders was to build Christianity into the heart of the nation;
    3. The role of the Enlightenment is not as significant as the role of Christianity in the founding;

- and from a theological perspective:
    1. A providential view of history;
    2. American exceptionalism as evidence of God's unique blessing on the nation;
    3. America as God's chosen nation, a new Israel
    4. Liberty as a biblical notion finding its consummate application in the civic life of America;
    5. The Bible as the primary source of the founding national documents.

Finally, the commonly held belief among all the CA works surveyed is that America must recover its Christian heritage from a culture that is drifting deeper into secularism.

Prior to the presentation of the critique of CA, the book will briefly acknowledge the role of Christian theology in the American notion of liberty. This will take place in chapter 3. It is important to recognize that the Christian religion, as an intellectual source for American revolutionary and founding ideas, played an important role alongside other intellectual sources. Primary and secondary sources are consulted in order to show that Christian theology, particularly Puritanism, was an important contributor to the idea of freedom in America.

The fourth chapter presents the critique of the CA thesis as it has been articulated in the works surveyed in chapter 2. The critique follows six lines of argument:

1. The CA thesis is ambiguous on the definition of "Christian nation;"
2. The CA thesis is ambiguous in defining the contours of the Enlightenment;
3. The Protestant consensus which was predominant in America from its founding until the early twentieth century is no more;
4. Religious pluralism was the intent behind the First Amendment; and it dominates contemporary American culture;
5. The Bible is not the primary source of the American founding
6. American exceptionalism, if it is defined in terms of divine national choice and preference, is not sustainable theologically or historically.

The fifth chapter offers closing arguments in critique of the CA thesis. Much of the work of evangelicals in the past thirty years has been devoted to defending the idea that America is a Christian nation, either because of its founding or because God chose it out of other nations for a special purpose. Rather than standing on the CA thesis, evangelicals can and ought to defend the idea that religious freedom is central to the identity of the American nation. After the closing arguments are made, the chapter concludes by offering suggestions for further research and study.

Acknowledgments

A PROJECT OF THIS scope is never simply the work of a single individual. This book is no exception. Over the course of the past four years, many helpful people have given me useful counsel in the process of thinking through the issues represented in this work. I have been challenged by insightful questions and encouraged by gentle admonitions to persevere by many thoughtful friends.

Of all those who helped me through producing this book, no one has been more insightful than my teacher and mentor Dr. Bruce Little. Dr. Little was my PhD advisor and this book's first form was as my dissertation; he is one of the most consistent thinkers I have encountered, and he applied his incisive logic to sharpen and strengthen my arguments. It was he who, through countless conversations in person, over the phone, and through emails challenged my thinking, offered ideas, exhibited patience, answered hosts of questions, guided my direction, and calmed many fears. It was Dr. Little who, after the death of my first PhD advisor, Dr. L. Russ Bush, III, stepped in on my behalf and took me with my project under his leadership. Dr. Bush was important to me, both personally and academically, and I have acutely felt his loss. He passed away at a critical point in the formulation of my ideas for this book, of which he provided instrumental guidance. I honor him and his memory. And I will not forget Dr. Little's graciousness in lifting me up during that time of loss and uncertainty. I owe him a profound debt of gratitude.

Dr. Richard Land has also been most helpful to me in not only affirming the positions I defended in the book, but also in challenging some of my conclusions. He has pushed me to think in a more focused way about the notion of American exceptionalism. His admonitions have helped me to hone my understanding of what American exceptionalism means, and what it does not mean. I have seldom met a more persuasive arguer with a broader knowledge base in both theology and history than Dr. Land.

Dr. David Puckett, whom I have known for many years, is responsible for sowing the initial seeds of this project in my mind. Over breakfast one morning in 2006, David suggested to me how interesting a work would be that would systematically critique the primary contentions of the Christian America thesis. My good friend Dr. James K. Dew Jr. was very encouraging to me, especially during times of mental block and self-doubt. Through many hours of dialogue on the issues of the book, Jamie helped me to organize and clarify my thoughts and also gave me the courage to assert myself when faced with thorny problems. I owe Dr. Richard A. Holland Jr. a debt of gratitude, too, for he also served as a faithful friend and sounding board for me at crucial points in my writing and research.

Dr. Mark Beliles graciously allowed me to interview him, and even consented to read my second chapter to assess my treatment of authors embracing the Christian America thesis. As you will see in the book, Mark is one of the authors with whom I took issue. At the time of our meeting, Mark knew that the direction I was taking on Christian America was not the same as his. Yet he magnanimously assisted me to understand the position I had set out to critique. He is truly a gentleman and a scholar.

I also want to express my gratitude toward the people of my church, First Baptist Church of Charlottesville, VA. They allowed me as their youth pastor to spend many hours away from church business to complete the book. My secretary, Emily Moody, gave me invaluable assistance in the organization of relevant materials from stacks of books and articles. My pastor, Dr. J. Lindsay Sadler Jr., generously offered me several weeks off from duties at the church, because he believed in me and in the Lord's work in my life.

No person has helped me more with the completion of this book than my wife, Mandy. Her sacrifices, encouragements, and support have sustained me during the most challenging moments this book has presented. Without her love and commitment to me, none of what I have produced would have come to fruition. During the course of my working through the requirements of the PhD degree, she held various jobs to support us financially, has endured two interstate moves, and has raised our two daughters, Caroline and Sally, in the nurture and admonition of the Lord. She is indispensable to me as a wife, friend, and partner as well as in bringing our children up to be wonderful

Christian girls, and devoted to their father. I owe her more than words can describe.

Finally, I thank God through the Lord Jesus Christ, who has given me the abilities to work for His glory. It is God who has been faithful to give me every gift, not the least of which is my salvation through Christ, for the completion of this book. All praise and thanks to Him, because He is kind and faithful to all those who put their trust in Him. As Ps 100:4 says, "Enter into His gates with thanksgiving and into His courts with praise! Be thankful unto Him, and bless His name!"

Introduction

THIS BOOK CRITIQUES THE idea of a Christian America (CA). More specifically, the book critiques what Mark Noll has termed "the strong, or exalted view of Christian America,"[1] which is an interpretation asserting that God, by a special act of providence, set America apart for a particular identity and mission in the world. The strong view of Christian America goes beyond simply affirming that American history and identity have at certain times been in keeping with Christian principles, or acknowledging the debt that America owes to Christianity in its founding and socio-political development. Rather, as Noll describes, it concludes "that the story of our land is in some sense an extension of the history of salvation.... And so, for them [advocates of the Christian America thesis], America today must still be an anointed land, set apart by a divine plan for an extraordinary existence as a nation and an extraordinary mission to the world."[2] Furthermore, CA minimizes secular influences upon American history and identity in order to portray the nation's heritage as singularly Christian.

The thesis of this study is that America was established as a nation with religious liberty and not as a Christian nation. Furthermore, the historiographical construal of Christian America in the strong sense is defeated by two assumptions commonly held by its proponents: that America is a uniquely Christian nation by virtue of its singular Christian heritage and God's special choice. Not all proponents of CA hold to both assumptions simultaneously, although some do. Still, both of these assumptions, whether connected or not, are unsubstantiated and will be critiqued on historical, philosophical, and theological grounds.

---

1. Noll, *One Nation*, 8. The term "Christian America" (CA) will be used henceforth as an appellation that specifically refers to the idea of the United States being a Christian nation in the strong sense.

2. Ibid., 7.

1

The Relationship between Religion and the State, 1630–1789

JUST OVER ONE AND a half centuries prior to the enactment of the U.S. Constitution in 1789,[1] the Massachusetts Bay Colony established how the relationship between religion and the state would be defined there. In 1630, Governor John Winthrop explained this model in his sermon entitled "A Model of Christian Charity." He said that the colonists who were about to establish Massachusetts Bay were entering into a covenant with God. Winthrop's expectation was that if they were obedient to the covenant, God would "please to hear us, and bring us in peace to the place wee desire, [and] hath hee ratified this Covenant and sealed our Commission. . . ."[2] If they were to fail in their commitment to the covenant, if they were to become more enthralled with the things of this world, then God would "surely break out in wrathe against us, be revenged of such a perjured people and make us knowe the price of the breache of such a Covenant."[3] In short, the Puritans were establishing a Christian colony: religion and the state would be unified on the basis of a covenant with God.

A great shift in the American conception of religion's role in the state would take place over the course of the next 160 years. In 1787, when the delegates to the Constitutional Convention met in Philadelphia, they did not intend to follow the Puritan model. Rather than uniting religion and

---

1. The Constitution was drafted in 1787 and the ratification process began after it was signed by the delegates of the Constitutional Convention on September 17 of that year. After the required nine states had ratified the Constitution, the document went into force and the government began to function. Thus, the First Congress assembled on March 4, 1789, and the Constitution went into effect on that day.
2. Winthrop, "A Modell of Christian Charity," 39.
3. Ibid., 40.

the state, thereby creating a Christian nation, the Convention intended to establish an environment in the new republic wherein the state would not interfere with the individual consciences of its citizens in religious matters. Religious freedom[4] was therefore guaranteed in the United States. This idea would mature between 1630 and 1789, championed by luminaries such as Roger Williams, William Penn, George Whitefield, John Leland, Thomas Jefferson, James Madison, and George Washington, among many others. The English philosopher John Locke (1632–1704), writing in 1689, stated in his *Letter Concerning Toleration*, that "the care of souls cannot belong to the civil magistrate, because his power consists only in outward force; but true and saving religion consists in the inward persuasion of the mind, without which nothing can be acceptable to God."[5] While this statement affirming individual religious freedom (without any compulsion by the state) is a well-known idea today, it was a revolutionary idea by eighteenth-century standards. Western society, since at least the empire of Constantine in the fourth century, had agreed that religion and the state were partners in bringing order and providing identity to a nation. Edwin Gaustad drew a stark contrast between that time and our own: "We of today ask where the state left off and the church began; they of yesterday can only shake their heads in wonderment at so meaningless a question."[6] Locke's statement in the *Letter* is passed over today as a given, but it was radical to Locke's readership in 1689, and was still innovative at the time of the founding of the United States.

The question addressed in this chapter is: what caused the shift in the American conception of the role of religion in the state between the Puritan model of 1630 and the enactment of the American Constitution in 1789? Or, as Frank Lambert put it, "How did the Puritan Fathers erecting their 'City upon a Hill' transform into the Founding Fathers drawing a distinct line between church and state"[7] and guaranteeing religious liberty? Lambert asserted that three major developments occurring in the eighteenth century changed the American conception of religion's role in the state to evolve from the Puritan model of a Christian state in the

---

4. The terms "religious freedom" and "religious liberty" will be used synonymously throughout the work. The term "freedom of conscience" will also refer to religious freedom unless otherwise specified.

5. Locke, *Letter Concerning Toleration*, 3.

6. Gaustad, *Faith of the Founders*, 12.

7. Lambert, *The Founding Fathers*, 3.

1600s to the Constitutional model which disestablished religion from the state and guaranteed uninhibited religious liberty:

1. The Great Awakening
2. The English Enlightenment
3. Radical Whig ideology.[8]

The chapter will examine each of these developments to show just how the American idea of the place of religion in the state progressed from the time of the Puritans in colonial New England until the American Constitution took effect. After these three developments are examined, the last part of the chapter will give a brief description of selected Founders'[9] conceptions of religion's role in the state, that which ultimately defined the American society, and set it apart as a standard that much of the world later followed.

THE PURITAN CONCEPTION OF RELIGION'S ROLE IN THE STATE IN THE SEVENTEENTH CENTURY

The Puritan colonies[10] were unique among the other English[11] eastern seaboard colonies. The Puritan colonies of New England in the seventeenth century included Massachusetts, Connecticut, Plymouth, New Haven, and New Hampshire. Rhode Island began as a Puritan colony, but was considered by the other Puritans as a maverick colony, and was not invited to cooperate in defense against the Indians or the French. New Haven would become part of Connecticut in 1665 and Plymouth would become part of Massachusetts in 1691. New Hampshire both united to and separated from Massachusetts twice between 1641 and 1691.

---

8. Ibid.

9. The terms "Founder" and "Founders" will be used to identify major figures who contributed to the establishment of the United States through the processes of developing the first American state papers that remain in force under the constitutional system: the Declaration of Independence, the Constitution, and the Bill of Rights.

10. For the purposes of this section of the chapter, the term "New England colonies" will refer to all the Puritan colonies except Rhode Island, unless otherwise stated.

11. The Act of Union of 1707 united England and Scotland into the Kingdom of Great Britain. The terms "England" and "English" will be used when referring to periods prior to 1707, and the terms "Britain," "Great Britain," and "British" will be used to refer to the same nation when referring to periods after 1707 unless otherwise stated.

John Montgomery cited Daniel Boorstin in observing the differences between the colonists of Virginia, Georgia, Pennsylvania, and the Puritans of New England. He summarized Boorstin by writing, "The Virginia colonists held the dream of the transplanter; the Georgia settlers, the dream of the philanthropist; the Pennsylvania Quakers, the dream of the perfectionist; and the New England Puritans, the grand vision of a New Zion."[12] The Puritan colonies of New England were based on religious purposes, above all else.[13]

The Puritans who set sail from England to America in the first part of the seventeenth century were escaping official persecution begun by James I in 1604. While the Protestant Queen Elizabeth I pursued a policy of toleration, upon her death in 1603 and the end of the Tudor line, a new set of political and religious realities descended upon England that would end the toleration the Puritans enjoyed. The Stuart line was initiated in James I. Almost immediately after ascending the throne he began an anti-Puritan policy at the Hampton Court conference of 1604. According to David Gelernter, "James proclaimed of the Puritans that 'I shall make them conform themselves or I will harry them out of the land.'"[14] This policy of persecution would ultimately lead to the English Civil War, the execution of Charles I, the Puritan rule under Oliver Cromwell, the restoration of the monarchy in 1660, and finally, the shift of power from the crown to the Parliament after the Glorious Revolution and the installation of the joint rule of William and Mary in 1688. By the end of James' rule and the beginning of the reign of Charles I in 1625, conditions had grown so intolerable to many Puritans that they left England to colonize America rather than submit themselves to rule under Charles I, or even to submit themselves to a form of toleration handed down by a what they viewed as an autocratic ruler. Perry Miller wrote,

> They had not been fighting in England for any milk-and-water toleration, and had they been offered such a religious freedom as

---

12. Montgomery, *Shaping*, 39.

13. For primary sources from and treatments of the seventeenth–century Puritans of New England, see McKenna, *Puritan Origins*; Miller, *Errand into The Wilderness*; Miller, *Nature's Nation*; Miller, *New England Mind*; Stout, *New England Soul*; Miller and Johnson, *Puritans*; Adair, *Founding Fathers*; Vaughan, ed., *Puritan Tradition*; Hall, ed., *Puritans in the New World*; Marsden, *Religion and American Culture*; Noll, *Old Religion*; Noll, *America's God*; and Bercovitch, *Puritan Origins*.

14. Gelernter, *Americanism*, 49.

> dissenters now enjoy in Great Britain, they would have scorned to accept the terms.... The Puritans were assured that they alone knew the exact truth, as it was contained in the written word of God, and they were fighting to enthrone it in England and to extirpate utterly and mercilessly all other pretended versions of Christianity. When they could not succeed at home, they came to America, where they could establish a society in which the one and only truth should reign forever.[15]

Thus, the Puritans had a very certain understanding of the kind of colonial society they were coming to establish in America. George Marsden wrote that "even ... moderate Puritans ... were willing to brave the high seas and the wilderness to found an alternative society based on Puritan principles. This society, the Massachusetts Bay Colony, would be, as Governor John Winthrop put it in 1630, 'a city upon a hill,' a model Christian state that all the world could imitate."[16]

It is important to note here that while the Puritans were escaping religious persecution and seeking to worship God as they chose, they were not establishing their colony on the basis of religious liberty. Noll wrote that "the first colonies actually instituted a tighter governmental control of religion than existed in the Old World."[17] This point will be further developed below, but Noll's broader point is to differentiate between positive and negative religious liberty. He wrote, "In both New England and the Chesapeake, the kind of freedom that mattered most turned out to be 'positive liberty' that enabled colonists to structure their lives as they had been prevented from doing in Great Britain, not 'negative liberty' where all were free to do as they pleased."[18] To summarize, the Puritan colonies of New England were exercising freedom to leave England and worship God on their own terms in America. They were not, however, establishing their colonies wherein everyone would be free to worship as they chose. So what was their goal in establishing overseas colonies? If they were not establishing their colonies on the basis of negative religious freedom, on what basis did they intend to establish them? Simply put, the goal was to form a pure society, one that integrated biblical theology into all areas of life and grounded in the idea of covenant. According to

15. Miller, *Errand into The Wilderness*, 144.
16. Marsden, *Religion and American Culture*, 22.
17. Noll, *Old Religion*, 74.
18. Ibid.

Stephen Keillor, "they came to advocate two ideas in precarious, paradoxical combination: a state church of all the English people, yet a pure one led by the pious alone."[19] Further, Keillor wrote, "They sought to have a purified church that controlled family, economy, and government. Not a church hierarchy but church members who were truly converted would truly integrate this society."[20] This society would then be fully Christian and would be an example for others, particularly England. The goal was to create, as Winthrop called it in his *Model of Christian Charity*, a "city upon a hill," a beacon that would be a source of inspiration to the world. Conrad Cherry asserted that the Puritans sought "to build a holy commonwealth in which the people were covenanted together by their public profession of religious faith and were covenanted with God by their pledge to erect a Christian society."[21]

Noll presented an astute explanation of the Puritan goal of theological integration in his work, *America's God: From Jonathan Edwards to Abraham Lincoln*. He stated, "They were the one group of colonists who aspired to establish an entire society on the basis of their theology, and the only ones to have partially succeeded."[22] The key element that would hold the integration of church, state, economy, family, and self would be the biblical notion of the covenant.

Winthrop's belief that the Massachusetts Bay Colony was entering into a covenant with God has already been mentioned. But it is worth noting again the significance of the idea of covenant to the Puritan conception of the role of religion in the state. Because the Puritans strictly followed the Calvinist theological tradition, they had a high view of election. They affirmed both the election of individuals to salvation, and of nations to carry out God's expressed purposes. Their model for this was the nation of Israel in the Old Testament. Here, however, the Puritans went beyond Calvin's understanding of election. Miller described this as "the saint [being] redeemed not simply by an infusion of grace, but by being taken into a league with God, an explicit compact drawn up between two partners, wherein the saint promised to obey God's will and God promised infal-

---

19. Keillor, *This Rebellious House*, 64.
20. Ibid.
21. Cherry, ed., *God's New Israel*, 26.
22. Noll, *America's God*, 21.

libly to grant him salvation."[23] According to Noll, "it seemed natural that the first work of faith should be covenanting with God and other believers to form individual churches."[24] When regenerate colonists came together to form churches, they did so under the covenant model, forming church covenants at each individual church. The society, made up of a cohesive system of church covenants, would thus be one where all aspects of life would be systematically and biblically knit together.[25]

As the colonists in New England were members of a covenanted society, all of life was submitted to the sovereignty of God and the authority of Scripture. Noll wrote, "the Reformed commitment to the theological significance of everyday life led to the development of something like Protestant metaphysics, Protestant epistemology, Protestant science, Protestant politics, Protestant social and economic theory, Protestant art, and Protestant poetics."[26] The Puritans were thus attempting to apply the integration of these units into a practical whole.

Where did this desire for integration originate? Miller identified the Puritan worldview as being fully Augustinian, in that all the questions of life could be answered in "the relation of the individual to the One. The substance of Augustine's message was this: '*Deum et animam scire cupio. Nihilne plus? Nihil omnino.*' If man once achieved knowledge of God and of his soul, the answer to all other questions would soon follow."[27] Furthermore, Miller noted the fact that Puritan anthropology was defined by the notion of total depravity. Because of this reality, humanity cannot hope to achieve order in society without limited government. But limited

---

23. Miller, *Nature's Nation*, 17.

24. Noll, *America's God*, 38.

25. This synthesis was undermined by the Half-Way Covenant as envisioned by Solomon Stoddard (1643–1729) of Northampton, Massachusetts. Among other things, Stoddard maintained that individual church covenants were unbiblical. As long as the majority of the populace was Christian, a national covenant existed and the seal of this covenant was the Lord's Supper. Thus, all persons were duty-bound to receive communion for the sake of being faithful to the covenant. Noll wrote, "Stoddard's proposals kept the language of covenant to describe personal salvation and to show how God cared for nations. But by pulling church order out of the stem of interlocking covenants, he moved away from the Puritans' historic integration of theology and society" (ibid., 42). The undermining of the synthesis begun in the Half-Way Covenant would lay the groundwork for its being torn apart as a result of the Great Awakening.

26. Ibid., 36.

27. Miller, *New England Mind*, 8. Augustine's statement is translated, "I long to know God and Spirit. Nothing more? Nothing altogether."

government did not mean democratic government. There was no modern idea of equality to be found among the Puritans. The notion of democracy was dismissed by Puritan anthropology as being nothing but anarchy. According to Montgomery, John Cotton's position was that "If the people be governors, who shall be governed?"[28] Rather, the limited government of the Puritans was centralized. Miller wrote, "it was a dictatorship, not of a single tyrant, or of an economic class, or of a political faction, but of the holy and regenerate."[29]

As a result of this view of humanity's nature and of government's consequent structure, the Puritans' understanding of religious liberty was radically different than the modern view. Their understanding of religious liberty was, to use Noll's term, "positive liberty," rather than "negative liberty." Just as they were free to leave England's shores to set up a colony to worship God as they saw fit, any dissenters living in Puritan New England were also free to leave. If they stayed, they were giving assent to the Puritan way. Dissenters did not enjoy negative liberty, the freedom to worship God according to the dictates of their consciences. The New England Puritans were overtly intolerant, in that they did not offer religious sanctuary to those who would disagree with them. They saw themselves in exceptional and exclusive terms, as God's new chosen people, bound to Him by covenant agreement. As Sacvan Bercovitch asserted, "The New World, like Canaan of old, belonged wholly to God. The remnant that fled Babylon [England] in 1630 set sail for the new promised land, especially reserved by God for them."[30] Because they believed that they were especially chosen by God, they sought to teach and model what they understood as pure biblical doctrine in their colony to the exclusion of other beliefs.

But they were not hypocritical. They did not deny negative religious liberty to persons within their own realms, having previously demanded it in their former home of England. Prior to setting sail for America, the Puritans' first desire was to transform England, to rid it of the last vestiges of Catholicism and restore pure worship there. When it became obvious that this would not come to pass, they came to America. Miller expressed this with crystal clarity: "To allow no dissent from the truth was exactly the reason they had come to America. They maintained here precisely

---

28. Montgomery, *Shaping*, 43.
29. Miller, *Errand into the Wilderness*, 143.
30. Bercovitch, *Puritan Origins*, 100.

what they had maintained in England, and if they exiled, fined, jailed, whipped, or hanged those who disagreed with them in New England, they would have done the same thing in England could they have secured the power...."[31] Miller also quoted Samuel Willard, minister of the Third Church in Boston, who said in 1681, "I perceive they are mistaken in the design of our first Planters, whose business was not Toleration; but were professed Enemies of it, and could leave the World professing they died no Libertines. Their business was to settle, and (as much as in them lay) secure Religion to Posterity, according to that way which they believed was of God."[32]

Thus was the nature of the Puritan conception of religion's role in the state. Religion and the state were knit together based on the idea that they had entered into a covenant with God, one not unlike that described in the Old Testament between ancient Israel and God. Ministers would not necessarily be magistrates, but the magistrates would be heavily influenced by the ministers. New England would be a Christian nation in every respect, because its people were supposed to be, on the whole, regenerate. Miller's statement, that "for the Puritan mind it was not possible to segregate a man's spiritual life from his communal life"[33] is essential in understanding the Puritan view of the place of religion in the state. If this was the initial view, what might explain why, over time, this view gave way to a commitment to negative religious liberty in America? The following is an attempt to answer that question.

THE GREAT AWAKENING (CA. 1730–CA. 1750) AND ITS ROLE IN THE SHIFT

The Great Awakening of the eighteenth century was a religious movement that swept North America and Great Britain as a result of influential preaching that stressed the individual's relationship to God.[34] It represented a move away from formal, state-sponsored religion to evangelicalism,[35]

---

31. Miller, *Errand into the Wilderness*, 145.
32. Ibid.
33. Ibid., 142.
34. Excellent treatments of the Great Awakening include Heimert, *Religion and the American Mind*; Lambert, *The Founding Fathers*; Noll, *Old Religion*; Noll, *America's God*; Noll, *History of Christianity*; Gaustad and Schmidt, *Religious History of America*; and Kidd, *Great Awakening*.
35. This term should be understood in its historical context in order to avoid anach-

which stressed the importance of the new birth, described by Christ in John 3. Noll described the Great Awakening as being the impetus for "Western Protestantism... moving from establishment forms of religion, embedded in traditional, organic, premodern political economies, to individualized and affectional forms, adapted to modernizing, rational, and market-oriented societies."[36]

This focus on the individual was an extension of the larger cultural dynamic of the English Enlightenment, which sought to demonstrate that one can decide for himself on religious matters with no reliance upon traditional external authorities. Old structures of religion, such as the parish system, were dismantled by the itinerant preachers of the Awakening. This meant that people now heard the word of God preached outside the boundaries of the parish and even the four walls of the church. Also, and very significantly, the Puritan integration which sought to join all of society together under pure theological doctrine broke up, and the place of religion in society began to take on a new meaning. Thus, Noll pointed out, "the Awakening marked a transition from clerical to lay religion, from the minister as an inherited authority figure to self-empowered mobilizer, from the definition of Christianity by doctrine to its definition by piety, and from a state church encompassing all of society to a gathered church made up only of the converted."[37] Moreover, the Awakening would create a fertile environment for revolutionary ideas that would inform the American colonies by the end of the eighteenth century. The extent of the Awakening's impact on the American Revolution is debated, but its role in laying the groundwork for political and religious liberty cannot be disputed, for reasons which will be discussed later.

Before examining how the Awakening brought changes to the place of religion in American society, it is appropriate to assess briefly the pre-Awakening religious landscape in America. How was the religious landscape of the British colonies defined prior to the Awakening? The religious landscape south of New England just prior to the Awakening was predominately Anglican, with the exception of Pennsylvania.[38] Much of

---

ronisms. Eighteenth-century evangelicalism is to be somewhat distinguished from twentieth and twenty-first century evangelicalism.

36. Noll, *America's God*, 4.
37. Ibid., 44.
38. The charter for Pennsylvania was granted to William Penn in 1681 by Charles II. It was set up as a Quaker colony which offered, using Noll's term, "negative" religious

that territory was divided into parishes, geographical partitions in which a particular Anglican minister carried out his ministry. People who lived within a particular parish attended church services officiated by that parish minister, who was educated and ordained by the Church of England. The parish system was meant to maintain the integrity and influence of the Church of England in the colonies. Each minister in the parish system offered a united front against heresies and preachers not recognized by the Church. Lambert stated, "They [parishioners] met at fixed times and sat in assigned pews. Their services followed the familiar patterns that their particular church or sect deemed authoritative. And they were protected from heretics and schismatics who might threaten their orderly worship."[39]

Still, fundamental changes were coming to the American colonies—intellectual-theological changes, demographic changes, and socio-economic changes. These changes would lay the groundwork for the Awakening's vast impact on the religious culture of the colonies. First, the intellectual-theological challenge of the English Enlightenment, specifically in the form of the philosophical religion known as deism. Deism called into question traditionally held beliefs about Christian doctrine, specifically, the doctrine of the Trinity, the doctrine of humanity and the doctrine of revelation. Deism began to undermine traditional religious belief and practice in America. It posited a transcendent God which was understood neither to be immanent nor triune. David Holmes wrote, "Deists postulated a distant deity to whom they referred with terms such as 'the First Cause,' 'the Creator of the Universe,' 'the Divine Artist,' 'the Divine Author of All Good,' 'the Grand Architect,' 'the God of Nature,' 'Nature's God,' 'Divine Providence,' and (in a phrase used by Franklin) 'the

---

freedom to all. According to Lambert, "In 1720, most Americans lived in colonies with an established church. Approximately 85 percent of the almost half a million inhabitants of British North America lived in provinces where either the Church of England or the Congregational churches constituted the official church. The Anglican Church was established in Virginia, Maryland, Delaware, North Carolina, and South Carolina; it was also loosely established in New York, although a Dutch Reformed preponderance weakened its hold there. Congregational churches were established in Massachusetts, Connecticut, and New Hampshire. While Pennsylvania had no official church, the Quakers had sufficient numbers to control the legislative assembly. New Jersey and Rhode Island were similar to Pennsylvania in that there numerous sects coexisted, albeit not harmoniously" (Lambert, *The Founding Fathers*, 129).

39. Ibid., 131.

Author and Owner of our System."[40] The God of the deists was viewed as the Creator, the author and giver of human reason and natural rights as well as the absolute source of morality. While deism did not gain a significantly large following in America in the eighteenth century, it did serve to challenge prevailing paradigms of religious faith and practice that had been carried over from England.

Another change laying the groundwork for the impact of the Awakening was the unique reality of religious pluralism in the colonies. The pluralism of the eighteenth century American colonies did not include the truly global elements of twenty-first century times. There was not a wide plurality of different worldviews, nor was there much diversity in racial or ethnic backgrounds. Free colonists were made up of Europeans holding to a set of basic Christian commitments. Still, the religious pluralism that existed in the colonies was not familiar to Europeans who were accustomed to one church for one place for one people group. Noll wrote, "By the mid-eighteenth century, however, the European pattern was breaking down fast. Not only were Baptists, Presbyterians, Methodists, and others seeking their own space in Congregationalist Massachusetts and Anglican Virginia, in the middle colonies of New York, New Jersey, and Pennsylvania, so many different Protestant groups had taken root that it had become a practical impossibility to favor anyone of them over the others."[41] The result of this growing pluralism in colonial society was to break down the traditional religious paradigm of the parish system under the established state church and present a number of religious choices to people.

Choice was itself another novel idea in the eighteenth century, and was a particularly unique factor in the British colonies. Whereas the Spanish and French colonial empires in America were devoted to extraction of wealth in some form, the British were the first to discover other methods of drawing wealth from their colonial assets, particularly in America.

Merchants discovered in the early 1700s that colonies were not only valuable for the resources extracted, but they would also be extraordinarily valuable as a source of new markets in which to sell their goods. The Second British Empire of the late nineteenth and early twentieth cen-

---

40. Holmes, *Faiths of the Founding Fathers*, 47.
41. Noll, *Old Religion*, 50.

turies would develop this idea to its fullest extent, but the British began to learn this valuable economic lesson early in the eighteenth century, just before the height of the First British Empire.[42]

The population of the British colonies would reach one million subjects by the middle of the eighteenth century, and this burgeoning population enjoyed greater financial independence than their counterparts in England. Gordon S. Wood pointed out that "Two-thirds of the white colonial population owned land, compared with only one-fifth of the English population. In no case was the overall situation of property-owning in America comparable to that of England, where more than 60 percent of the population owned no property of any kind. Freehold tenure in America was especially widespread. . . ."[43] So, this new economic reality presented the evangelicals of the Awakening with an uncommon opportunity. Lambert wrote that the "consumer revolution in the English Atlantic provided evangelicals with new models for defining their audiences and new techniques for conveying the gospel to them."[44]

One of the new models utilized by merchants to expand their market among American consumers was advertising. A merchant would advertise his product in a newspaper, being careful to accentuate its value dramatically. Lambert observed that "Josiah Wedgewood became a master of extolling his pottery in this fashion. Rather than assuming that buyers would seek them out and come to them for merchandise, merchants now pursued consumers wherever they were."[45]

Thus, the development of the open market in the American colonies presented compelling object lessons for itinerant preachers carrying the gospel from town to town. Instead of waiting for people to fill a pew on the assigned day at the assigned hour to hear a carefully scripted sermon written along the lines of a strict Anglican perspective, itinerant preachers of the Awakening would enter a town on any day and preach a message directed to the individual, often outside the four walls of a church. Like the merchants who were discovering new ways to profit from sales by going to the consumers rather than waiting for the consumers to come

---

42. The high water mark of the First British Empire was the defeat of the French and the absorption of their overseas empire in America and India at the conclusion of the Seven Years War/French and Indian War and the signing of the Treaty of Paris in 1763.

43. Wood, *Radicalism*, 123.

44. Lambert, *Founding Fathers*, 138.

45. Ibid.

to them, evangelicals were adopting those methods to carry the gospel to the people.

George Whitefield (1715–1770), the incomparable figure of the Awakening, used advertising masterfully in order to gather enormous crowds for his sermons. According to Lambert, "Advance publicity begun months before he arrived in a particular location served to build anticipation to a fever pitch."[46] Additionally, "evangelicals penetrated parish lines by sending itinerant preachers all over the Anglo-American world. Where they found a sympathetic parish minister, they preached from his pulpit. Where parish ministers opposed them, they preached wherever they found space within the parish: in market squares, from courthouse steps, at racecourses, in public parks, and even in taverns."[47]

In this new environment of an open religious market, religion began to flourish as it never had previously in the colonies. This open market forced religious leaders to compete for new congregants for the first time. Prior to the Awakening, the union of religion and state set up a culture wherein the people went to the church to receive spiritual guidance. The open market dynamic introduced during the first half of the eighteenth century along with religious pluralism reversed that traditional reality. Rodney Stark explained this phenomenon plainly:

> ...religious economies usually have been distorted by state regulations that either impose a monopoly firm or constrain the market by subsidizing a state church and making it difficult for other religious groups to compete. But religion languishes in a monopolized religious economy, not only because so many find their religious tastes unserved but because, as with commercial monopolies, monopoly religious firms become lazy and inefficient. In contrast, religion thrives in a free market, where many religious groups vie for followers and those firms lacking energy or appeal fall by the wayside.[48]

Therefore, the combination of the influence of English Enlightenment religious thought manifested most clearly in deism, and the growing religious pluralism in the colonies along with the development of a market-oriented religious environment made the impact of the Awakening felt throughout the colonies. The key to understanding the significance of the

---

46. Ibid., 139.
47. Ibid.
48. Stark, *Victory of Reason*, 199.

Awakening in colonial America is found in one word: *choice*. For centuries, Western culture offered little in terms of religious choice, indeed discouraged it. For the first time, religious choice was thrust upon ordinary people. Choice itself was a key development in the West leading to religious liberty and also a significant factor in changing American conceptions of the role of religion in the state from the premodern view of the Puritans to the modern view of the Founding Fathers.

The impact of the Awakening upon the colonies was all-encompassing. This religious movement was perhaps the first real force serving to unite the British colonies from thirteen disparate colonies to a league which would eventually confront Britain in 1775. Noll stated that the Awakening "tended to break down the provincialism of the various colonies and to aid in the process of inter-colonial communication which would one day lead to the formation of United States. From Charlestown to Boston, Whitefield's name was in the air."[49]

Whitefield was mentioned earlier. Among all the personalities of the Awakening of the eighteenth century, none compare with Whitefield in terms of miles travelled, sermons preached, and the numbers of people who heard him. He travelled between England and America seven times before his death in 1770 and while in America, he travelled up and down the Eastern seaboard. Brian Moynahan offered this brief example of Whitefield's energy:

> He preached at a frenetic pace. On October 12, 1740, a crowd of twenty thousand came to Boston Common to hear him, "a sight," he claimed immodestly but truthfully, "perhaps never seen before in America." Whitefield spoke almost until dusk fell and many were moved to tears; it was said that he could make hard men weep merely by pronouncing the word "Mesopotamia." The following Sunday, he was in Northampton, lodging with Jonathan Edwards. He preached in the morning, with Edwards in tears throughout; "'The people were equally affected," he wrote, "and in the afternoon the power increased yet more." By November 9, Whitefield was in Philadelphia, and several thousand came to listen to him in a new hall whose roof was not yet in place. He urged them to "go to the grammar school of faith and repentance" and to spurn "Christless talkers."[50]

---

49. Noll, *Christians in the American Revolution*, 45.
50. Moynahan, *History of Christianity*, 587.

The message that Whitefield preached was captivating because it offered a fresh perspective on biblical doctrine in a way that was defined by dramatic flair. He, along with Jonathan Edwards, emphasized the importance of the individual's relationship to God through the saving work of Jesus Christ. He urged his listeners to be born again. Noll called Whitefield "the most visible symbol of the new evangelicalism"[51] which represented a shift in religious understanding in terms of an emphasis on the intellect, outward formalism, and the corporate bodies of church and state to one of an emphasis on the heart-centered affection for Christ, inward piety, and the individual soul. Noll wrote, "the shift represented by Whitefield marked the passing of Puritanism and the rise of evangelicalism as the dominant Protestant expression in America. In this new form, loyalty to a particular church was less important that a vibrant religion of the heart."[52]

Another aspect of Whitefield's message was a test of previously unchallenged sources of authority. One effect of preaching outdoors and away from parish churches was that it separated people from the social hierarchies that dominated church culture. Wood described the situation this way: "There were the few who were sometimes called 'the reverend' or 'right reverend,' 'the honourable,' or 'excellent,' or 'noble,' or 'puissant,' or 'royal,' and there were the many who were often called 'the Mob,' 'the Vulgar,' or 'the Herd.'. . . . Southern squires entered their churches as a body and took their pews only after their families and the ordinary people had been seated."[53] When Whitefield, or any itinerant preacher who was not welcomed by the parish priest preached outside of the church, social barriers were wiped away and all stood as equals before God, sinners needing personal redemption by Christ. This breakdown of social status was most stark when Whitefield addressed clergymen who were not true believers. According to Keillor, "When Whitefield and other itinerants criticized unconverted ministers, that undercut the clergy's presumed superiority to the lay person. If the minister had to answer to God, then all people must, regardless of social standing."[54]

---

51. Noll, *Old Religion*, 51.
52. Ibid., 52–53.
53. Wood, *Radicalism*, 24–25.
54. Keillor, *This Rebellious House*, 76.

The impact of the Awakening was felt in at least one more way. The Puritan integration that had been constructed in New England was dismantled for all time. The Awakening split the New England Puritans from one group into four groups, each defined by its response to the phenomenon of the revivals sweeping the colonies. One group, the Old Calvinists, sought to maintain the theologically integrated society which had been from the beginning. The moderate New Lights, of which Edwards was one, sought to purify New England churches from within. The Separates, or radical New Lights welcomed the revivals and formed their own churches in reaction against the dry religiosity of the New England churches. They identified themselves with Baptists, Methodists, and Presbyterians, and grew very quickly. Finally, the Old Lights were against the revivals, seeing them through the lenses of the Enlightenment and deism and condemning their doctrines as childish relics. Mark Noll, George Marsden, and Nathan Hatch wrote, "Those who opposed the revival took over the Puritan conception of unified society, but greatly deemphasized the need for personal faith to ground the society. On the other hand, those who promoted the revival retained the Puritan conviction about the need for personal salvation, but largely abandoned the Puritan concern for a united commonwealth. The Great Awakening forced a choice. The result was the end of Puritan ideas about society, state, and politics."[55]

Thus, the Awakening's impact was felt most pointedly in the presence of real religious choices for ordinary people in an open market of ideas. By the time of the signing of the Declaration of Independence only forty or so years after the beginning of the Awakening, Lambert wrote, "the fast-growing population of dissenters lobbied legislators to bring laws into conformity with the new religious economy, by disestablishing state churches and guaranteeing complete religious freedom."[56]

THE ENGLISH ENLIGHTENMENT AND ITS ROLE IN THE SHIFT

The English Enlightenment represented a dramatic shift in the overall pattern of Western thought.[57] Simply put, it marked the division between

55. Noll et al., *Search*, 60.
56. Lambert, *Place of Religion*, 208.
57. For treatments of Enlightenment philosophy, see Ahlstrom, *Religious History*; Heimert, *Religion and the American Mind*; Holmes, *Faiths of the Founding Fathers*; Lambert, *Founding Fathers*; May, *Enlightenment*; Noll, *History of Christianity*; Noll, *America's God*; Ericson, *American Freedom*; Bewkes et al., *Western Heritage*; Van Doren,

premodernity and modernity in the Western world. It was a revolution in human intellectual life and it is far beyond the scope of this book to provide a comprehensive treatment of it. Still, it is necessary to devote some attention to the relevant aspects of the Enlightenment's impact on the shift of American conceptions of religion's role in the state because it is one of the most important dynamics contributing to this shift.

The mindset of the premodern West was marked by humility before authority, submission to and acceptance of the supernatural, recognition of limits to the human capacity for understanding God and His creation (mystery), and acquiescence to the notion of the fallen state of man in sin. In contrast, the modern mind rejected external authorities, such as royal majesty or priestly command. It threw off old trepidation before mystery and the supernatural. It rejected the idea of limits to human understanding of the world as well as that of the universal sinfulness of humankind. It was the Enlightenment that brought about this intellectual sea change in the West. Eugene Bewkes, et al., identified the significance of the Enlightenment in this way: "... men faced life with a new confidence in themselves, with a new recognition of human power and achievement, with a new appreciation of present values, and with a new conviction of the onward progress of their race in past and future."[58]

The role of reason in the human encounter with the world was one of the primary concerns of Enlightenment thought. Prior to the Enlightenment, reason was widely accepted as a useful supplement to revelation, a means of gaining further insight into matters of faith, what Martin Luther referred to as ministerial reason. Reason did not challenge revelation or ecclesiastical authority, but supported them, according to the premodern mind. After the Enlightenment, according to Bewkes, et al., "Reason now was not satisfied to deny the authority of the church or the pope; it attacked the fundamental concepts of Christianity, like the Trinity, incarnation, and the sinfulness of man."[59] Furthermore, according to Charles Van Doren, "The ancients had had no concept of progress, at least in the sense of a steady improvement over the centuries and millennia.... The eighteenth century not only believed in progress, it even began

---

History of Knowledge; Russell, *History of Western Philosophy*; and Hamlyn, *History of Western Philosophy*.

58. Bewkes et al., *Western Heritage*, 553.

59. Ibid., 554.

The Relationship between Religion and the State, 1630–1789   19

to believe in *necessary* progress; things *had* to get better, because that was the nature of things."[60]

Contrasting American intellectual life, prior to and after the English Enlightenment, demands that one give attention to the curriculum of universities in New England, particularly Yale and Harvard. In the early eighteenth century the curriculum was defined by a method known as the "Old Learning." This method was based on the Ramist system, a system of neo-Platonic, Augustinian epistemology. Petrus Ramus (1515–1572), a French philosopher, believed that all things existed as ideas in God's mind. The goal was to discover those ideas, and as Lambert stated, "Yale students like Samuel Johnson (1696–1772) kept notebooks meticulously classifying all knowledge into 'innumerable divisions and subdivisions,' which managed to 'put the mind of God in 1,267 propositions.'"[61] The authority of Scripture was at the heart of this method, because the presupposition was that all questions could be answered by appealing to the Bible. This method fit well with the Puritan belief that all aspects of life are unified under the sovereignty of God, and that Scripture is the absolute moral, ontological and epistemological authority. It also fit well into the premodern mindset, which accepted *a priori* statements as authoritative.

Harvard at the beginning of the eighteenth century was a thoroughly Puritan institution, and was formed with the goal of training students to interpret Scripture, but also to study great theologians of the past. All knowledge was unified, and texts such as William Ames's *Medulla Sacrae Theologiae*, John Wollebius's *The Abridgement of Christian Divinity*, and Petro van Mastricht's *Theoretico-Practica Theologia* were studied in order to demonstrate this unity. Lambert quoted Cotton Mather who recommended van Mastricht's work to Harvard describing the work as, "the whole of Christian theology and morality, theory and practice, is laid out with a minuteness and precision that bring a hundred years of methodizing to a stupendous fulfillment."[62]

Thus, the Old Learning was a representation of premodern and Puritan epistemology and methodology. A new method would come in the form of the "New Learning," which would be heavily influenced by English Enlightenment—modern—thought. Henry May wrote, "The

---

60. Van Doren, *History of Knowledge*, 217. Emphasis in the original.
61. Lambert, *Founding Fathers*, 163.
62. Ibid., 164.

New Learning of Newton and Locke, which had arrived with dramatic suddenness in the Dummer gift of books to Yale in 1714, had almost everywhere gained the victory over Protestant scholasticism by the middle of the century."[63] The New Learning followed Francis Bacon's rejection of *a priori* speculation in favor of methods that derive knowledge from evidence. Thus, students were taught to call the authority of Scripture into question as the path to certainty.

A powerful example of the contrast between the Old and New Learning is found in Benjamin Franklin's discovery of electricity in 1752. Natural phenomena had always been interpreted as acts of God, whose purposes were disclosed in divine mystery. Lightning, to the premodern mind, was God's way of warning or punishing wayward people. Franklin, however, believed that lightning and electricity were identical, and that studying lightning was another way of studying the behavior of electric currents. After he conducted his experiment which demonstrated the truth of this hypothesis in Philadelphia, he was acclaimed as one of the greatest and most forward-thinking men of his time. Lambert wrote, "Some persons around the world hailed Franklin as 'a sort of demigod who had invaded the supernatural realm and by harnessing lightning had exercised a huge liberating control over nature.' Franklin chose to interpret his discovery less dramatically. 'It has pleased God in his Goodness to Mankind,' he wrote, 'at length to discover to them the Means of securing their Habitations and other Buildings from Mischief by Thunder and Lightning.'"[64]

The Enlightenment worldview has been succinctly described by May: "Let us say that the Enlightenment consists of all those who believe two propositions: first, that the present age is more enlightened than the past; and second, that we understand nature in man best through the use of our natural faculties."[65] Gaustad observed that "any description of the Enlightenment must, however, confront two words that are themselves both intricate and diffuse: *Reason* and *Nature*."[66] Simply put, reason referred to the ability of humans to know without the aid of divine revelation. Indeed, revelation and reason most often affirm the same moral

---

63. May, *Enlightenment*, 33.
64. Lambert, *Founding Fathers*, 169.
65. May, *Enlightenment*, xiv.
66. Gaustad, *Faith of the Founders*, 86.

conclusions, so Scripture is not necessary as the sole authority. Nature referred to that which was universal in the human race, providing guidance to human morality and epistemology. It was viewed as the source of the human mind and human reason. Locke wrote concerning reason and nature this way: "The state of Nature has a law of Nature to govern it, which obliges everyone, and reason, which is that law, teaches all mankind who will but consult it, that being all equal and independent, no one ought to harm another in his life, health, liberty or possessions...."[67] Thus, the English Enlightenment of the seventeenth and early eighteenth centuries emphasized *a posteriori* over *a priori* method, the present over the past, reason over revelation, and nature over God.

The Enlightenment in England influenced the British colonies more than the Continental Enlightenment for obvious reasons, and the works of Francis Bacon, Isaac Newton, and John Locke were especially prominent. Thomas Jefferson held these three thinkers in such high regard that he had the artist John Trumbull paint a portrait of them and he placed it in his home at Monticello. Lambert quoted Jefferson as having called them, "the three greatest men that have ever lived, without any exception, and as having laid the foundation of those superstructures which have been raised in the Physical and Moral Sciences."[68]

Bacon, author of *Novum Organum*, said that human knowledge rests on experience and observation systematically and inductively interpreted, not *a priori* principles arrived at through deduction. This represented a major reversal. Bacon observed that the human mind was at a distinct disadvantage when it came to arriving at any given conclusion, because it was plagued by four "idols": the idols of the tribe, the den, the market, and the theatre.[69] The only way to overcome these habits of the mind that hindered the understanding of truth, for Bacon, was to arrive at conclusions

---

67. Locke, *Concerning Civil Government*, II.6.
68. Lambert, *Founding Fathers*, 161.
69. The meaning of the four idols is as follows: the tribe, the intellectual preference for *a priori* explanations over experience; the den, mental preference for excesses over the mean; the market, confusion about the meaning of terms, either of those that refer to things which do not exist or of those that do exist and yet unfocused in their meanings; the theatre, two methods of arriving at conclusions, either by flawed views of philosophy or by false argument. An example of a flawed philosophy would be a superstitious use, whereby philosophy is used to prove a particular theology. An example of a false argument would be a reliance on dogma without reliable or reasonable basis. See Magill, ed., *Masterpieces of World Philosophy*, 216–23.

through a studied process of induction. He stated, "There are and can exist but two ways of investigating and discovering truth. The one hurries on rapidly from the senses and particulars to the most general axioms, and from them, as principles and their supposed indisputable truth, derives and discovers the intermediate axioms. This is the way now in use. The other constructs its axioms from the senses and particulars, by ascending continually and gradually, till it finally arrives at the most general axioms, which is the true but unattempted way."[70]

Newton utilized Bacon's method in his study of science, and showed that the universe is governed by unchanging laws. For example, the law of gravity which governs the rotation of the planets and the track of comets is the same law that governs motion on the earth. This law, however, did not come into existence on its own, but was established by God, who is over and above all things. Newton said in the conclusion to his *Mathematical Principles of Natural Philosophy* that,

> Bodies projected in our air suffer no resistance but from the air. Withdraw the air ... and the resistance ceases; for in this void a bit of fine down and a piece of solid gold descend with equal velocity. And the same argument must apply to the celestial spaces above the earth's atmosphere; ... but though these bodies may, indeed, continue in their orbits by the mere laws of gravity, yet they could by no means have at first derived the regular position of the orbits themselves from those laws.... This most beautiful system of the sun, planets, and comets, could only proceed from the counsel and dominion of an intelligent and powerful Being.... This Being governs all things, not as the soul of the world, but as Lord over all; and on account of his dominion he is wont to be called *Lord God pantokrator*, or *Universal Ruler*;....[71]

The immediate ramifications of what Newton was showing in his study of science were that the universe was governed by forces which were discoverable and discernable by the human mind. The movements of the sun, planets, comets, and other heavenly bodies were not divine mysteries that only God could reveal, but were comprehended by mathematical principles. Newton showed that the universe was one of order, and that this ordered universe welcomed human inquiry. Wrote Carl Becker, "Perhaps after all God moved in these clear ways to perform his wonders; and it

---

70. Bacon, *Novum Organum*, 108.
71. Newton, *Mathematical Principles*, 369–70. Emphasis in the original.

must be that he had given man a mind ingeniously fitted to discover these ways. Newton, more than any man before him, so it seemed to the eighteenth century, banished mystery from the world."[72]

Locke's thought built on the writings of Bacon and Newton. Locke's philosophical, social, and political contributions to the West cannot be understated. Next to the Founders themselves, it is possible that no other thinker contributed more to the establishment of the United States than did Locke. But Locke could not have made his impact alone. Bertrand Russell stated, "the victory of Locke's philosophy in England and France was largely due to the prestige of Newton. . . . The victory of Newtonian cosmogony diminished men's respect for Descartes and increased their respect for England. Both these causes inclined men favorably towards Locke."[73] Newtonian cosmology was inherently optimistic, because it pointed to an ordered and intelligible state of things in the universe. If humans could understand the universe, then perhaps they could harness its power for the common good. If humans were not bound by intellectual limits by authorities based on *a priori* assertions, there was no limit to the potentialities of human discovery and endeavor. As Bewkes, et al., pointed out, "the fact that Newton had demonstrated the harmony and intelligibility of physical nature suggested that the 'natural' could be discovered and other fields as well. As compared with Newtonian nature, for example, the realm of politics was decidedly chaotic. This chaos, eighteenth century thinkers believed, was the result of the blunders of men. Undoubtedly a true social system in which men can live together in a well-ordered society was discoverable."[74]

Locke thought he had presented an idea for such a society. He believed that humankind, in its natural state, was free to dispose of its life and property as it deemed proper. Humans also naturally existed in a state of absolute equality. Because nature dispersed its gifts of reason and freedom to all equally, no one person could lord over another as a result of being endowed more generously with others. Locke described this natural state of equality among all in this way: "wherein all the power in jurisdiction is reciprocal, no one having more than another, there being nothing more evident than that creatures of the same species and rank,

---

72. Becker, *Declaration of Independence*, 41.
73. Russell, *History of Western Philosophy*, 641.
74. Bewkes et al., *Faith and Reason*, 566.

promiscuously born to all the same advantages of Nature, and the use of the same faculties, should also be equal one amongst another, without subordination or subjection...."[75]

Based on these assertions, Locke proposed his idea of the social contract. Since each individual human being was free and independent, any form of government would have to be consented to by every free and independent person. Thus, government must always be by consent of the governed for common security and protection of property. Once the government is installed by the governed, the government is ruled by the will of the majority of its citizens. Locke wrote,

> Men being . . . by nature all free, equal, and independent, no one can be put out of this estate and subjected to the political power of another without his own consent, which is done by agreeing with other men, to join and unite into a community for their comfortable, safe, and peaceable living, one amongst another, in a secure enjoyment of their properties, and a greater security against any that are not of it. This any number of men may do, because it injures not the freedom of the rest; they're left, as they were, in the liberty of the state of Nature. When any number of men have so consented to make one community or government, they are there by presently incorporated, and make one body politic, wherein the majority have a right to act and conclude the rest.[76]

Locke's positions on political theory are inextricably connected to his theory on religious practice and the role of religion in the state. Simply put, he was an exponent of full religious freedom. He defined the church in terms that are similar to his social contract theory. His view of the church was that it is a voluntary organization. For Locke, a person's faith is just that, a personal decision that involves no one else except that person and God. He said of the church in his *Letter Concerning Toleration*, "I say it is a free and voluntary society. Nobody is born a member of any church; otherwise the religion of parents would descend unto children by the same right of inheritance as their temporal estates, and everyone would hold his faith by the same tenure he does his lands, than which nothing can be imagined more absurd."[77] The role of the state is to secure the liberty of its citizens to worship how they choose, not to compel them

---

75. Locke, *Concerning Civil Government*, II.4.
76. Ibid., VIII.95.
77. Locke, *Letter Concerning Toleration*, 4.

to worship how it chooses. The state cannot compel faith because the role of the state is to implement law by force and faith does not arise out of force but out of persuasion. Thus, the state must protect an environment where religious reasoning and persuasion may flourish. Locke illustrated this point by presenting Christ as the model Persuader:

> If, like the Captain of our salvation, they sincerely desired the good of souls, they would tread in the steps and follow the perfect example of that Prince of Peace, who sent out His soldiers to the subduing of nations, and gathering them into His Church, not armed with the sword, or other instruments of force, but prepared with the Gospel of peace and with the exemplary holiness of their conversation. This was His method. Though if infidels were to be converted by force, if those that are either blind or obstinate were to be drawn off from their errors by armed soldiers, we know very well that it was much more easy for Him to do it with armies of heavenly legions than for any son of the Church, how potent soever, with all his dragoons.[78]

Locke's intellectual consistency between his political theory, his theory of the state, and his positions on religious liberty are clearly seen. What is also clear is the impact of the Enlightenment on the value Locke placed upon personal liberty. For Locke, personal liberty was the natural state of every human being. It was the basis for the social contract, and it was also the basis for the church. Both the church and the state were organizations set up by the free and voluntary choice of individuals.

This is in stark contrast to the Puritan conception of the state and the church. Recall that for the Puritans, the basis for both state and church was the covenant which humans entered into with God. The authority of God's word revealed and obedience to it were at the very center of the notion of the covenant for the Puritans. Not so for Locke. Locke's social contract was not centered on God, but on humankind in the natural state. Becker wrote, "The older version, which was a compact between the people and God in person, Locke could not use because, as we saw, nature had stepped in between God and man. Locke, like everyone else, had therefore to make his way, guided by reason in conscience, through Nature to find the will of God; and the only version of the original compact from which he could derive governmental authority, was such a compact as men, acting according to their nature, would enter into among themselves...."[79]

---

78. Ibid., 2.
79. Becker, *Declaration of Independence*, 63.

The Enlightenment emphasis on the authority of reason would have a profound impact on the Founders. First, deism emphasized ethical concerns because of its focus on the goodness of the Supreme Being and His having created humans with the capacity to reason. Also, even though deists rejected the divinity of Jesus, they extolled His moral example and teachings. Locke's statements on the role of religion and the state fit well within the deistic value system acclaiming freedom of religious choice. Holmes wrote, "Their fundamental belief in reason and equality drove them to embrace liberal political ideals. In the eighteenth century, many Deists advocated universal education, freedom of the press, and separation of church and state. These principles are commonplace in the twenty-first century, but they were radical in the eighteenth."[80] Deism would also influence many of the Founders' views of God. This point is most clearly seen in Jefferson's references to God in the Declaration of Independence as he refers to Him in impersonal terms, such as "Creator," "nature's God," "Supreme Judge of the World," and "Divine Providence." It is also seen in the fact that the U.S. Constitution in no way references God meaningfully,[81] which in itself is an unembellished distinction from the Puritan way of establishing a government.

Second, the New Learning was well established in the universities by the time the Founders' generation was being educated. May wrote that while the universities still maintained a desire for deference to tradition, "Everywhere periodic student riots showed that these rules roused to resentment. In their classes, their clubs, and their libraries, students encountered books and ideas that aroused more disturbing questions than their elders intended. The Founding Fathers were products of colleges which were conservative and didactic in intent but, fortunately, somewhat confused in practice."[82] The New Learning emphasis shifted from theology to morality as its authority moved from revelation to reason, and as it did, it imported the value system of the Enlightenment which was squarely centered on personal liberty. As Lambert stated,

> At the heart of Calvinism was the notion that God's grace, not good works, was the means of salvation. Now the Enlightenment

---

80. Holmes, *Faiths of the Founding Fathers*, 25.

81. The phrase "in the year of our Lord" is used in Article VII at the closing of the document. The expression does not meaningfully refer to God because it was an idiomatic way of referencing the date.

82. May, *Enlightenment*, 33–34.

boldly put the focus on human acts and dismissed as abstractions or superstitions ideas that God somehow "saved" people. In constructing their "Christian Common-wealth," the Puritan Fathers had been guided by Christian principles, more specifically, those of the Calvinist turn. Now many of the most influential men who would become the Founding Fathers became severe critics of the Puritans' most cherished beliefs, including that of God's central role in shaping the course of human existence.[83]

RADICAL WHIG IDEOLOGY AND ITS ROLE IN THE SHIFT

When one considers the sum of American revolutionary thought, his mind is really being drawn toward what scholars have called radical, or real, Whig ideology.[84] Radical Whig ideology was developed by the English Dissenters of the early eighteenth century. Its roots lie in the English Civil War which culminated in the execution of Charles I in 1649, the Commonwealth period under Oliver Cromwell during the 1650s, and the Glorious Revolution of 1688.

Simply put, the controversies of the 1600s in England were based on the power struggle between Parliament and the crown. After the installation of William and Mary in 1688, it was clear that Parliament was to have the upper hand in the mixed monarchy of England. But by the 1720s, weaknesses in the system were showing themselves. The king (with whom the Church of England was closely aligned) was using bribery to control the Parliament. Thus, to "Commonwealth men" of the early eighteenth century, the tide of power was shifting away from rule of the people through the Parliament and toward the arbitrary rule of the dually aligned monarchy and Church. The Dissenters were those who opposed this perceived shift in power. Marsden effectively described the fundamental belief system of radical Whig ideology when he wrote, "[Dissenters] shared with the Puritans the belief that high-handed monarchical power is always supported by ecclesiastical privilege. Therefore, the Commonwealth men championed both the inalienable rights of humanity to life, liberty,

---

83. Lambert, *Founding Fathers*, 172–73.

84. For treatments of radical Whig ideology, see Robbins, *Eighteenth Century Commonwealthman*; Maier, *From Resistance to Revolution*; Bailyn, *Ideological Origins*; Colbourn, *Lamp of Experience*; and Bonomi, *Under the Cope of Heaven*. For works by radical Whigs, see Sidney, *Discourses Concerning Government*; Trenchard and Gordon, *Cato's Letters*; and Milton, *Areopagitica*.

and property, in the tradition of John Locke, and the inalienable rights of conscience in the traditions of English religious dissent."[85]

The Commonwealth men viewed the Church of England with great suspicion, because to them it closely resembled Catholicism, a system which represented superstition, arbitrary privilege, and authoritarianism. These undesirable features were also marks of the monarchy, in contrast to dissenting Protestantism which championed common-sense reason as well as individual liberty under God. Thus, as Noll wrote, the notion that "unchecked power led to corruption and corruption to unchecked power, and that the arbitrary exercise of unchecked power must by its very nature result in the demise of liberty, law, and natural rights"[86] were at the center of radical Whig ideology.

Radical Whig ideology had some notable connections with Christianity, including some equally notable departures from it. The Commonwealth men shared a low view of human nature with the Puritans, as well as a disdain for despotic authority and an emphasis on liberty as bestowed by God. But they did not garner these convictions from Scripture, nor did they submit to Scripture as their authority as the Puritans did.

Like the Puritans, the Commonwealth men were opposed to monarchical/ecclesiastical rule. But they did not define liberty in the same way the Puritans did. As Noll observed, "Puritanism had grown out of a particular understanding of the way in which men were freed *from* sin; the overriding concern of the Whigs was to preserve freedom from tyranny."[87] Still, because radical Whig ideology and Christianity were closely linked through the English dissenting tradition, it became difficult to discern where one ended and the other began. Again, Noll stated, "In the crisis atmosphere of the Revolution the Whig struggle to preserve natural rights and the Christian struggle to protect God-given privileges often became the same thing."[88]

The primary source of radical Whig ideology was English Enlightenment thought. Newton and Locke were particularly important to Whig

---

85. Marsden, *Religion and American Culture*, 45. Religious dissenters in England were those not aligned with the Church of England: Baptists, Quakers, Puritans, etc. Many came to America, but many also stayed in England.

86. Noll, *Christians in the American Revolution*, 23.

87. Ibid., 55. Emphasis in the original.

88. Ibid., 56–57. This will become a salient point in later chapters.

thinkers. John Milton was an important source for Radical Whig ideology as well, particularly his *Areopagitica*, which he wrote in 1644. This work sought to press the issue of freedom of speech, since at the time the government required licenses of authors for the publication of written works. His work is also relevant to the issue of freedom of conscience, but the points he pressed were all based on the idea of individual liberty.

Newton's scientific discoveries and Locke's political theory underscored the notions of the power of human reason over arbitrary authority and the natural state of humankind in liberty and equality. Locke's work on social contract theory and freedom of conscience were also central to radical Whig ideology. Caroline Robbins wrote of Newton's influence on radical Whig ideology: "He connected earth and heaven in a vast unity working according to discoverable laws. Descartes had done much to free inquiry from restrictions. Newton freed scientists from Cartesian assumptions. His principles made dogmatism and intolerance impossible. They imposed upon philosophers new responsibilities and new methods. They must now reexamine the unity of Creation. They must have courage to avoid arbitrary conclusions."[89] Her assessment of Locke's influence on radical Whig thinkers was that, "[Whigs] found a revolutionary potential in Locke's philosophy, as well as in his *Treatises*."[90]

This potential was particularly evident in Locke's views on the right of the governed to overthrow despotic rulers. Locke's position, adopted and enshrined in the Declaration of Independence, was that if a government abuses the natural liberty of the governed, the people have the right to overturn it. Locke wrote, "exceeding the bounds of authority is no more a right in a great than a petty officer, no more justifiable in a king than a constable."[91] Following this statement, he anticipated an objection: "May the commands, then, of a prince be opposed?"[92] His answer was that "force is to be opposed to nothing but to unjust and unlawful force. Whoever makes any opposition in any other case draws on himself a just condemnation, both from God and man; and so no such danger [of anarchy or chaos] or confusion will follow, as is often suggested."[93]

---

89. Robbins, *Eighteenth Century Commonwealthman*, 70.
90. Ibid., 87.
91. Locke, *Concerning Civil Government*, XVIII.202.
92. Ibid., XVIII.203.
93. Ibid., XVIII.204.

To appreciate the radical element in Whig thought, it is appropriate to pause and briefly assess the social situation that radical Whig ideology addressed, particularly just prior to the American Revolution. Wood has made a remarkable contribution to American revolutionary history. His work *The Radicalism of the American Revolution* is important because in it, Wood demonstrated that the Revolution was not merely a war of secession, but was rather driven by truly radical ideas, ideas that would forever change the political, economic, religious, and social fabric of the West.

First, it is important to note that political liberty was a hallmark of English life, even before the strife of the 1600s. It was assumed by English subjects, and it did not exist anywhere else in Europe as prominently as it existed in England. The French monarchy, for example, was based squarely on the principle of the divine right of kings and absolute monarchy. Nothing close to English liberty existed there. Wood observed that, "Even the young Prince of Wales, soon to be George III, shared in this unmonarchical celebration of liberty. 'The pride, the glory of Britain, and the direct end of its constitution,' he said, 'is political liberty.' No unruly American provincial could have put it better."[94] Still, eighteenth century Englishmen and American colonists alike knew full well that they were subjects to the British monarch.

The notion of personal freedom was still foreign to most ordinary people of the eighteenth century. It is widely taken as a given in today's society but to eighteenth century people, personal freedom was not for ordinary folk but was a mark of the upper class. The aristocracy had the freedom to pursue lives of leisure, but everyone else had to work for subsistence. As Wood observed, "The liberality for which gentlemen were known connoted freedom—freedom from material want, freedom from the caprice of others, freedom from ignorance, and freedom from having to work with one's hands."[95] The idea of labor being the source of wealth or of happiness had not yet become commonplace. Wood wrote, "Hard, steady work was good for the character of common people: it kept them out of trouble; it lifted them out of idleness and barbarism; and it instilled in them the proper moral values; but it was not thought to expand the prosperity of the society."[96] Emphases upon individual lib-

---

94. Wood, *Radicalism*, 14.
95. Ibid., 33.
96. Ibid.

erty, social equality, and the reasonable natural faculties of the intellect placed by Enlightenment and Whig thinkers took hold among the general American populace after the Revolution. Until then, personal freedom was commonly understood to be solely for the upper ranks of society. According to Wood, "Traditionally consumption was regarded as both the privilege of the gentry and as an obligation of their rank. Gentlemen responded to unemployment among the laboring ranks by ordering another pair of boots or a new hat.... 'To be born for no other Purpose than to consume the Fruits of the Earth,' wrote Henry Fielding in 1751, 'is the Privilege (if it may be really called a Privilege) of a very few.'"[97]

Republicanism assailed this mindset. Republicanism was a notion birthed and developed by radical Whig ideology, indeed a notion that brought the United States into existence. Republicanism brought representative government, separation of powers, free-market economy, and religious liberty to Western culture. Republican ideas are at the heart of radical Whig ideology. Wood stated, "[republicanism] offered new conceptions of the individual, the family, the state, and the individual's relationship to the family, the state, and other individuals. Indeed, republicanism offered nothing less than new ways of organizing society. It defied and dissolved the older monarchical connections and presented people with alternative kinds of attachments, new sorts of social relationships."[98] It was the radical Whigs and their ideas that birthed and nurtured republicanism in America, and to the consequent views on religion's role in the state the study now turns.

American colonists in the eighteenth century, especially after the Treaty of Paris concluded the French and Indian War in 1763, were not intimately acquainted with the injuries and insults against individual liberties suffered by their forefathers long ago and far away in England during the 1600s. They were barely aware of the intricacies of all that being subjects to a king entailed, since that king was separated from them by three thousand miles of cold ocean. However, they did know something of dissent, particularly religious dissent, many of them having come to America to escape the Church of England. Although radical Whig ideology had subsided after the 1720s in England, it continued to gain an increased following in the colonies. Patricia Bonomi wrote, "In the

---

97. Ibid., 34.
98. Ibid., 96.

American colonies, a number of which had been settled at least in part by refugees from the religious politics of the Old World, two-thirds or more of the people fell under the designation of dissenters. This created a receptive environment for literature that denounced ecclesiastical tyranny and promoted freedom of conscience."[99]

There were several radical Whig writers in England during the course of the eighteenth century: Richard Cumberland, Robert Molesworth, Joseph Addison, Algernon Sidney and Walter Moyle to name a few. Of all the radical English Whig writers, none had a greater following than John Trenchard and Thomas Gordon because their journal, *The Independent Whig*, was the only major publication that was printed in American editions before the Revolution.[100] This journal appeared in London from 1720–1723 and was republished over the next twenty-five years.[101] It was dedicated to, among other things, complete religious liberty. Its subtitle was "a Defense of Primitive Christianity, and of Our Ecclesiastical Establishment, Against the Exorbitant Claims and Encroachments of Fanatical and Disaffected Clergymen." Trenchard and Gordon published another set of writings together entitled *Cato's Letters*, subtitled "Essays on Liberty, Civil and Religious, And other important Subjects." *Cato's Letters* had a more secular focus, but as seen in the title, still addressed issues related to religious liberty.

The Roman Republic (ca. 509–27 BC) was used as a source by Whig writers because it was seen as a model of a virtuous state, one which had for centuries protected the liberty of its citizens, but which was destroyed by the forces of tyranny in the Roman revolution of the first century BC. Keillor stated, "Though Radical Whigs came out of a zealous, militant Protestant tradition, they could not go to the New Testament for political blueprints for society. It had none. So they turned to Roman writers who praised the Roman Republic and deplored the lack of virtue leading to its downfall: Sallust, Tacitus, Cicero, Plutarch."[102] According to Trenchard

---

99. Bonomi, *Under the Cope of Heaven*, 195.

100. Ibid. A pamphlet by John Milton was printed in America, but this was not as influential as the writings of Trenchard and Gordon.

101. Robbins, *Eighteenth-Century Commonwealthmen*, 115.

102. Keillor, *This Rebellious House*, 87. The ancient republics, Athens, Carthage, Sparta, and Rome, were exceptions to the Enlightenment view that humankind can learn nothing valuable from the past. The Roman Republic was particularly so. Wood states, "The eighteenth century was particularly fascinated by the writings of the golden age of

and Gordon, the Roman Republic owed its rapid rise in economic and military power to its protection of liberty. As Robbins noted, "It stimulated its citizens to greater exertions. Nothing was too hard for liberty. Great discoveries in arts and sciences occurred in countries where free inquiry was allowed. Preservation an extension of liberty was all important."[103]

Given the ancient example of a noble republic which was destroyed by neglecting the protection of its first principles, Trenchard and Gordon sought to prevent such destruction from happening in their own country. A great deal of optimism was expressed in the efficacy of liberty in securing progress. There was therefore a consistent attack upon the Church of England, which Trenchard and Gordon viewed as a twin of Catholicism. Robbins wrote, "The anticlericalism of the *Independent Whig* is its most striking characteristic.... First of all, so long as the exiled Stuarts continued to exist and to profess Catholicism, there persisted a strong and vigorous prejudice against the Protestant but High-church group that were suspected of Jacobitism and of a belief in divine right."[104]

Trenchard and Gordon's writings on liberty are reminiscent of Locke's writings on the subject. Indeed, the influence of the Enlightenment upon radical Whig ideology is detected most unmistakably at this point. This quote from a passage in *Cato's Letters*, provided by Robbins, demonstrates the debt radical Whig ideology owed to Locke:

> [*Cato's Letters* asserted] without the right of resistance men cannot defend liberty, the chief topic of his letters. All Men are born free. Liberty is a Gift which they receive from God himself, nor can they alienate the same by Consent, though possibly they may forfeit it by Crimes. No man has Power over his own Life, or to dispose of his own Religion, and cannot consequently transfer the Power of either to anybody else; much less can he give away the Lives and Liberties, Religion or acquired Property of his posterity, who will be born free as himself was born, and can never be bound by his wicked and ridiculous Bargain.[105]

Roman literature—'the First Enlightenment,' as Peter Gay has called it—the two centuries from the breakdown of the republic in the middle of the first century B.C. to the reign of Marcus Aurelius in the middle of the second century A.D." (Wood, *Radicalism*, 100).

103. Robbins, *Eighteenth-Century Commonwealthmen*, 125.

104. Ibid., 116.

105. Ibid., 124.

In this passage we find Locke's ideas that humans are free in their natural state, liberty is not surrendered when a government is consented to, and the equality of all on the basis of an equal bestowal of gifts upon all by nature. Moreover, Noll demonstrated how Trenchard and Gordon's writings provide another example of the fine line between Christian values and radical Whig ideology. Noll pointed out that, though Trenchard and Gordon regularly used Christian language, they based their convictions upon human reason, not Scripture. Noll quoted Trenchard and Gordon as writing, "Why did we, or how could we, leave *Popery*, and embrace the *Reformation*, but because our own *private Reason* told us; and *Scripture*, of which we made *our selves the Judges*, told us? . . . As we must judge from Scripture what is Orthodoxy; so we must judge from Reason, what is Scripture."[106] This passage gives further evidence that Enlightenment philosophy was at the core of radical Whig ideology because of its unreserved commitment to the authority of reason, which was so important to the rise and spread of the notion of religious liberty and disestablishment of religion from the state.

THE CONCEPTION OF RELIGION'S ROLE IN THE STATE BY 1789

A great distance was traversed in American conceptions of religion's role in the state between the founding of Massachusetts Bay Colony in 1630 and the enacting of the Constitution in 1789. This chapter has attempted to demonstrate that the Great Awakening, the English Enlightenment, and radical Whig ideology were critical to the shift from the Puritan to the Constitutional model of the role of religion in the state. The Puritans established a Christian state, one that united civil and ecclesiastical life.

The Puritan view of religious freedom was, as Noll called it, positive rather than negative, in that they escaped the persecution of the Church of England to American shores in order to establish a system of religion and government on their own terms. They were not intending to offer complete freedom of religion to every colonist, or negative religious freedom, to again use Noll's term. This would have effectively separated religion from the state and would recognize religion as a matter of private conscience. Lambert stated, "To the Puritans who fled persecution, Massachusetts Bay represented the freedom to practice without interfer-

---

106. Noll, *America's God*, 61.

ence the one true faith, which they based solely on the Bible, correctly interpreted."[107]

After the Awakening, the Enlightenment, and radical Whig ideology had made their impacts upon religious, political, economic, and intellectual life during the late seventeenth and early to mid-eighteenth centuries, the shift in the American conception of the place of religion in the state was complete. The model the Founders sought to preserve as a fundamental part of American political and social life was that of disestablishment and of religious freedom, and they did so both in the text of the Constitution and in the First Amendment.[108] According to Lambert, "...the United States Constitution created the framework for a secular state open to all persons regardless of religion.... Rather than viewing religion as an integrative force, the Founding Fathers considered it to be divisive, threatening their desire to form a 'more perfect union.' American society had grown more pluralistic and sectarian from the Great Awakening to the Revolution."[109]

Clearly then, in contrast to the Puritans, the Founders did not seek to create a Christian state, but a state marked by a plurality of faiths. They sought to establish a nation in which the individual conscience could be free to choose from an open market of religious ideas, a market not unlike that presented by the itinerant preachers of the Great Awakening of the eighteenth century. The flourishing of faith would be encouraged, not by the volubility, but the silence of the state in religious affairs.

This study has already noted the pluralism which marked the American colonies during the period of the Great Awakening. By the time the American Revolution commenced in 1775, the Awakening had made religious pluralism in the colonies even more pronounced. According to Holmes, the major religious groups found during this time in the colonies were Quakers, Moravians, Mennonites, Congregationalists, Presbyterians, Baptists, Anglicans, Roman Catholics, Lutherans, and the Dutch Reformed.[110] Methodism would begin to grow as a distinct denomination

---

107. Lambert, *Founding Fathers*, 3.

108. For treatments of the founders and the role of religion in the state, see Gaustad, *Faith of the Founders*; Holmes, *Faiths of the Founding Fathers*; Lambert, *Founding Fathers*; Bowen, *Miracle at Philadelphia*; West, *Politics of Revelation*; Wood, *Radicalism*; and Wood, *Creation of the American Republic*.

109. Lambert, *Founding Fathers*, 238.

110. Holmes, *Faiths of the Founding Fathers*, 5–25.

as a result of the preaching of John Wesley during the Great Awakening, but it would not become a major one until the Second Great Awakening in the early nineteenth century.

The Founders were conscious of the plurality of faiths that existed in the colonies and the religious choices that the Awakening presented to individuals. Whitefield died in 1770, just five years before the battles of Lexington and Concord, thus they all were acquainted with his enormous evangelical influence on the colonial religious life. Taken as a whole, the Founders were not uncomfortable with this pluralism. Writing on the Constitutional Convention of 1787, Catherine Drinker Bowen assessed the contemporary social climate by asserting, "if Virginia had started out as Anglican, Massachusetts as Puritan, Pennsylvania as Quaker, they had gradually won to a wider conception and wider liberty—within Protestant limits, that is—a limit defined with nice but unconscious irony by President Ezra Stiles of Yale College as 'universal, equal, religious, protestant liberty.' Within these boundaries the states quite early practiced a surprising diversity—presbyter and priest alike would have called it an anarchy—which was to become a strength to the nation rather than a weakness."[111]

While it is not within the scope of this work to analyze and explain the views of each Founder related to the issue of religion and the state, it is appropriate to give special attention to some of the aspects of the positions held by Jefferson (1743–1826) and Madison (1751–1836). Because of their early work in ensuring religious liberty in Virginia, and seeing Virginia's model of religious liberty adopted into the Constitution, these two Founders are particularly relevant. Before delving into Jefferson and Madison on religion and the state, however, it is interesting to note and valuable to bear in mind how close some of the other influential Founders were in their positions on religion and the state. John G. West did a study on several Founders' positions, including Benjamin Franklin, John Witherspoon, George Washington, James Wilson, Alexander Hamilton, John Adams, John Jay, Thomas Jefferson, and James Madison. He noted a number of common themes in their positions, but most striking was their commonly held view that religious freedom ought to be one of the distinguishing marks of the new American society. He wrote,

---

111. Bowen, *Miracle at Philadelphia*, 215.

> First and foremost is the Founders' attachment to religious liberty. Evangelicals such as Witherspoon and Jay, no less than freethinkers such as Franklin and Jefferson, believed in the right of all sects to worship God as their consciences dictate. Regardless of personal religious preferences, none of the Founders wished the government to interfere with the religious opinions of the citizenry to promote either evangelical orthodoxy (in the case of Witherspoon and Jay) or a rational Unitarianism (in the case of Franklin and Jefferson). All were content to allow competing sects to flourish in America free from government encumbrance. Religious obligation was considered separate and distinct from civic obligation, though it was not regarded as inferior to it.[112]

If anyone can be said to have followed the Enlightenment values of reason, nature, and optimism, it would be Jefferson. One can almost hear Locke speaking through Jefferson in the Declaration of Independence. The statement "... they are endowed by their Creator with certain inalienable rights; that among these are life, liberty, and the pursuit of happiness. That, to secure these rights, governments are instituted among men, deriving their just powers from the consent of the governed; that, whenever any form of government becomes destructive of these ends, it is the right of the people to alter or abolish it...." reads very much like Locke's *Second Essay Concerning Civil Government*. Marsden wrote, "When Jefferson proclaimed in the Declaration that rights to life and liberty were beyond doubt, or 'self-evident,' he was summarizing views of Locke that had become commonplace in eighteenth-century political thought."[113]

Jefferson, as is widely known, was not an orthodox Christian but a deist. Deism, that "single banner"[114] of the Enlightenment as Montgomery asserted, was a powerful basis for Jefferson's desire to see religion disestablished and freedom of religion guaranteed. As a deist, Jefferson believed that freedom of conscience was a natural right that the state could not touch.

In 1779, he proposed a "Bill for Establishing Religious Freedom" in Virginia, and it was seven years later, with a great deal of help from his fellow Virginian and friend Madison, before it would become law. When it did become law in 1786, Jefferson had the privilege as governor

---

112. West, *Politics of Revelation*, 73–74.
113. Marsden, *Religion and American Culture*, 42.
114. Montgomery, *Shaping*, 48.

of signing it and it became known as the Virginia Statute for Religious Freedom. Most of the language Jefferson used in the bill was preserved in the Statute. Gaustad and Schmidt quoted an important passage from the Statute that reflects Jefferson's sentiments on disestablishment and freedom of conscience: "Be it enacted … that no man shall be compelled to frequent or support any religious worship, place, or ministry whatsoever, nor shall be enforced, restrained, molested, or burthened [sic] in his body or goods, nor shall otherwise suffer on account of his religious opinions or beliefs."[115] Thus, the year before the Constitutional Convention was assembled to craft a stronger government over the old system under the Articles of Confederation, Jefferson's bill overturned Anglican establishment in Virginia that started with the inception of the colony nearly two centuries earlier in 1607.

Jefferson's role in helping to define the role that religion would have in the United States under the Constitution was, at best, indirect. He was not present at the Convention assembling in Philadelphia in May, 1787. He was representing the United States as the American ambassador to France in Paris. Still, through his correspondence with Madison, Jefferson was able to keep abreast of the debates and issues the delegates to the Convention were discussing. In October of 1787, Madison sent Jefferson a copy of the newly signed Constitution to Paris for his perusal.

Jefferson replied in a letter dated December 20, 1787 that there was much to admire about the document, but there were still some problems. After listing some of the aspects of the document he liked, Jefferson famously remarked, "There are other good things of less moment. I will now add what I do not like. First the omission of a bill of rights providing clearly and without the aid of sophisms for freedom of religion, freedom of the press. . . ."[116] He explained the seriousness of the need for such a statement of basic rights: "Let me add that a bill of rights is what the people are entitled to against every government on earth, general or particular, and what no just government should refuse, or rest on inference."[117] The Bill of Rights had begun to be drafted in 1788 and satisfied Jefferson's desire. It was also a key element in winning over states reluctant to ratify the Constitution without such a clear statement of basic liberties.

115. Gaustad and Schmidt, *Religious History of America*, 125.
116. Jefferson to Madison, 90.
117. Ibid., 91.

The Relationship between Religion and the State, 1630–1789

Jefferson's high view of natural liberties is clearly seen, as well as his work in disestablishing religion in Virginia. Although he was not a delegate to the Convention, his correspondence with Madison urging the drafting of a bill of rights that should be added to the Constitution seems to have had a significant impact on his younger colleague. Madison did have some differences with Jefferson on the Constitution, and some of these are outlined in *Federalist* no. 49. But Madison and Jefferson were in fundamental agreement on the role of religion in the state, as evidenced by their work together on the Virginia Statute and the Constitution.

Madison's views on disestablishment and freedom of conscience were established as a young man of twenty years old, when in the summer of 1771 in Caroline County, Virginia, a Baptist preacher named John Waller was horsewhipped by the local parish priest for preaching without a license. John Waller was an associate of John Burruss, the first pastor of Polecat Church, which erected its own church building two years after the whipping. Polecat Church would later become Carmel Baptist Church and is still in existence in Caroline County, and is, in fact, one of the oldest churches in continuous service in the county. (I was a member of Carmel Baptist Church in the early 1990s as well as the church's Christian school principal.)

The account of this event was given by Lewis Peyton Little:

> In the spring of 1771 as he was holding divine worship in Caroline County, the minister of the parish (Morton) and his clerk (Thomas Buckner) with the sheriff (William Harris) came to the place. Mr. Morton strode up to the stage on which he stood and with his whip tumbled over the leaves of the book as Mr. Waller was giving out the psalm; but Waller held his thumb on the place until the whole was sung; then Mr. Waller began to pray; and his reverence Morton ran the butt of his whip into Waller's mouth and silenced him. After that the clerk, Buckner, pulled him down and dragged him and whipped him in so violent a manner (without the ceremony of a trial) that poor Waller was presently in a gore of blood and will carry the scars to his grave. However, Waller, sore and bloody as he was, remounted the stage and preached a most extraordinary sermon.[118]

Madison heard of the incident and deeply sympathized with the plight of persecuted Christians such as Waller. Michael Novak wrote that,

---

118. Little, *Imprisoned Preachers*, 229.

"As a member of the Church of England, he was morally offended when members of his church indulged like 'imps of Satan' in the persecution of other believers."[119] As a student at Princeton, he was influenced by the teachings of John Witherspoon, the sole clergyman to sign the Declaration of Independence and a champion of religious liberty. Witherspoon's teaching and the experience of the persecuted Baptists in Caroline County gave Madison a fervent desire to see religious liberty take hold in Virginia. In 1776, Madison was a delegate to the Virginia Convention, which under the leadership of George Mason, framed the Virginia Declaration of Rights. Section 16 of that document affirmed that faith is compelled only by individual reason and private conviction, and is not the concern of the state. The Virginia Declaration would be very influential in disestablishment in Virginia, and was also an important source for Madison as he began drafting the Bill of Rights in 1788.

Madison's role in the development of the Constitution is virtually unmatched by any of his contemporaries and his views on preserving natural liberties through a republican style of government are outlined in many of his writings. In *Federalist* no. 10, he expressed his belief that a representative government, as opposed to a pure democracy, would better protect the people from the tyranny of the majority. A pure democracy, by definition, must be small. The majority produced by a democracy would be monolithic in its position, and would then be in a position to lord over the minority. He wrote that in a democracy, "a common passion or interest will, in almost every case, be felt by a majority of the whole; a communication and concert result from the form of government itself; and there is nothing to check the inducements to sacrifice the weaker party or an obnoxious individual. Hence it is that such democracies ... have ever been found incompatible with personal security or the rights of property."[120] By contrast, a representative government, such as a republic, can grow in population and territory without the limits that a democracy has. With growth in size, a republic's free marketplace of ideas also grows.

Even a majority will have a range of opinions that will keep it from exercising tyrannical lordship over a minority. Madison said, "Extend the sphere, and you take in a greater variety of parties and interests; you make it less probable that a majority of the whole will have a common motive

---

119. Novak, *On Two Wings*, 52.
120. Hamilton, Madison, and Jay, *Federalist*, 51.

to invade the rights of other citizens; or if such a common motive exists, it will be more difficult for all who feel it to discover their own strength, and to act in unison with each other."[121] Thus, no one religious sect will be able to impose its will upon the whole. Religious groups must compete for adherents in a free marketplace ruled by individual choice, just as other religious groups do. Madison further clarifies this point in a letter written to Jefferson during the fall of 1787. He wrote, "In a large society, the people are broken into so many interests and parties, that a common sentiment is less likely to be felt, and the requisite concert less likely to be formed, by a majority of the whole. The same security seems requisite for the civil as for the religious rights of individuals. If the same sect form a majority and have the power, other sects will be sure to be depressed."[122]

Jefferson and Madison, because of their work in Virginia disestablishing religion from the state, were very influential in guiding the Constitutional debates toward disestablishment and religious freedom in all the states. And this is one of the great achievements of the American Constitution. For the first time, a Western nation divided religion and the state, based on the conviction that personal religious belief was not the concern of the state and had no jurisdiction over it. It was a revolutionary idea whose time had indeed come. The Great Awakening demonstrated to the colonists living in British North America that they could choose what religion they would follow from a variety of competing sects. The English Enlightenment thinkers Newton and Locke taught Americans that their world was not one shrouded in divine mystery and that God had bestowed reason upon the whole human race that they might understand His universe. Along with reason, God had given to humans basic rights, one of which was freedom of conscience which transcended all forms of outside human compulsion. Finally, radical Whig ideology took the Enlightenment notion of liberty and introduced it to ordinary people, seeking to throw off all royal and ecclesiastical authorities, which were seen as inherently tyrannical.

The Puritan model of an integration of religion and state, no matter how logically formulated or well-intentioned, could never survive against such powerful ideas that had decades to mature and develop around the ever-changing circumstances of colonial America in the eighteenth cen-

121. Ibid., 52.
122. Madison to Jefferson, 72–73.

tury. The difference between the Puritan and the Constitutional models of religion's role in the state is the difference between two distinct modes of thought: one is premodern, the other, modern.

The Founders were not attempting to do the same thing as the Puritans. They were not seeking to create a Christian state. They realized that to do such a thing would be to step backward into the premodern world, when they knew they were introducing a form of society that was different than any which had preceded them.

When Patrick Henry attempted to have Christianity recognized as the state religion of Virginia in 1785, he was met with the furious resistance of Madison who rebutted him in his famous Memorial and Remonstrance, which championed religious freedom. The Virginia Statute of Religious Freedom was the final outcome of that debate in Virginia, paving the road to the Bill of Rights. While the Puritans may have seen themselves as a new Israel establishing a theologically pure society, the Founders had no such notion in mind. As Montgomery said,

> In certain circles at the far right of the religious spectrum it is customary to wax eloquent on the "Bible religion of our Founding Fathers." We are implored to "return to the simple Gospel that made our Founding Fathers great," etc. Unhappily, though we might fervently wish that these sentiments were accurate, the fact is that they express a pure mythology. The idea of believing Christian Founding Fathers is very largely a pious myth, and if we want to arrive at a balanced and mature understanding of the relation between scriptural religion and our national heritage, we must rigorously carry out a process of demythologization at this point.[123]

Instead of contending for the idea of a Christian America as an apologetic for evangelical Christianity, evangelicals can and ought to demonstrate that religious liberty is at the heart of American heritage. This is an argument that is easily won, and an argument that lays the ground work for a much more effective apologetic based on the reliable authority of Scripture.

---

123. Montgomery, *Shaping*, 50–51.

2

The Thematic Landscape of the Christian America Thesis, 1977–2007

THE PREVIOUS CHAPTER ATTEMPTED to demonstrate that an important shift took place in American[1] views on the relationship between religion and the state between 1630 and 1789, from the Puritan model of a Christian state with positive religious freedom to that of a secular state offering negative religious freedom. The Puritan model of a Christian state was used in all the New England colonies in the seventeenth century except Rhode Island, which was a haven of religious freedom. As the proponents of Christian America have accurately observed, the establishment of colonies for the Puritans was a Christian, not a secular, enterprise. This model, while not precisely duplicated, was approximated by the Middle and Southern colonies. Thus, while strictly speaking the Puritan model was a local reality, its Christian basis serves as a paradigm for the other British colonies. At least three developments accounted for the shift: the impact of the Great Awakening, the English Enlightenment, and radical Whig ideology upon the social, political, and religious fabric of the colonies.

In the last thirty years, however, a large number of evangelical writers have presented a somewhat different viewpoint. Rather than interpreting America's religious identity in terms of being a secular state with uninhibited religious freedom, these writers have attempted to define the American identity according to a biblical paradigm. More specifically, they have understood the United States to have been founded as a Christian nation.

---

1. The term "American" in this context refers to the thirteen British North American colonies that would become the United States of America in 1776.

Two noteworthy events occurring in the late 1970s formed the impetus for the spread of CA in its contemporary form. First, in 1977, Peter Marshall and David Manuel produced a work entitled *The Light and the Glory*, a work which concluded that America is a new Israel which God founded based upon a covenant between Him and the nation. The second was the establishment of the Moral Majority in 1979 by Charles Stanley, D. James Kennedy, Jerry Falwell, and Tim LaHaye as a reaction against what they perceived as then-President Jimmy Carter's anemic response to a cultural drift toward secularism.[2]

Since that time, the CA thesis has gained in popularity as evidenced by the continuing publication of works to the present day which espouse the idea and are dedicated to its promulgation. The chapter will survey the contemporary CA thesis in terms of the historical, philosophical, and theological themes as presented by its proponents since 1977.[3] For each of these three thematic categories, the survey will examine a representative sample of writers demonstrating how the themes are used to promote the CA thesis. The survey will show that the CA thesis is not a simplistic argument, but has been developed into a multi-faceted contention by a wide range of evangelical writers over the last three decades.

HISTORICAL THEMES FOR THE CA THESIS

When drawing from history to defend the CA thesis, writers commonly addressed five common major themes:

---

2. Moyer, "Battle for the City," 2.

3. The evangelical proponents of CA to be treated in this chapter are as follows in order of publication date: Marshall and Manuel, *Light and the Glory*; Falwell, *Listen, America*; Whitehead, *Second American Revolution*; Robertson, *America's Dates With Destiny*; Eidsmoe, *Christianity and the Constitution*; LaHaye, *Faith of Our Founding Fathers*; Hart, *Faith and Freedom*; Amos, *Defending*; DeMar, *God and Government*, vol. 1; Beliles and McDowell, *America's Providential History*; Barton, *Myth of Separation*; Barton, *America's Godly Heritage*; DeMar, *America's Christian History*; Kennedy and Newcombe, *What If?*; Barton, *Original Intent*; Hutson, *Forgotten Features*; McDowell, *America, a Christian Nation?*; Beliles and Anderson, *Contending*; Lillback and Newcombe, *George Washington's Sacred Fire*; McDowell and Beliles, *American Dream*.

1. The faith of the Founders[4]
2. The sources appealed to by the Founders
3. The Christian character of colonial documents and early state constitutions
4. The Christian character of early colleges
5. The influence of the Great Awakening.

Faith of the Founders

Perhaps no other theme pertinent to the CA thesis is more hotly debated than whether or not it is appropriate to style the Founders "Christians." All proponents of CA, no matter how they defined the idea, insisted that, at the very least, the Founders shared a Christian metaphysical and ethical belief system. David Barton intended to prove this rhetorically by asking, "Did you realize that 52 of the 55 Founding Fathers who worked on the Constitution were members of orthodox Christian churches and many were evangelical Christians?"[5]

The majority of the books espousing CA presented a list of major and minor figures involved in the national founding and summarized their religious beliefs using primary source material. For example, Barton prided himself on this methodology in attempting to demonstrate that the Founders, with the exception of a very few, were boldly professing Christians. Contrasting his work *Original Intent* with the book *In Search of Christian America* by Mark Noll, George Marsden and Nathan Hatch, Barton wrote, "While allegedly examining the Founding Era, strikingly, 88 percent of the 'historical sources' on which they rely postdate 1900, and 80 percent postdate 1950! Conversely, in *Original Intent* the numbers are dramatically different. This book, unlike *In Search of Christian America*, examines not only the Founding Era but also the situation today . . . only 34 percent (rather than 88 percent) of its sources postdate 1900, and only 21 percent (rather than 80 percent) postdate 1950."[6]

---

4. When using the term "Founders," it is helpful to distinguish between the colonial Founders of the seventeenth century and the national Founders of the eighteenth century. The chapter is referring to the national Founders of the eighteenth century when using the term "Founders" unless otherwise specified.

5. Barton, *America's Godly Heritage*, 3.

6. Barton, *Original Intent*, 306–7.

Stephen McDowell also carefully cited the writings of selected Founders in his work, *America, A Christian Nation?* Some of the notable Founders McDowell quoted and identified as Christian were James Otis, Samuel Adams, John Jay, James Wilson, John Quincy Adams, Alexander Hamilton, Noah Webster, and Rufus King. McDowell quoted these particular individuals because of their contributions to the basis of American law. He cited Jay, the first chief justice of the Supreme Court, as stating, "the . . . natural law was given by the Sovereign of the Universe to all mankind."[7] Samuel Adams, described by McDowell as "signer of the Declaration and Father of the American Revolution," was quoted as saying, "In the supposed state of nature, all men are equally bound by the laws of nature, or to speak more properly, the laws of the Creator."[8] He also quoted Noah Webster, author of the first Webster's Dictionary: the "'Law of nature' is a rule of conduct arising out of the natural relations of human beings established by the Creator and existing prior to any positive precept [human law]. . . . These . . . have been established by the Creator and are, with a peculiar felicity of expression, denominated in Scripture, 'ordinances of heaven.'"[9]

Figures such as those above appeared in many of the CA works, but they are minor in comparison to luminaries such as George Washington, Thomas Jefferson, James Madison, or Benjamin Franklin. Minor figures which are cited by CA proponents are many: Barton himself defined a Founding Father as any person "who exerted significant influence in, provided prominent leadership for, or had a substantial impact upon the birth, development, and establishment of America, as an independent, self-governing nation."[10] By this standard, about 250 figures stood out as Founding Fathers in Barton's works. Other minor figures cited in CA works as believing Christians include Patrick Henry, Gouverneur Morris, John Adams, John Witherspoon, Roger Sherman, and William Findley.

These minor figures are not designated as such to minimize their contributions to the founding of the United States. Some, such as Witherspoon, exerted great influence on James Madison. John Adams was, of course, the second President of the United States and instrumental in the adop-

---

7. McDowell, *America, a Christian Nation?*, 8.

8. Ibid.

9. Ibid., 9.

10. Barton, *Original Intent*, 5.

tion of the Declaration of Independence before the Second Continental Congress. Still, their work, while greatly significant and indispensable to the cause of the early Republic, is dwarfed by that of George Washington (Generalissimo of the Continental Army, President of the Constitutional Convention, and first President of the United States), Thomas Jefferson (author of the Virginia Statute of Religious Freedom and the Declaration of Independence, and third President), James Madison (Father of the Constitution, author of the Bill of Rights, and fourth President), and Benjamin Franklin (signer of the Declaration and the Constitution and almost universally recognized then and now as embodying the spirit of the new nation).

What of the faith systems of the major figures? How did the CA proponents account for their beliefs? With the exception of Tim LaHaye, who described Jefferson as "the closet Unitarian who had nothing to do with the founding of our nation (he was in France being humanized by the French skeptics of the Enlightenment at the time),"[11] the CA writers affirmed that while all may not have been professing Christians, they at least shared a Christian ontological and ethical system. Peter Lillback and Jerry Newcombe wrote an extensive work entitled *George Washington's Sacred Fire*, in which they contended that Washington was clearly an observable Christian and not a deist as he is sometimes characterized. They wrote, "He was generally very quiet about anything pertaining to himself, including his faith, yet he was always concerned to respect the faith of others, attempting to practice his Christian faith privately, even while he at times openly affirmed his Christian beliefs in public. There are numerous accounts from family and military associates—too numerous to be dismissed—of people coming across Washington in earnest, private prayer."[12]

It was generally agreed upon by CA proponents that Thomas Jefferson was not an orthodox Christian in the sense that he accepted all the historic doctrines of the faith. Still, many CA proponents counted Jefferson as holding firmly to a form of the Christian tradition. John Eidsmoe created a list of nine points which summarized Jefferson's beliefs. Included in this list were a belief in monotheism, Jesus as the supreme moral example, the Bible as authoritative on ethical matters, and man having been

---

11. LaHaye, *Faith of Our Founding Fathers*, 13.
12. Lillback and Newcombe, *George Washington's Sacred Fire*, 34–35.

created by God as a free and rational creature.[13] While these beliefs by themselves certainly did not qualify Jefferson as an evangelical Christian (and Eidsmoe did not claim this for him), they did qualify him as being in alignment with basic Christian teaching.

James Madison was generally claimed by CA proponents as a Christian of the Calvinist sort. Having been heavily influenced by John Witherspoon, President of the College of New Jersey (now Princeton University) while he was a student there, Madison benefitted from theological teaching as well as classics, history, and philosophy. According to Eidsmoe, "One thing is certain: the Christian religion, particularly Rev. Witherspoon's Calvinism, influenced Madison's view of law and government."[14]

CA writers conceded that Benjamin Franklin, like Jefferson, was not an orthodox Christian, but his views were still in line with basic Christian teachings. The most commonly cited speech of Franklin's by CA writers was his motion on the floor of the Constitutional Convention on June 28, 1787 to adjourn for prayer during the controversy over which plan of the Constitution should be adopted. Below is a relevant portion of the speech taken from Mark Beliles and Douglas Anderson:

> I have lived, Sir, a long time, and the longer I live, the more convincing proofs I see of this truth: that God governs in the affairs of men. And if a sparrow cannot fall to the ground without his notice, is it probable that an empire can rise without His aid? We have been assured, Sir, in the Sacred Writings that 'except the Lord build the house, they labor in vain that build it (Psalm 127:1).... I therefore beg leave to move that, henceforth, prayers imploring the assistance of Heaven and its blessing on our deliberation be held in this assembly every morning... and that one or more of the clergy of this city be requested to officiate in that service.[15]

Because of Franklin's call to prayer, he was regarded as one of the great examples of piety and submission to God, and as one who did not shrink from calling upon His aid in urgent matters of state.

Much more could be drawn from CA writings on the faith of the Founders. Suffice here to say that it was universally agreed among the proponents of CA that the Founders as a whole were not irreligious, and the

13. Eidsmoe, *Christianity and the Constitution*, 245.
14. Ibid., 101.
15. Beliles and Anderson, *Contending*, 27.

vast majority of them were orthodox Christians. The conclusion drawn from this belief, as stated by Lillback and Newcombe, is "to substantiate the critical role that Christians and Christian principles played in the founding of our nation."[16]

Sources Appealed to by the Founders

While the Founders' individual and collective faith in Christian teachings was a powerful basis upon which CA is constructed, the sources consulted by the Founders in their own private and public writings were presented by CA writers as forming an equally firm basis for their assertions. Their contention was that the vast majority of these sources did not originate from the Enlightenment, but from biblical Christianity.

Eidsmoe and Barton both cited an ambitious study by Donald Lutz and Charles S. Hyneman. These scholars sifted through 3,154 references to sources used by the Founders. These references were found in books, articles, pamphlets, and so forth written between 1760 and 1805. This study found that the Bible accounted "for 34 percent of the direct quotes in the political writings of the Founding Era."[17] Barton's conclusion was that "The fact that the Founders quoted the Bible more frequently than any other source is indisputably a significant commentary on its importance in the foundation of our government."[18]

While the CA proponents affirmed that the Founders drew heavily upon Scripture as a source in their political writings, they also widely pointed to numerous other important sources. D. James Kennedy and Jerry Newcombe, for example, are among several of the Reformed CA writers who focused upon John Calvin as a significant contributor to the Founders' ideas on the Constitution. Calvin's theology was said to have played a major role through not only later political philosophers in England, but also through the collective civil thought and practice of the New England Puritans. Furthermore, since Calvin's work, *Institutes of the Christian Religion*, was his attempt to systematize the doctrines of the Bible, Kennedy and Newcombe were led to draw a truly bold conclusion. They wrote, "If we are going to get back to the principles that made America great, then we are going to have to get back to the principles of

---

16. Lillback and Newcombe, *George Washington's Sacred Fire*, 27.
17. Ibid. See also Eidsmoe, *Christianity and the Constitution*, 51.
18. Ibid., 226.

John Calvin, because it is precisely his principles that made this nation great. John Calvin is considered to be one of the greatest original thinkers of all time; however, this is really not accurate, because Calvin was not so much an originator as he was an expositor of the Scriptures—an expounder of the teachings of Jesus Christ. So, in an indirect sense, the virtual founder of this nation was Jesus Christ and His teachings."[19]

Gary DeMar asserted some conclusions of his own regarding Calvin and Calvinism's influence upon the framers of the Constitution. The depravity of man, one of the fundamental doctrines Calvin treated in his *Institutes*, is clearly seen in the constitutional separation of powers, according to DeMar. In order to prevent centralization of power in the hands of one man, or even one body of men, the framers' dividing of powers into three branches and establishing a system of checks and balances was derived directly from Calvin's thought on man's fallen nature and proclivity to seek and abuse power. DeMar wrote, "The framers of the Constitution were also aware of the biblical doctrine of the depravity of man. Man, left to his own desires, seeks to place himself in places of power and authority unless there are certain checks and balances to stop him.... In order to circumvent a movement toward centralized tyranny, a system of checks and balances was instituted patterned after biblical law."[20]

William Blackstone, Samuel Rutherford, and John Locke were each claimed by CA writers as some of the most important Christian sources used by the Founders. John Whitehead, in his work entitled *The Second American Revolution*, gave a thorough treatment of Blackstone and Rutherford. Blackstone was an English jurist and a contemporary of most the Founders. His *Commentaries on the Laws of England* was published in the late 1760s and was popular in the American colonies. As Whitehead explained, Blackstone's understanding of law was firmly rooted in God's revelation in nature and in Scripture. All human activity is governed by law, and every person is answerable to law, which is revealed expressly by God. According to Whitehead, "In Blackstone's view, and in the eyes of those who founded the United States, every right or law comes from God, and the very words *rights, laws, freedoms*, and so on are meaningless without their divine origin."[21]

19. Kennedy and Newcombe, *What If?*, 59.
20. DeMar, *God and Government*, 142.
21. Whitehead, *Second American Revolution*, 31; emphasis original.

Samuel Rutherford, the seventeenth-century scholar and author of *Lex, Rex or, the Law and the Prince* wrote his work in 1644. Rutherford, Whitehead claimed, is responsible for handing down to the Founders the ethical standards of the Reformation through his influence upon Locke and John Witherspoon. *Lex, Rex* was written at the beginning of the English Civil War in order to counter the doctrine of the divine right of kings which affirmed that the king was above the law. Whitehead wrote that Rutherford's influence was most widely felt in the colonies in the form of two principles: "First, there was the concept of the covenant or constitution between the ruler and God and the people. This covenant, Rutherford argued, could not grant the state absolute or unlimited power without violating God's law. . . . Rutherford's second principle declared that all men are created equal. Since all men are born sinners, Rutherford reasoned that no man is superior to any other man. He established the principle of equality and liberty among men, which was later written into the Declaration of Independence."[22] Thus, Whitehead saw a direct line of thought on the nature of law from the Reformation view based upon Scripture to the English Civil War of the seventeenth century, to the adoption of the Declaration of Independence and establishment of the United States in 1776.

Locke was also claimed by CA proponents as an important biblical thinker who helped establish the Founders' Christian-based conclusions about the nature and role of government. Benjamin Hart wrote of Locke, that "His 'social compact' theory was not really a theory at all, but was derived mainly from Scripture and his experience with the Congregational church, or 'conventicle,' which was patterned after the example of the apostolic churches."[23] Locke's authorship of a Christian apologetic work (*The Reasonableness of Christianity*, 1695) and paraphrases of Romans, Galatians, Ephesians and 1 and 2 Corinthians was further encouragement for CA proponents. Hart claimed that it was Locke's reading of Genesis that contributed to his idea of the social contract. The free state of nature enjoyed by man was for Locke, according to Hart, a condition which existed prior to the Fall. After Adam's sin, civil government would be necessary for the protection of private property. Furthermore, Hart

---

22. Ibid., 29–30.
23. Hart, *Faith and Freedom*, 76.

connected Locke's position on the individual's freedom of conscience to the individual's relationship to the government. He wrote,

> Locke was merely applying Protestant religious principles to the world of politics. If the individual has the authority to interpret Scripture for himself, without a human agent acting as intermediary, isn't it also up to the individual to determine his own relationship to the government and indeed to the rest of society? Under extreme circumstances, thought Locke, the conscience of the individual, informed by Scripture and right reason, can supersede the government and even the collective judgment of the group because society is a voluntary union, from which anyone can exit if he so chooses.[24]

The social compact theory of Locke that was heavily drawn upon by the Founders in their public writings and clearly seen in the founding documents was less the product of Enlightenment thought and much more the product of Locke's own Protestant interpretation of the Bible. Hart declared, "He was himself a devout Christian. Locke's notions about government have their foundation in the Scriptures. The Declaration has been called a revolutionary document. But its power came from its affirmation of truths long established."[25] Barton cited a quote from James Wilson, an associate justice on the first Supreme Court and a signer of the Constitution in denying that Locke was anything less than a committed Christian: "I am equally far from believing that Mr. Locke was a friend to infidelity [a disbelief in the Bible and in Christianity].... The high reputation which he deservedly acquired for his enlightened attachment to the mild and tolerating doctrines of Christianity secured to him the esteem and confidence of those who were its friends."[26]

The Founders drew from a plethora of sources, as demonstrated particularly by Eidsmoe and Barton in their discussions of the study by Lutz and Hyneman. Other prominent thinkers cited by the Founders included Montesquieu, Hume, Plutarch, Beccaria, Cato, De Lolme, Trenchard and Gordon, and Pufendorf. Less frequently cited authorities included Cicero, Hobbes, Grotius, Rousseau, Bacon, Milton, Plato, Machiavelli, and Voltaire. According to CA proponents, the Christian faith was the key contributor to these sources. To underscore the significance of the Christian nature of

---

24. Ibid., 187.
25. Ibid., 285.
26. Barton, *Original Intent*, 219.

the Founders' sources, Barton wrote, "Of the Founders' most frequently invoked political authorities, Hume was the only non-Biblical theorist; and for those views he was attacked and discredited by many of the Founders."[27]

Christian Character of Colonial Documents and Early State Constitutions

One of the primary contentions of the CA thesis is that the Founders were informed by their own committed faith in the Bible as well as political authorities who were mostly explicitly Christian. They claimed the Founders were also heavily influenced by the historical and cultural realities of the Christian character of the colonies' founding documents dating back to the seventeenth century in addition to the early state constitutions which were developed concurrently and subsequent to the Revolution. The language in many of these documents has led the CA proponents to conclude that the colonies were established on Christian principles, and that these principles did not fade when the U.S. Constitution was drafted and ratified. Kennedy and Newcombe asserted that "the Founders of this country never heard or thought of any such thing as a secular nation. There had never existed anywhere on the face of this planet such a thing as a secular nation. When it finally did come into existence in France shortly after the founding of America, the Founding Fathers of this country were appalled."[28]

Jerry Falwell, in his book *Listen, America!*, cited the First Charter of Virginia, the Mayflower Compact, and the Fundamental Orders of Connecticut to demonstrate that there was a distinctly evangelical Christian motive behind the establishment of the first colonies. He wrote, "One has only to research all the early documents of American history to find that, time and again, our Puritan Pilgrim heritage was centered around advancing the Kingdom of God."[29] For example the First Virginia Charter, dated April 1606, stated, "We, greatly commending, and graciously accepting of, their Desires for the Furtherance of so noble a Work, which may, by the Providence of Almighty God, hereafter tend to the Glory of His Divine Majesty, in propagating of *Christian* Religion to

---

27. Ibid., 222.
28. Kennedy and Newcombe, *What If?*, 65.
29. Falwell, *Listen, America!*, 33.

such People, as yet live in Darkness and miserable Ignorance of the true Knowledge and Worship of God, and may in time bring the Infidels and Savages, living in those Parts, to human Civility, and to a settled and quiet Government."[30] Falwell pointed out that this document clearly shows that one of the purposes for the Virginia colony established at Jamestown in 1607 was to present the gospel to the Indians in order to convert them to Christianity. Moreover, Falwell contended that the Mayflower Compact is no less explicit in this regard: "In The Name of God, Amen. We, whose names are underwritten . . . , Having undertaken for the Glory of God, and Advancement of the Christian Faith and the Honor of our King and Country, a Voyage to plant the first colony in the northern Parts of Virginia: . . ."[31] Falwell's conclusion related to these documents was that from America's inception, evangelical Christianity was at the heart of the colonists' motive for coming to the New World and establishing colonies.

Kennedy and Newcombe also attempted to demonstrate that the motive for the early colonists was to convert the native peoples of America. They cited the New England Confederation of 1643, specifically this document's definition of the purpose for the existence of the colonies which were forming a partnership: "We all came into these parts of America, with one and the same end and aim, namely, to advance the Kingdom of our Lord Jesus Christ."[32] Contrary to the common misperception that the New England colonies were established merely on the basis of free religious expression denied them in England, DeMar asked, "These early settlers were doing more than fleeing religious persecution. A goal was settled upon that would see the kingdom of God manifested in a wilderness. When is the last time you read this in a history book?"[33]

John Winthrop's 1630 sermon, "A Model of Christian Charity," was frequently advanced as another important example of the early Christian motive for establishing the first colonies to advance God's kingdom. In this sermon, called by Hart "the keynote of American history,"[34] Winthrop taught the settlers of the Massachusetts Bay Colony that they were about to establish their own "city upon a hill," borrowing from Christ's imag-

---

30. Ibid., 31–32.
31. Ibid., 32.
32. Kennedy and Newcombe, *What If?*, 64.
33. DeMar, *America's Christian History*, 38.
34. Hart, *Faith and Freedom*, 90.

ery in Matt 5:14.³⁵ Winthrop desired that the Massachusetts Bay Colony would be an example of a community based upon God's righteousness and justice for the whole world to see. So for Winthrop, not only were the colonists attempting to advance God's kingdom among the Native Americans, but also to all the nations through their example. Hart stated, "Winthrop believed his role in God's plan was to show the world what a truly Christian community would look like. He wanted to make sure New England would be an astounding success so that all the world would want to imitate its example."³⁶

What basis did the early state constitutions provide for the CA thesis? McDowell looked to the state constitutions of Massachusetts (1780), New Hampshire (1784), South Carolina (1776), Tennessee (1797), and even to the Northwest Ordinance of 1787. He stated that the primary source for these documents was Scripture.³⁷ He also cited phrases from each document in an attempt to demonstrate this basic assertion. Some examples: Massachusetts' early constitution affirmed "the goodness of the great Legislator of the universe . . . His providence. . . . and devoutly imploring His direction" and Tennessee's stated, "No person who denies the being of God, or a future state of rewards and punishments, shall hold any office in the civil department of this State."³⁸ Article III of the Northwest Ordinance of 1787, arguably the most important act of the government under the Articles of Confederation, and the organizational basis for the ensuing westward expansion of the United States, was quoted by McDowell as stating, "Religion, morality, and knowledge being necessary to good government and the happiness of mankind, schools and the means of education shall forever be encouraged."³⁹ Barton quoted the first state constitution of Delaware in order to underscore the same point. He wrote, "For example, notice Delaware (the other states were very similar): 'Every person appointed to public office shall say 'I do profess faith in God the Father, and in Jesus Christ His only Son, and in the Holy Ghost, one God, blessed for evermore; and I do acknowledge the holy scriptures of the Old and New Testament to be given by divine inspiration.' This

---

35. Winthrop, "Christian Charity," 39.
36. Hart, *Faith and Freedom*, 90.
37. McDowell, *America, a Christian Nation?*, 12.
38. Ibid., 14–15.
39. Ibid.

was not a requirement for seminary (it would be wonderful if it were!); this was the requirement to be a politician—a requirement set up by the Founding Fathers!"⁴⁰ Thus, the fact that many early state constitutions as well as the Northwest Ordinance made statements affirming God's providence, calling upon Him for aid, requiring office holders to be men of faith, and encouraging Christian education provided DeMar, Barton, and others with what they saw as indisputable proof of the CA thesis.

Christian Character of Early Colleges

The fact that most colleges that were formed in colonial America made their start as religious institutions was certainly not missed by the proponents of CA. It was their contention that these early schools laid the foundation for the Founders' attitudes regarding the relationship between the Christian faith and the state. Furthermore, the very notion of the value of education is a product of Puritan theology—and it was the Puritans who first established many of the early institutions of higher learning. McDowell wrote, "Education in America has reflected a Christian philosophy. Schools were started to teach people to read the Bible; almost all early colleges were started by a particular Christian denomination or for a religious reason; the most influential textbooks in the first three plus centuries of our history were thoroughly Christian."⁴¹ Hart stated, "In the Puritan mind literacy was important not only to ensure a reasonably informed electorate, essential for the survival of democratic government; but it also played an important role in the individual's walk with the Lord."⁴²

Harvard College was the first institution of higher learning established in the English North American colonies. In 1636, the school began with the donation of a library and funds from John Harvard "for the purpose of training Puritan ministers."⁴³ Barton noted that the school's two mottos were "For the Glory of Christ," and "For Christ and the Church."⁴⁴ To underscore the significance of the influence that Harvard's Christian education had upon the founding generation, Barton stated, "This school

---

40. Barton, *America's Godly Heritage*, 25.
41. McDowell, *America, a Christian Nation?*, 16.
42. Hart, *Faith and Freedom*, 107.
43. Ibid., 108.
44. Barton, *Original Intent*, 81.

and its philosophy produced signers John Adams, John Hancock, Elbridge Gerry, John Pickering, William Williams, Rufus King, William Hooper, William Ellery, Samuel Adams, Robert Treat Paine, and numerous other illustrious Founders."[45]

Harvard was not the only college established with Christian theology at its heart. The College of William and Mary was founded in 1692 in Williamsburg, VA to spread the gospel. As late as 1792, Barton noted that the school was continuing to train students in personal Christian piety: "The students shall attend prayers in chapel at the time appointed and there demean themselves with that decorum which the sacred duty of public worship requires."[46] Yale was founded in 1701 "for the purpose of training Congregational clergy, in response to the emergence at Harvard of what some thought to be erroneous Arminian theology (that opposed strict Calvinist predestination, but favored election and salvation by grace),"[47] according to Hart. Barton listed several Founders who were educated at Yale: "It was this school and its philosophy which produced signers Oliver Wolcott, William Livingston, Lyman Hall, Lewis Morris, Jared Ingersoll, Philip Livingston, William Samuel Johnson, and numerous other distinguished Founders."[48] Princeton was founded in 1746 as a Presbyterian school. John Witherspoon was president of Princeton while James Madison was a student there, and exerted a great deal of influence upon this important founder. "Its president immediately preceding the Revolution was the Rev. Dr. John Witherspoon, later a signer of the Declaration of Independence and a venerated leader among the patriots. Signers James Madison, Richard Stockton, Benjamin Rush, Gunning Bedford, Jonathan Dayton, and numerous other prominent Founders, graduated from Princeton (a seminary for the training of ministers),"[49] according to Barton. Dartmouth College was established in 1754. Barton cited the charter of the school which states its purpose in these terms:

> Whereas... the Reverend Eleazar Wheelock... educated a number of the children of the Indian natives with a view to their carrying the Gospel in their own language and spreading the knowledge

---

45. Ibid.
46. Ibid., 82.
47. Hart, *Faith and Freedom*, 109.
48. Barton, *Original Intent*, 83.
49. Ibid.

of the great Redeemer among their savage tribes. And . . . the design became reputable among the Indians insomuch that a larger number desired the education of their children in said school. . . . [Therefore] Dartmouth-College [is established] for the education and instruction of youths . . . in reading, writing and all parts of learning which shall appear necessary and expedient for civilizing and Christianizing the children.[50]

King's College, later Columbia University, was founded the same year as Dartmouth. William Samuel Johnson, a signer of the Constitution, was appointed as its first president. Barton stated of King's College, "Columbia's admission requirements were straightforward: No candidate shall be admitted into the College . . . unless he shall be able to render into English . . . the Gospels from the Greek. . . . It is also expected that all students attend public worship on Sundays."[51]

These schools do not represent the whole number of schools founded during the colonial period upon Christian theology. They do represent an important sampling, and they illustrated the point made by proponents of CA that higher education during the colonial period was not only influenced by Christianity, but was overtly and expressly Christian, and dedicated to spreading the Christian gospel. Furthermore, proponents of CA stressed that these early schools were highly significant in the formation of the minds of the Founders of the nation. Because these schools were founded for the sake of training students to be highly proficient in Christian orthodoxy, many CA writers drew the conclusion that the Founders sought to build Christianity into the heart and soul of the United States.

Influence of the Great Awakening and Radical Whiggism

The Great Awakening and radical Whig ideology were seen in the previous chapter to be very significant in the formation of the value placed on freedom of conscience in the American colonies. CA proponents went a bit further. They viewed these two movements as being significant in preparing the founding generation for the great trial of the American Revolution and for the creation of a Christian nation (or, at least, a nation built upon Christian principles). Beliles and McDowell commented on

---

50. Ibid., 83–84.
51. Ibid., 84.

this by writing, "George Washington, Samuel Adams, Thomas Jefferson and others who guided us throughout independence and beginnings as a nation were young men during this time period. The Godly environment of the Awakening deeply affected and helped prepare them for their destiny."[52] LaHaye concurred with this view: "Another factor that influenced the thinking of the American people was the Great Awakening revivals from 1738 to 1760. According to many historians, they provided the colonists with the mental and moral toughness to declare their independence from England and endure the rigors of the Revolutionary War, which lasted for seven long years. That victory was attributed by many to 'the strong hand of Providence'—hardly the reaction of a nation of deists and secularists."[53] Without the religious, social, and political impact of the Awakening, the American Revolution would not have benefitted from the moral and spiritual high ground provided by the Awakening that ultimately gave impetus to its success.

The decentralizing motive of the Great Awakening and radical Whig ideology served as a stimulus to the development of revolutionary thought in America. Hart described the two movements in terms of a political-religious alliance dedicated to throwing off old forms of authority much the same as what happened in seventeenth century England under Cromwell. The Awakening would strike at the heart of dead orthodoxy embodied in the Church of England. Radical Whiggism would strike at the centralized authority of British governing bodies which killed individual initiative and creativity. Accordingly, Hart wrote,

> The Great Awakening was not explicitly a political movement, but it had many important political implications. It meshed well with the American trend toward democracy, and complemented the Whig political tradition of Locke, Sydney, Montesquieu, and Blackstone, who were suspicious of all governing establishments. The alliance that emerged between these extreme Protestants and the radical Whig libertarians was analogous to Cromwell's co-option of the supporters of Parliamentary supremacy in 17th-century England to triumph over royal authority. The drama of England's Puritan Revolution was about to be replayed in the colonies. Only this

---

52. Beliles and McDowell, *America's Providential History*, 127.
53. LaHaye, *Faith of our Founding Fathers*, 32–33.

time, the Whig/dissenting-Protestant alliance would achieve a complete victory.[54]

These five historical themes were not the only ones used in the CA thesis. For example, Barton held up examples from the discovery of America, acts of the Continental Congress, the Revolutionary War, and the government under the Articles of Confederation in addition to the above five themes to show that, "The quantity of organic utterances (historical material) available for proving that this is a Christian nation are such that one might be tempted to say, as did the Apostle John when writing about Jesus, that if everything 'were written down, I suppose that even the whole world would not have room for the books that would be written' (John 21:25)."[55] These five themes did, however, form the main historical basis for the CA thesis, and were presented by proponents of the CA thesis in order to demonstrate unequivocally that America's Christian roots run deep, and that Christianity can be shown from history to be the main intellectual and spiritual force bringing this nation into existence. The chapter now turns from the historical themes for the CA thesis to the philosophical themes.

PHILOSOPHICAL THEMES FOR THE CA THESIS

The most common philosophical themes appealed to by CA advocates included the following:

1. The original intent of the Founders may be accurately discerned by applying the same evangelical hermeneutical method as used when interpreting Scripture.

2. The original intent of the Founders was to build Christianity into the heart of the nation.

3. The role of the Enlightenment is not as significant as the role of Christianity in the founding.

There may be several other arguments put forward by proponents of CA, but these three are the most significant because they provide the primary intellectual justification for the CA thesis.

---

54. Hart, *Faith and Freedom*, 223.
55. Barton, *Myth of Separation*, 83.

Evangelical Hermeneutical Method: the Logos Paradigm

A universally acknowledged tenet among CA proponents was that the Founders of the American nation clearly expressed their original intent in their writings, and that America has deviated from it. The assumption undergirding this tenet is that the original intent of the Founders can be accurately discerned in the first place. As evangelicals who are committed to the inerrancy and infallibility of the Bible, proponents of CA have imported their hermeneutical method for interpreting Scripture to that of the founding documents. This they believed is the key to understanding exactly what the Founders intended in the eighteenth century, how far the nation has strayed from original intent, and how it can be recovered.

William Andrew Moyer's Ph.D. dissertation entitled "Battle for the City on a Hill: Evangelical Interpretations of American History, 1960–1996" is most helpful on this point. Moyer called the evangelical hermeneutical method used by CA proponents "the Logos paradigm."[56] The Logos paradigm is centered on the notion of verbal inspiration, that God used the human authors of the Bible to write down the exact words He intended. Biblical interpretation is the attempt to arrive at God's intended meaning as presented by the human author of the text. Referring to Scripture, Moyer explained, "For the evangelical, the Word is not merely a guideline, suggestion, or good counsel. It is divine instruction and it is verbally inspired."[57] He presented a brief history of the impact of the Reformation and modernism on the hermeneutical methodology of Protestants in order to demonstrate that the Logos paradigm has become the prevalent means of interpretation of Scripture by evangelicals. Since the founding documents are, according to Moyer, "schematically akin to sacred scripture . . . hermeneutical principles which evangelicals apply to the Bible also provide the paradigm by which the evangelical nationalist interpret [sic] the meaning and purpose of the Constitution and the history of America."[58]

Moyer stated that since the Logos paradigm is simultaneously applied to the interpretation of Scripture and the founding documents, CA writers believed that discerning original intent is possible. "For the

---

56. See Moyer, "Battle for the City," 290–339.

57. Ibid., 291.

58. Ibid., 290. Moyer's term "evangelical nationalist" is synonymous with the term "CA proponent" used in this book.

evangelical, Biblical revelation is ascertained by discerning the intended meaning of Scripture in its originating context.... There is not much of a leap to apply these same methods to interpreting the 'sacred' documents of American history,"[59] wrote Moyer. He asserted that what is gained in the use of this method of interpretation, both in the study of Scripture and in the study of the founding documents, is authority: "... original intent is tied to the idea of authority."[60] Thus, biblical exegesis is the act of drawing authorial intent from the text and applying its meaning to a contemporary situation. Since the Bible is taken to be the Word of God by proponents of CA, the original intent of the author is authoritative because God inspired that author to record that particular text. The same principle would apply to the writings of the Founders. Whatever was written by the Founders is authoritative and binding upon the American system for all time, just as the Bible is binding at all times.

The practical application of this hermeneutic is clear: just as CA writers would use specific passages from Scripture to demonstrate the truth and authority of a particular action or dogma, quoting from specific passages from the Founders' writing demonstrates the authority of their original intent. Moyer stated it this way: "Evangelicals prove the legitimacy of their ideas by citing appropriate verses of Scripture as their authority. This is often been referred to as 'proof texting.' Evangelical nationalists utilize this same technique in establishing the Christian origins of America by quoting the founding fathers. Quotations carry a great deal of weight in the strategy to persuade America that it is the principles of Christianity that gave birth to the new nation and, therefore, should continue to be practiced."[61]

What are some examples of CA proponents employing the Logos paradigm in their writings? One can see this as Eidsmoe wrote, "Those who believe in original intent would say the Convention ended in 1787, and from that point on the letter of the Constitution was fixed (except for the ratification and amendment processes), just as the canon of Scripture was complete when the last book of the New Testament was written."[62] Here Eidsmoe saw a clear analogy between the authority of the founding

---

59. Ibid., 302.
60. Ibid., 304.
61. Ibid., 309.
62. Eidsmoe, *Christianity and the Constitution*, 397.

documents and Scripture. Barton also employed the Logos paradigm in his use of direct quotations, or proof texting as Moyer would say, from the Founders. He claimed that

> there is an unhealthy tendency in many current books on the Founders—a tendency confirmed in their concluding bibliographies-to cite predominately contemporary "authorities" speaking about the Founders rather than citing the Founders' own words. Such evidence is termed "hearsay" and would never stand up in a court of law; *Original Intent*, however, has pursued the practice of "best evidence": it lets the Founders speak for themselves in accordance with the legal rules of evidence. *Original Intent* will provide hundreds of the Founders' direct declarations on many of the constitutional issues which America continues to face today. Their words, their conclusions, and especially their intent is clear and their wisdom is still applicable for today.[63]

Original Intent had as its purpose the gathering together of a host of primary source material from the founding period in order to demonstrate what the Founders intended and how America drifted away from their intent. Barton's work, *The Myth of Separation*, also set out to demonstrate original intent by citing a host of court cases which identified America as a Christian nation in different ways. Another example can be found in Hart's work. His assumption was that knowledge of the Founders' original intent was so certain and authoritative that it is possible to predict exactly how they would respond to how their writings were interpreted today. He demurred, "Men such as Jefferson and Madison would recoil in horror if they could see how their words, ideas, and actions have been so misrepresented to inhibit rather than expand religious freedom; that while the words of the Constitution seem to be intact, they bear little resemblance to the ever-expanding government now in existence."[64] Hart's exportation of biblical interpretation to the interpretation of historical documents led him to believe he knew the minds of Founders, as well as their emotional reaction to how the founding documents are applied in the twentieth and twenty-first centuries.

Not surprisingly, proponents of CA embraced a strict constructionist view of the Constitution, and were suspicious of the court's practice of judicial review over the past fifty or so years. As Scripture was taken by CA

---

63. Barton, *Original Intent*, 5–6.
64. Hart, *Faith and Freedom*, 355.

writers as the basis for truth, the founding documents were understood to be the basis for American law and freedom. Also, according to CA writers, just as moral relativism results when the Bible is removed as the basis for truth, arbitrary rule by an oligarchic state results when the founding documents are not interpreted along the lines of original intent. Hart put it this way: "If unchecked, the state will inexorably set itself up as the absolute authority in all areas of life, beyond which there can be no appeal. The law becomes whatever suits those who hold the levers of power, who proceed unrestricted even by their own consciences."[65] Beliles and Anderson agreed with this view. They asserted, "Law needs an unchanging standard. Without it, America is at the mercy of whatever radical element is able to take over and convince a court of its point of view."[66]

Original Intent of the Founders

Given the hermeneutic methodology of CA proponents, how have they argued for the Founders' original intent? Perhaps no CA writer has championed the notion more strenuously than Barton. Barton's organization, known as WallBuilders, is dedicated to educating people on the basis of the founding of the United States. The website stated,

> WallBuilders' goal is to exert a direct and positive influence in government, education, and the family by (1) educating the nation concerning the Godly foundation of our country; (2) providing information to federal, state, and local officials as they develop public policies which reflect Biblical values; and (3) encouraging Christians to be involved in the civic arena. . . . In the first part of this goal, we develop materials to educate the public concerning the periods in our country's history when its laws and policies were firmly rooted in Biblical principles.[67]

WallBuilders is the publisher for all of Barton's writings, and it makes dozens of books, pamphlets, video recordings, and other materials available through its website which forwards the CA thesis. Barton's most significant works are primarily dedicated to arguing that the original intent of the Founders was to establish a Christian nation. Furthermore, Barton

---

65. Ibid., 23, 26.
66. Beliles and Anderson, *Contending*, 139.
67. *WallBuilders: Our Goal.*

strenuously contended throughout his writings that America has drifted far from the original intent of the Founders.

In *Original Intent*, Barton used the 1892 U.S. Supreme Court decision *Holy Trinity v. United States* as a model for demonstrating the Founders' original intent, among other things. This decision is portrayed as among the most powerful evidences for the United States having been established as a Christian nation because the decision itself appeals to a wide range of historical evidences ("organic utterances") starting with Columbus' discovery of America through the late nineteenth century. Barton wrote, "When the *Holy Trinity* Court described America as a 'Christian nation,' it did so because, as it explained: 'This is historically true. From the discovery of this continent to the present hour, there is a single voice making this affirmation.... [T]hese are not individual sayings, declarations of private persons: they are organic utterances; they speak the voice of the entire people.... These and many other matters which might be noticed, add a volume of unofficial declarations to the mass of organic utterances that this is a Christian nation.'"[68]

The *Trinity* decision was only one of the authorities appealed to by Barton. In his book, *The Myth of Separation*, Barton actually turned to dozens of court decisions in order to demonstrate the original intent of the Founders. For example, Barton pointed to the Pennsylvania Supreme Court decision *Updegraph v. The Commonwealth* (1824) to show that blasphemy against Christ was punishable by law. As shown above, Blackstone was held up as one of the most powerful legal influences upon the Founders. Barton wrote in explaining the *Updegraph* decision, "The number of times that our Founders quoted Blackstone testifies to the impact that he had on their thinking and to the respect they paid him."[69]

Another example is the decision handed down by the South Carolina Supreme Court, *City of Charleston v. S. A. Benjamin* (1846). As Barton quoted it, this decision asserted, "Christianity has reference to the principles of right and wrong... it is the foundation of those morals and manners upon which our society is formed; it is their basis. Remove this and they would fall.... [Morality] has grown upon the basis of Christianity [emphasis added to the text of the decision by Barton]."[70] The issue in this

---

68. Barton, *Original Intent*, 75.
69. Barton, *Myth of Separation*, 52.
70. Ibid., 73. Emphasis is in the original.

case, according to Barton, related to religious pluralism. The court was affirming that Christianity defined the meaning of religious tolerance, and since this was the case, no other religious commitment could supersede it in legal importance.

A final example given is the decision in *United States v. Macintosh* (1931), handed down by the U.S. Supreme Court. Barton quoted its declaration: "We are a Christian people... according to one another the equal right of religious freedom, and acknowledging with reverence the duty of obedience to the will of God."[71] The fact that this decision was made so recently in American history was not lost on Barton. His consistent message was that the intention of the Founders was to establish America as a Christian nation, and the courts upheld that intention for the first 150 years of the nation's history. He wrote, "These cases (and hundreds like them), the records of the early Supreme Court Justices, and the writings of the pioneers of American legal practice, leave no doubt where our Founders stood on Christian principles in government, education, and public affairs. Our Fathers intended that this nation should be a Christian nation, not because all who lived in it were Christians, but because it was founded on and would be governed and guided by Christian principles."[72]

For Barton, there is a clear line in history when the courts ceased to affirm this original intent of the Founders. The U.S. Supreme Court decision of 1947, *Everson v. Board of Education*, cited Jefferson's 1802 letter to the Danbury Baptists in which he wrote to assure them that there would be no nationally-recognized denomination. In this letter is found the oft-repeated phrase, "wall of separation," referring to the First Amendment's disestablishment clause. According to Barton, this phrase was seldom used in legal discourse, until 1947 and the handing down of the *Everson* decision. Once this happened, the original intent of the Founders regarding the relationship between Christianity and the state was distorted. Barton wrote,

> ... in *Everson v. Board of Education*, the Court, for the first time, did not cite Jefferson's entire letter, but selected only eight words from it. The Court now announced: 'The First Amendment has erected "a wall of separation between church and state." That wall must be kept high and impregnable.' The courts continued on this track so steadily that, in 1958, in a case called *Baer v. Kolmorgen*, one of the

71. Ibid., 76.
72. Ibid., 82.

judges was tired of hearing the phrase and wrote a dissent warning that if the court did not stop talking about the "separation of church and state," people were going to start thinking it was part of the Constitution. That warning was in 1958 [emphasis original]![73]

By the time school prayer was outlawed in 1962 as a result of the *Engel v. Vitale* decision, Barton noted that the term "church" was legally redefined to mean a public religious activity rather than a Christian denomination. This amended definition would have disastrous effects upon religious liberty in America, according to Barton. He wrote, "This was the turning point in the interpretation of the First Amendment."[74]

While Barton has researched and written far more on this point of original intent, he is by no means a lone voice in the wilderness. Several other proponents of CA have followed Barton's lead in attempting to demonstrate that the Founders' original intent was to base the nation upon Christianity, and especially that American courts have led the culture away from original intent. LaHaye wrote, "Lest you think that's an oversimplification of the issues, let me point out that for 150 years this nation was built on Biblical principles that assured freedom, community decency, and domestic tranquility. Today, particularly since the Supreme Court has resolutely misinterpreted the Constitution so as to increase the scope and power of the federal government and to separate it almost entirely from God and Biblical principles, it has become both secular and hostile to religion."[75] DeMar insisted that "A wealth of historical evidence points to the fact that our forefathers knew nothing about an absolute separation as is being promoted by present-day court decisions."[76] Beliles and Anderson asserted that the Founders built five principles into the Constitution, each of which was biblical in origin, which would provide the document its formal integrity: elected representative government, separation of powers, federalism, prohibition of government interference in religious matters, and permanent union with amendment process.[77] These authors contended that for most of this nation's history, American laws recognized the foundation of Christian integrity established by the

73. Barton, *America's Godly Heritage*, 15.
74. Ibid., 16.
75. LaHaye, *Faith of Our Founding Fathers*, 190.
76. DeMar, *God and Government*, 119.
77. Beliles and Anderson, *Contending*, 126–30.

Founders. Now, that foundation has been slowly but surely eaten away. What is the danger, according to Beliles and Anderson? They wrote, "Without God's word as our anchor for law, we are ultimately governed by activist judges and their judicial whims.... Without the Bible as our ultimate basis for law, our legal system has no anchor and the nation will drift ultimately into anarchy as small, yet powerful and active minority groups insist on their own way with their own interpretation of what the law is. Law needs an unchanging standard. Without it, America is at the mercy of whatever radical element is able to take over and convince a court of its point of view."[78]

This chapter's limited treatment of this argument from original intent is not a comprehensive treatment of the extensive writing on this subject. CA proponents, especially Barton, drew from a myriad of sources to argue this point, and believed that the evidence overwhelmingly supports CA. The point here has been to present a representative sample of how CA proponents have used original intent to argue for their position.

The Role of the Enlightenment Compared to the Role of Christianity in the Founding

Secular thought, specifically the ideas of the Enlightenment, does not deserve to be counted as a significant factor in the founding, according to the CA thesis. This argument can be found in almost all the of the CA writings treated in this chapter, but only a sampling will be addressed.

Gary Amos's thesis in his work, *Defending the Declaration*, was that the Bible served as the primary source of the Declaration rather than the secular ideas of the Enlightenment.[79] Thus, even though Locke was an important Enlightenment thinker, Amos contended that Locke's theories on the social compact and on inalienable rights were informed by his Christianity rather than secular thought. Amos also referred to Locke's use of the term "self-evident," a term which on the surface seems to be from the Enlightenment, but on closer inspection, conforms neatly to biblical orthodoxy. Amos asserted that the term's use by Richard Hooker (1554–1600), the Anglican theologian and latitudinarian, and Thomas Aquinas was fully in line with Scripture, and it was according to Hooker's and Aquinas's understanding that Locke employed the term in his own

---

78. Ibid., 138–39.

79. This contention will be more thoroughly treated in the theological themes section.

writings. Thus, Amos stated, "Locke's views of reason are not of the Enlightenment, unless we are willing to make Hooker in 1593 the epistemological father of the Enlightenment rather than Locke."[80]

Deism as a faith system gained a significant following as a result of English Enlightenment epistemology and ontology. Eidsmoe and Hart sought to undermine the belief that deism as a faith system influenced the Founders more than Christianity. According to Eidsmoe, "Deism, while it existed in America and was even accepted by a few leading Americans (Thomas Paine, Ethan Allen, and possibly James Wilson), was (1) less influential than Christianity and (2) fundamentally compatible with Christianity in its view of law and government."[81] Hart wrote, "Contrary to popular conception, deist beliefs played almost no role in America's founding."[82] He cited the historian Perry Miller and Timothy Dwight, president of Yale (1795–1817), in asserting that deism, while popular in Europe, was never a widely held belief in America.

It is significant that the French Revolution followed the American Revolution by less than a decade, and that the American revolutionary theme of liberty was an influential factor in the French Revolution. Hart, along with several other CA writers, compared the American Revolution with the French Revolution. The CA argument from this comparison was that, while the French Revolution was primarily influenced by Enlightenment thought, the American Revolution was mainly informed by the Bible. The consequences of these ideas are thus clearly seen. Hart wrote, "Liberation of the individual was not an idea of the *philosophes*; it was a Christian idea, and specifically a Reformation idea, as America was settled overwhelmingly by fundamentalist Protestants."[83] Barton, in comparing America to other nations formed out of revolutions, pointed to the success and staying power of the U.S. Constitution. He wrote, "Two hundred years under the same document—and under one form

---

80. Amos, *Defending*, 100.

81. Eidsmoe, *Christianity and the Constitution*, 45. Eidsmoe's statement here is consistent with the view expressed by Amos, that even if certain Enlightenment ideas found their way into the Founders' thought or the founding documents themselves, those ideas were actually imported by Enlightenment thinkers from Christianity. This is one reason why many CA writers believe in the appropriateness of minimizing the impact of the Enlightenment on the founding, and stressing that of Christianity and the Bible instead.

82. Hart, *Faith and Freedom*, 339.

83. Ibid., 28.

of government—is an accomplishment unknown among contemporary nations. For example, Russia, Italy, France, and other nations underwent revolutions about the same time as the American Revolution, but with very different results. Consider France: in the last 200 years it has gone through seven completely different forms of government; Italy is now in its 51st; yet we are still in our first."[84] The reason for the success and longevity of the American Constitution, according to Barton, is that the Founders drew most heavily from the Bible in order to establish a Christian nation. This fact contrasted starkly with those other nations drawing primarily from anti-Christian sources to establish secular governments.

This practice of looking to the failures of other nations to sustain a republican form of government in order to underscore the success of the American experiment with constitutional government was not uncommon among CA writers. The practice was one way that the theological themes of the CA thesis were expressed. The chapter now turns to a discussion of these theological themes.

THEOLOGICAL THEMES FOR THE CA THESIS

This chapter has provided a modest treatment of the themes and arguments justifying the CA thesis as presented by its supporters over thirty years. The CA thesis is a deeply ingrained and closely held belief maintained by a number of leading evangelicals, and a powerful point of controversy in the contemporary culture. This may not have been the case if the CA thesis were simply an historical/philosophical assertion. Since there are powerful theological elements to the CA thesis, its proponents understood it to have a transcendent quality for which a body of mere historical evidences and philosophical arguments could never give a satisfactory account.

In light of this, it is important to examine five common theological themes to CA:

1. A providential view of history.
2. American exceptionalism as evidence of God's unique blessing on the nation.
3. America as God's chosen nation, a new Israel.

---

84. Barton, *America's Godly Heritage*, 8.

4. Liberty as a biblical notion finding its consummate application in the civic life of America.
5. The Bible as the primary source of the founding national documents.[85]

Providential History

A providential view of history is at the core of the CA thesis. If there is one theological point that is indispensable to the CA thesis, it is that history is moving toward the fulfillment of God's purpose. This point can be seen in the title of Kennedy and Newcombe's book, *What If Jesus Had Never Been Born?* Their answer was, of course, that if Jesus had never been born, the American nation would never have come into existence: "Had Jesus never been born, there never would have been an America."[86]

To further illustrate this point, the chapter will use David Bebbington's work, *Patterns in History*. Bebbington examined five ways in which humans have sought to understand history's meaning. He juxtaposed four of these views in light of what he identified in his final chapter as a Christian view of history. These included cyclical, Marxist, and historicist views of history as well as a view embracing the idea of inevitable progress. In defining the Christian view, Bebbington wrote, "Christians, then, have normally adhered to these three convictions about history: that God intervenes in it; that he guides it in a straight line; and that he will bring it to the conclusion that he has planned. The three beliefs together form the core of the Christian doctrine of providence."[87]

In contrasting the Christian view of history with the four other views, Bebbington argued that it is the cross of Christ that sets it apart from all others. He contended that, "The major claims of Christianity about history are summed up by the cross. There Jesus, in fulfilling the prophecies of the Old Testament and creating the theme of the church's preaching, confirmed the vision of history as an ongoing line. The work of Jesus, by opening the kingdom of heaven to all believers, established a Christian hope that God will bring history to a triumphant conclusion."[88]

---

85. That is, the Declaration of Independence, the Constitution, and the Bill of Rights.
86. Kennedy and Newcombe, *What If?*, 58.
87. Bebbington, *Patterns in History*, 43.
88. Ibid., 175.

How, then, should the Christian historian present history? Bebbington's answer to this question was expressive of the motive of many proponents of CA. Bebbington stated, "History on Christian premises has the apologetic task of revealing as credible the belief that God stands behind and acts within the historical process. It also serves the evangelistic task of proclaiming Jesus Christ as the one whose victorious work assures us that God will bring history to a triumphant close."[89] In other words, Bebbington asserted that to a Christian audience, the historian can seek to demonstrate the outworking of God's providence on the stage of human history. To the secular audience, the historian is to write history to show how God answers the problem of human suffering through Christ's cross, and that death does not have the final word.

Bebbington's point that Christian historians ought to write with an apologetic/evangelistic motive was evident throughout Kennedy and Newcombe's work. Here is an example of how the authors engaged in their apologetic task: they asked, "If the Founders of the new nation intended this to be a secular state, then why did they, when governing, perform so many religious acts which were officially part of the government? The first act of the first Congress—the same men who wrote the first amendment—was to hire chaplains to say prayers before the sessions of the House and the Senate. The leaders of the new nation called for national days of fasting, prayer, and thanksgiving."[90] The goal here was to educate believers about their nation's Christian roots so that they might grasp the wonder of God's work in American history, and understand the connection between that history and the history of salvation.

Their evangelistic motive was expressed in this quotation: "The Old Testament tells the story of the fall of man into slavery; God's deliverance of His people; their bondage in Egypt; then God bringing them out after 430 years of slavery.... All of this is but mere foreshadowings of the great deliverance and of the great emancipator, Jesus Christ, who came to deliver us from bondage unto freedom, from slavery unto liberty, to set free the slaves and those who are imprisoned."[91] Secular readers here are shown how liberty in the Bible is expressed, and that the political liberty Americans enjoy is a direct result of that biblical liberty won through the

---

89. Ibid., 188.
90. Kennedy and Newcombe, *What If?*, 73.
91. Ibid., 78.

work of Christ.[92] Thus, Kennedy and Newcombe's apologetic/evangelistic tasks clearly revealed their commitment to writing providential history.

Beliles and McDowell clearly expressed their historiographical presupposition in their work, *America's Providential History*. As stated earlier, Beliles and McDowell began their history of America not at 1492, 1607, 1620, 1754, 1776, or 1787. Their history began at the Garden of Eden. Their explanation for this was, "We begin the history of America with Creation, and Adam and Eve, because if one does not understand God's plan and purpose for man from the beginning, he will not be able to understand how America fits into His overall plan. The history of America, or any country, cannot be studied as an isolated event."[93] Furthermore, the authors asserted, "we examine the history of America from a Christian perspective. Since God is the author of history and He is carrying out His plan in the earth through history, any view of the history of America, or any country, that ignores God is not true history."[94] For Beliles and McDowell, to fail to acknowledge the Christian doctrine of providence in the study of history will entail a fatally flawed understanding of the import of its content. This is the reason why America has lost sight of the meaning of its national history as well as its divinely ordained purpose.

Moreover, like Kennedy and Newcombe, Beliles and McDowell employed the apologetic/evangelistic formula for the Christian writing of history. Their stated purpose for writing was, "to equip Christians to be able to introduce Biblical principles into the public affairs of America, and every nation in the world, and in so doing bring Godly change throughout the world."[95] Their readership is to take God's message of the Bible as it relates to American history into the public sphere, while non-Christians the world over are to experience the regenerating change of Christ because of that message.

These examples represent two primary ways of how providential history was understood and applied in the CA thesis. The next three theological themes addressed in this section are entailed in this providential view of history.

---

92. The theological theme of liberty as a biblical notion applied in America will be addressed later more fully.

93. Beliles and McDowell, *America's Providential History*, vii.

94. Ibid.

95. Ibid., 1.

American Exceptionalism as Evidence of God's Unique Blessing

What is meant by the term "American exceptionalism?" Generally speaking, the term was understood by CA proponents to mean America's unique status in the world as the oldest constitutional democracy, the most powerful military, economic, and cultural force in history, the most religiously free, and the most engaged nation in the fulfillment of Christ's Great Commission in the world. LaHaye thought of America as a "miracle nation." He proclaimed, "And now at the time of the world's greatest population and the world's greatest technological explosion, it is no accident that millions of Christians are willing to send billions of dollars with their sons and daughters to proclaim God's message of love to the ends of the earth. Perhaps that is the main purpose for the existence of this miracle nation."[96] Stephen McDowell and Mark Beliles expressed American exceptionalism in these terms: "America is different than any nation in history.... America is the most free and prosperous nation to have ever existed. America is exceptional."[97] Falwell wrote, "... America has reached the pinnacle of greatness unlike any nation in human history...."[98] These sentiments about America's singular greatness echoed throughout the writings of CA proponents.

Credit was universally given to the nation's Christian origins and "godly heritage" by CA writers for its power and prestige, which were gained over a short time compared to many other nations. Because America's colonial roots are found squarely in Reformation theology, the rest of American history was set up to be blessed by God. The early colonists came to America bringing with them a firm commitment to glorify God and spread the gospel. They established their colonies in the wilderness and worked diligently to carve out a civilization on a new and barely explored continent. McDowell and Beliles put it this way: "The early settlers of America carried these seed ideas [of the Reformation] with them as they colonized the nation in the seventeenth and eighteenth centuries. These ideas were planted, grew, and began to bear great fruit. This seed determined the fruit of the American Christian Republic. It produced America as an exceptional nation, the most free and prosperous

---

96. LaHaye, *Faith of our Founding Fathers*, 65–66.
97. McDowell and Beliles, *American Dream*, 3.
98. Falwell, *Listen, America!*, 29.

in history."[99] This "seed principle" was an important theme for McDowell and Beliles. When a godly idea is sown as a seed in a civilization by the providence of God, God blesses that idea until it grows into maturity, thus defining that civilization. America's "seed," the ideas and theology of the Reformation, were planted in America by the earliest colonies, and God brought those Reformation ideas to maturity during the course of American history. According to McDowell and Beliles, "The seed principle is a common idea in Scripture. The Bible teaches that the Kingdom of God is like a seed (Mark 4:30–32). The seed determines the fruit, in nature and also in the sphere of ideas. Ideas determine what a culture or nation will be."[100] Specifically, the authors identified seven ideas which were planted as seeds in the colonies. They were the biblical notions of:God, man, the family, the truth, history, government, and education.[101] Thus, for McDowell and Beliles, God has blessed America because of the biblical ideas planted therein, and placed the nation in a unique position in the world so that it would bear witness to the truth of Jesus Christ.

Falwell also attributed America's meteoric rise to world power and prestige to the God's blessing and providential purposes. The signal reason for God's blessing was that the colonists and the Founders recognized that God had a special plan for America, and their motive in establishing the constitutional system was to form a Christian nation. "Any diligent student of American history finds that our great nation was founded by godly men upon godly principles to be a Christian nation" and the Founders "developed a nation predicated on Holy Writ,"[102] according to Falwell. Furthermore, since the Founders were all guided by the Bible, they expected God to be faithful to bless them and their nation as long as the nation remembered Him. Concerning this, he wrote, "Our Founding Fathers firmly believed that America had a special destiny in the world. They were confident that God would bless their endeavors because they did not forget to acknowledge Him in all their doings."[103]

Marshall and Manuel's stance on this issue was in a similar vein as the above CA writers, but they stated it in much stronger terms. Their

---

99. McDowell and Beliles, *American Dream*, 10.
100. Ibid., 13.
101. Ibid., 14–34.
102. Falwell, *Listen, America!*, 29.
103. Ibid.

view of God's plan for America was rooted in covenantal terms. God called America to fulfill His purposes through a covenant established first with the colonists and ultimately with the Founders. Through faithfulness to God's call upon America, the nation would be uniquely blessed among all the nations of the earth. In their opening chapter, Marshall and Manuel looked back nostalgically to the recent past and found an America experiencing the pinnacle of that state of blessedness: "*America, America*—until about fifteen years ago, the name by itself would evoke a feeling of warmth. . . . In general, we were the most steadying influence on an uneasy globe. And at home, we were supremely confident that we were indeed making the world a better place to live in. We believed that technologically and diplomatically, it was only a matter of time before this assignment would be satisfactorily completed."[104] But, the authors observed, because American power and international prestige had been eroded by the Vietnam War, the American economy had slowed in the 1970s, and American morality had been undermined during the upheavals of the 1960s, God's blessing and grace upon the nation were beginning to be removed. America was established as, according to Marshall and Manuel, "A new Jerusalem, a model of the Kingdom of Christ upon earth—we Americans were intended to be living proof to the rest of the world that it *was* possible to live a life together which reflected the Two Great Commandments and put God and others ahead of self."[105] As long as America was to honor its calling and covenant with God, America would be uniquely blessed. If America chose to abandon God, God's blessings would also be lifted. Still, it is always possible for America to be restored to her God-given greatness: "That grace seems to be lifting now, but as we look at our nation's history from His point of view, we begin to have an idea of how much we owe a very few-and of how much is still at stake. For God's call on this country has never been revoked."[106] America, like Israel of the Old Testament, has but to return to God and God will be faithful to restore its people. All we must do as a nation is trust this promise of God.

---

104. Marshall and Manuel, *Light and Glory*, 13; emphasis original.
105. Ibid., 23; emphasis original.
106. Ibid., 26.

America as the New Israel

While few proponents of CA were bold enough to openly embrace the view that America is not only a Christian nation, but God's specially chosen nation in contemporary times, Marshall and Manuel clearly did so and many others also seemed implicitly to hold the view. As the chapter has already shown, there is nothing implicit about Marshall and Manuel's claims about America's status. The thesis of Marshall and Manuel's book clearly stated that America was called of God to fulfill "a definite and extremely demanding plan" and that "In the virgin wilderness of America, God was making His most significant attempt since ancient Israel to create a new Israel of people living in obedience to the laws of God, through faith in Jesus Christ."[107] With the Constitution serving as the divinely inspired "institutionalization of the covenant's legacy"[108] America remains God's chosen people even though its people may have faltered in their commitment to the covenant. Still, when God's people in America fulfill what is written in 2 Chr 7:14, God will again show Himself faithful to restore America's greatness. Marshall and Manuel stated, "That a drought could be broken, or an Indian attack averted, by corporate repentance is an idea which sounds alien to many Christians today. Yet it was central to the faith which built this country, and is one of the most prominent, recurring themes in the Bible. One of the most familiar examples is, 'If my people who are called by my name humble themselves, and pray and seek my face, and turn from their wicked ways, then I will hear from heaven, and will forgive their sin and heal their land.'"[109] The idea that America must return to its Christian roots was a powerful one among all CA proponents, and the chapter will explore this theme below more deeply. Still, it was a central component to Marshall and Manuel's belief that America exists as God's chosen nation.

Marshall and Manuel forwarded the most boldly stated claim on this theological theme. But other CA writers seemed to have practically affirmed similar conclusions. The very notion of American exceptionalism was one of the most recurring theological themes in CA writings. McDowell and Beliles wrote, "This nation was, and in many ways still is,

---

107. Ibid., 22–23.
108. Ibid., 345.
109. Ibid., 25.

special."[110] B. F. Morris, the nineteenth-century writer whose work strongly impacted DeMar, wrote, "Whether we consider the colonial period, or that of the Revolution, or those of subsequent times, our growth in numbers, in territory, in wealth and power, has been almost unparalleled. ... Our example has long been an object of jealousy and fear to the oppressors of man."[111] Hart presented a similar view as Marshall and Manuel on the Constitution as the basis for a covenant between God and America: "Similarly, the U.S. Constitution has worked because there has been a sacred aura surrounding the document; it has been something more than a legal contract; it was a covenant, an oath before God. ... The American people are bound together by an oath; an oath between the people to form a government of 'just and equal laws' under God. When that oath is violated, the bond, too, is dissolved-which is the grave danger our nation faces today."[112] Beliles and Anderson concurred with this view. They insisted, "America's Constitution, like the Corinthian church the apostle Paul was referring to, was in many ways 'written not with ink, but with the Spirit of the living God.'"[113] To be fair, none of these writers explicitly took the position that America exists as a new Israel, but they did firmly espouse the idea of American exceptionalism.

American Liberty as a Biblical Notion

To many CA writers, the roots of American political liberty are found in Scripture, and that without the influence of Scripture, there would have been no notion of the liberties guaranteed in the Constitution. The chapter contended earlier that certain advocates of CA found a direct line between Reformation thought and the founding national documents. This particular theological theme—that American liberty is a biblical notion—is a specific example of how this line connects the Reformation to America's founding.

The Old Testament forms the basis of the CA idea that American liberty is rooted in Scripture. Pat Robertson contended, for example, that the Old Testament is the starting point for the whole structure of American government. He maintained that "The Old Testament stories of those first

---

110. McDowell and Beliles, *American Dream*, 3.
111. Morris, *Christian Life*, 23.
112. Hart, *Faith and Freedom*, 77.
113. Beliles and Anderson, *Contending*, 3.

kings of Israel gave our nation's forefathers the basis upon which to institute a more perfect government in this land."[114] By this he meant that when a wicked king ascended the throne, God established a way of limiting that king's power to infringe on the people's rights. This God-ordained limit, according to Robertson, is found in Deut 17:19–20, which commands the king to fear God, scrupulously obey His law, and not exalt himself above the people "that he and his sons may continue long in his kingdom in the midst of Israel." From this passage, Robertson concluded, "The covenant between God, the king, and the people was simple. The king would retain his office as long as he obeyed God and protected the unalienable rights of the people. But if he failed and elevated his own good above the people's good, he would be removed from office."[115] Thus, Robertson here contended that the liberty of the people to remove a corrupt leader from power is modeled in the Israelite monarchy.

Robertson also stressed that the notion of personal rights is found in Scripture. Citing the inalienable right to life defined in the Declaration, Robertson found biblical support in Gen 2:7, "Then the LORD God formed man of dust from the ground, and breathed into his nostrils the breath of life...." He also cited the New Testament in support of the concept of liberty. He wrote, "God is the giver of Liberty. The apostle Paul proclaimed it in the New Testament: 'Now the Lord is the Spirit: and where the Spirit of the Lord is, there is liberty.'"[116] Robertson found the right to pursue happiness in Eccl 3:13, "... that every man who eats and drinks sees good in all his labor—it is the gift of God." Man's inalienable rights are so not because the state guaranteed them, but because God has given them and He does not lie or change His mind. He stated, "Moses said it this way: 'God is not a man, that He should lie, ... Has He said, and will He not do it? Or has He spoken, and will He not make it good?'"[117]

Beliles and Anderson concurred with this view. In addition to turning to the Bible to find basis for American liberty, they also maintained that the Israelite monarchy was the model used by the framers of the Constitution. Their citation from Scripture was from 1 Sam. 8, the passage relating how Israel wanted to be like other nations and be ruled by

---

114. Robertson, *Dates with Destiny*, 70.
115. Ibid., 71
116. Ibid., 69. The Scripture verse is from 2 Cor 3:17.
117. Ibid., 70.

a king. They stated, "As a result of the people's will, their constitution was amended to establish a constitutional monarchy. Though this development led the Israelites away from liberty, it is crucial to note that this change was a direct result of free civic choice."[118]

Hart drew other conclusions as to how the Old Testament forms the basis for American liberty. He observed that the Puritans who colonized New England compared themselves to the Israelites under Moses, leaving a tyrannical empire and settling a new promised land. This observation was not directed at the Puritans only, but also to the revolutionaries who broke away from Britain and declared their independence. He wrote, "We find, in the Old Testament, God leading His people, the Israelites, out of bondage, just as Bradford, Winthrop, and their Christian followers had fled the Stuart tyranny. Pharaoh's yoke inhibited the Israelites from keeping God's commandments, just as the Puritans believed the English Church was an impediment to the true Christian faith. In a long catalogue of abuses, the Declaration made a case for why the Americans could no longer live under such a corrupt, dissolute, and tyrannical regime. . . ."[119] Not only did Hart trace the biblical roots of liberty, but he also traced the notion through Western history to eighteenth century America. He concluded that "freedom of conscience was hardly an Enlightenment or humanist notion; it is a Christian principle applied to politics—though a principle, sadly, that many Christians through the ages have failed to grasp."[120]

Rather than appealing to specific texts of Scripture, Amos's contention that American liberty is rooted in Scripture is grounded more generally. He pointed to the biblical model of law and authority, stressing that personal liberty and order in society does not come from an arbitrary use of power. Liberty, order and arbitrary power cannot exist simultaneously, but liberty and order do result in an environment defined by a biblical exercise of power. He wrote, "Whoever wields power can determine the content of laws, the extent, and even the existence of other people's freedoms. Biblical philosophy, on the other hand, admits to predetermined lines of authority which the civil government is not permitted to cross. Personal rights and freedoms are God-given and inalienable; they do not

---

118. Beliles and Anderson, *Contending*, 79.
119. Hart, *Faith and Freedom*, 281.
120. Ibid., 343.

exist merely for civil convenience or at the discretion of those who hold civil power."[121] So for Amos, the Declaration sets up the foundation for law which results in personal freedom, namely law which is not arbitrary but stems from that which God has ordained.

Beliles and McDowell, like Robertson, appealed to 2 Cor 3:17 in order to find the roots for American liberty in the New Testament. They equated the personal, spiritual liberty that results when God's Spirit enters and regenerates an individual with how God enters into a nation and brings the people liberty. They explained, "When the Spirit of the Lord comes into the heart of a man, that man is liberated. Likewise, when the Spirit of the Lord comes into a nation, that nation is liberated. The degree to which the Spirit of the Lord is infused into a society (through its people, laws, and institutions) is the degree to which that society will experience liberty in every realm (civil, religious, economic, etc.)."[122] While the authors stressed that the New Testament defined liberty in spiritual terms, they nevertheless affirmed that civil liberty comes about because of spiritual liberty. They wrote, "Though internal liberty was a primary focus of Jesus Christ, it must not be overlooked that His inaugural and farewell sermons both emphasized external civil liberty. In Luke 4:18, Christ's first public message focused on 'liberty' for 'the poor ... the captives ... [and] those who are oppressed ...' It is safe to assume that poverty, slavery, tyranny and injustice were on the Lord's mind when, in His final sermon, He commissioned His followers to 'Go therefore and make disciples of all the nations ...' (Matthew 28:19)."[123] Like Hart, Beliles and McDowell continued to trace the concept of liberty from the Bible through history, giving particular attention to documents such as the Mayflower Compact, the English Bill of Rights, and the Constitution. Their conclusion was that God providentially acted to bring liberty, which was grounded in the Bible, to American shores.

The conflation of liberty as defined in the Old and New Testaments with American political liberty is important to the CA thesis. For the advocates of CA, American liberty would not have been possible if Jesus Christ had not come to set people free from sin's condemnation. The spiritual liberty that Christ won is manifested in the state in the form

---

121. Amos, *Defending*, 126.
122. Beliles and McDowell, *America's Providential History*, 26.
123. Ibid., 3.

of political liberty. As Kennedy and Newcombe asserted, "Historian Dr. Charles Hull Wolfe observes that constitutional government and liberty are a heritage passed on from God, beginning with the Abrahamic covenant and climaxing with the American Constitution. When Moses made the covenant between God and the Hebrew people, it was the beginning of political liberty."[124]

The Bible as the Primary Source for the Founding Documents

The CA writers contended that the founding documents were not the product of English Enlightenment thought, but the Bible. This argument, like the argument for original intent, was commonly found throughout CA writings over the past thirty years. Here, the chapter will treat the writers who have argued the most strenuously for this point, namely, Amos, Eidsmoe, and Beliles and Anderson.

Amos' work, *Defending the Declaration*, is a carefully researched book forwarding the simple thesis that the Declaration can trace its roots to the Bible more than it can to the Enlightenment. While the ideas expressed in the Declaration may not be directly biblical, they at least "are not opposed to the teachings of the Bible or of mainstream Christianity. The popular notion that the intellectual heritage of the Declaration traces solely to deism, the Enlightenment, the Renaissance, and from there to pagan Rome and Greece is seriously flawed."[125] Even where ideas and terms found in the Declaration, such as "Nature and Nature's God," seem to be imported from Enlightenment thought, Amos contended that Enlightenment thinkers actually borrowed those ideas from the Bible, and therefore, Christianity is owed the final debt. Amos asserted that the Enlightenment, at its core, presents a secular worldview, and therefore, an anti-Christian, anti-biblical one. Critiquing Noll, Marsden, and Hatch, a popular target among CA proponents, Amos wrote, "I strongly disagree with those Christian writers who have set out to prove that the Founders rejected Christian principles and consciously built the American government on a non-Christian or an anti-Christian base.... I disagree with Noll, Hatch, and Marsden that all the Founders, including John Witherspoon, were infected with anti-Biblical rationalism."[126]

---

124. Kennedy and Newcombe, *What If?*, 80.
125. Amos, *Defending*, 20–21.
126. Ibid., 21.

Amos confronted the allegation that the Declaration was not founded on Christian principles by asserting that Jefferson and the Founders embraced a Christian view of law. For one thing, Locke, one of the primary sources for Jefferson as he penned the Declaration, was not a deist, asserted Amos, but a Christian. Also, Amos took the phrase "Nature and Nature's God" and attempted to demonstrate that these terms find their roots not in Enlightenment thought, but are consistent with orthodox Christian teaching. The phrase also cannot be described as sprouting from Greek and Roman stoicism, because according to Amos, it is not consistent with stoic teaching. He wrote that, ". . . only in the Judeo-Christian theological tradition, including both mainstream Catholicism and Calvinist Protestantism, and in the Christian common law do we find all the factors necessary to give rise to the concepts reflected in the phrase 'laws of nature and of nature's God.'"[127]

Amos also addressed rights theory in his work on the Declaration. He lamented, "Today, the rights theory of the founding fathers and the Declaration of Independence is routinely traced to deism, the Enlightenment, the Renaissance, and from there to ancient Rome and Greece."[128] Nothing could be farther from the truth, for Amos. It is the Bible that most clearly establishes what freedom under law means, and that government's role is to protect the freedom of the citizens who obey the law. Scripture teaches that freedom and personal rights are given by God and the government is not in a position to define those rights, but rather to protect them, according to Amos. "This is why only Biblical ethics maintain a proper balance between order in public life and individual freedom,"[129] wrote Amos.

Even the social compact theory which Locke articulated after the Glorious Revolution cannot be accurately termed secular, for Amos. Amos argued that the compact theory has its roots in Christian teaching as far back as the High Middle Ages. He contended: "Every idea in the Declaration's compact theory of government finds precedent in the Bible. Through the Catholic Church, especially during the Gregorian Reforms of the eleventh through thirteenth centuries, those Biblical precedents were infused into western culture and political thought. They underlie

---

127. Ibid., 74.
128. Ibid., 125.
129. Ibid., 126.

the Magna Carta in 1215, which has clear and direct historical links to the American Revolution and the Declaration of Independence."[130]

Amos' work reflected a more serious academic approach to the question of the origins of the Declaration than many other CA writings. Amos, however, was not alone in arguing that the Bible is the primary source for the founding documents. Eidsmoe also attempted to present a carefully researched work that traced the Christian roots of the Declaration and the Constitution. He compiled a list of what he called sixteen "biblical principles"[131] explicit in the founding documents. They included

1. God's providence
2. God's law
3. Law of nations
4. Man's equality
5. Human rights
6. Rights secured by the government
7. Consent of the governed
8. Man's sin nature
9. Limited powers
10. Rights of the accused
11. Property rights
12. Sanctity of contract
13. Two witnesses
14. Corruption of blood
15. Sundays excepted
16. Separation of church and state[132]

For each of these principles, Eidsmoe found specific biblical references in support. He also combed the Declaration and the Constitution to find support and concluded that there is a direct line between the Bible and the founding documents.

130. Ibid., 149.
131. Eidsmoe, *Christianity and the Constitution*, 362.
132. Ibid., 362–76.

For example, when Eidsmoe identified man's equality as a biblical principle, he wrote,

> Scripture states that "God is no respecter of persons" (Acts 10:34) and that in Christ "there is neither Jew nor Greek" (Gal. 3:28). . . . The framers of the Constitution had a firm basis for believing in equality for they believed in a Creator: "All men are created equal." If one accepts the evolutionary humanist model, what is to prevent one from concluding that some men, or some races, have evolved to a point of superiority over others? Lest that notion sound far-fetched, let us remember that the Nazis believed exactly that. This is not to suggest that evolutionists do not believe in equality, only that they lack a firm basis for believing in equality.[133]

Drawing from two verses in Scripture and cross referencing those verses with a statement from the Declaration demonstrated for Eidsmoe that the Bible is the primary sourcebook for the concept that all are created equal. This methodology was used for all the principles in Eidsmoe's list. On the divine origin of human rights, Eidsmoe first provided a very brief summary of Locke, Jefferson, and Vattel, then turned to the affirmations of human rights in the Declaration and the Constitution (specifically, the right of habeas corpus and the right not to be prosecuted ex post facto). Then, Eidsmoe stated, "Human rights find their basis in the Bible. . . . God also confers certain positive rights through the negative commands of Scripture. The commandment, 'Thou shalt not kill' (Exod 20:13), confers a right to life. The command not to kidnap or enslave confers a right to liberty (Exod 21:16; Deut 24:7). The command, 'Thou shalt not steal' (Exod 20:15) confers a right to property. The three rights of life, liberty, and property mentioned by Locke come from the Bible."[134] Eidsmoe's methodology was clearly intended to draw a clear line from the Bible to the founding documents. This line, for Eidsmoe, runs straight through the entire course of Western thought, even the Enlightenment. Since Enlightenment thinkers such as Locke were clearly borrowing from Scripture to formulate their own ideas, the Bible's first-tier influence on the founding documents is not minimized.

Following Amos in attempting to demonstrate the Bible's preeminent influence in the founding documents, and using Eidsmoe's methodology, Beliles and Anderson identified ten biblical principles in the Constitution,

133. Ibid., 364–65.
134. Ibid., 367.

and another five "structural framework principles."[135] The five principles were listed earlier in this chapter, but Beliles and Anderson's ten "internal principles" included:

1. "Man is of divine origin"
2. "Man has individual value"
3. "Government exists to serve the people"
4. "The source of individual rights is God, not government"
5. "God is sovereign over government"
6. "All men are created equal"
7. "Civil government is dependent upon successful self government"
8. "Government and law are based upon moral absolutes"
9. "Man's nature is sinful"
10. "External forms are a result of internal power."[136]

What was striking about Beliles and Anderson's list is its close similarity to Eidsmoe's, and that the exact methodology was used to reach the conclusion of the Bible's predominant influence on the founding documents. On the principle of the equality of man, for example, Beliles and Anderson used the same biblical references Eidsmoe used. They wrote, "This idea, too, originated with the Bible. In the Book of Acts 10:34, scripture tells us that 'God is no respecter of persons.' In Galatians 3:28, it says that in Christ, 'there is neither Jew nor Greek.' In fact, the entire legal code in the Bible demonstrates equal justice under law."[137] Thus, just as Amos and Eidsmoe contended that all the ideas contained in the founding documents are explicitly biblical, and therefore Christian, Beliles and Anderson affirmed the same contention and clearly followed their lead.

Before closing, a final issue needs to be addressed on this contention. CA writers openly acknowledged the objection that the Constitution does not mention God anywhere. They vigorously denied, of course, that this fact takes anything away from the Christian character of the Constitution. How they did so varied from writer to writer.

---

135. Beliles and Anderson, *Contending*, 126–30.
136. Ibid., 110–20.
137. Ibid., 115.

DeMar consistently pointed to a nineteenth-century work supporting CA by B. F. Morris entitled *The Christian Life and Character of the Civil Institutions of the United States*. He stated on the American Vision website[138] which offers the book for sale, "Be afraid ACLU. Be very afraid. Morris packs *The Christian Life and Character* with page after page of original source material making the case that America was founded as a Christian nation. The evidence is unanswerable and irrefutable. This 1,000-page book will astound you and send enemies of Christianity into shock."[139] How did Morris's book answer for the absence of God in the Constitution? Morris recounted a quaint story of an exchange on this very issue between a professor at Princeton, a Rev. Dr. Miller, and Alexander Hamilton. The exchange, according to Morris, went like this: "Rev. Dr. Miller ... met Alexander Hamilton in the streets of Philadelphia and said, 'Mr. Hamilton, we are greatly grieved that the Constitution has no recognition of God or the Christian religion.' 'I declare,' said Hamilton, 'we forgot it!'"[140]

Morris' answer to the omission of God from the Constitution obviously falls short, even when one considers a brief statement from Washington he included about how the Constitution was to protect free religious expression despite the omission. Thankfully, the CA writers who addressed the omission gave a more sophisticated treatment of it than the work by Morris.

Hutson, in his rebuke of Isaac Kramnick and Laurence Moore's *The Godless Constitution*, insisted that the Constitution does indeed mention God: "Done in Convention by the Unanimous Consent of the States present the Seventeenth Day of September in the Year of our Lord one thousand seven hundred and Eighty seven and of the Independence of the United States of America the Twelfth."[141] He also pointed to the acknowledgement of the Christian Sabbath in the Constitution: "If any Bill shall not be returned by the President within ten Days (Sundays excepted) after

---

138. DeMar is the president of American Vision, and its purpose is to advance the CA thesis among other things. It seems to be a counterpart to Barton's WallBuilders, although American Vision commits to reformed theology much more strongly than WallBuilders.

139. Morris, *American Vision*.

140. Morris, *Christian Life*, 296–97.

141. U.S. Constitution, art. 7.

it shall have been presented to him, the Same shall be a Law...."[142] Hutson wrote, "This language does nothing less than write the Christian Sabbath into the Constitution by presuming that the president will not work on Sunday. Does this section make the United States a Christian nation? Many Americans in the early nineteenth century would have argued that it did...."[143]

Eidsmoe's answer to the omission of God from the Constitution was that the framers wanted to avoid causing dissent among the thirteen states, dissent which might have jeopardized its ratification. He observed that "... most [states] had their own state churches. There was general agreement that the federal government would not establish anyone of those state churches as the new federal church thereby creating resentment among the others, or interfere with any of the state establishments. A religious reference could have created divisions."[144] Even if the Constitution made no reference to God, Eidsmoe reasoned, the Declaration made several references to "Nature and Nature's God," the "Creator," and "Divine Providence." "There is no indication that any delegate objected to any of these references,"[145] wrote Eidsmoe.

Robertson, a Republican candidate for president in 1988, attempted to answer for the omission in a similar way, but he went farther than Eidsmoe. His argument was that the Declaration serves as the basis for the Constitution and the Bill of Rights. Since the Declaration had already made several references to God, it was not the Constitution's place to do so. The Constitution was the pragmatic document expressing how the government was to function, while the Declaration formed the basis for that plan. Robertson stated, "That Constitution, as our manmade plan for government, is not an appropriate or necessary place to speak of God. The Declaration has said enough. God is the source and protector of our liberty, the judge of our good intentions. In His natural and revealed Law we find the purpose and foreshadowings of the plan of this government. But after that, the people make the decisions."[146] Robertson's point was that the American government was not established to be theocratic but

142. U.S. Constitution, art. 1, sec. 7.
143. Hutson, *Forgotten Features*, 114.
144. Eidsmoe, *Christianity and the Constitution*, 360.
145. Ibid.
146. Robertson, *Dates With Destiny*, 92–93.

democratic, so the plan for government should make no reference at all to God or to Jesus Christ.

While other CA writers, such as LaHaye and Beliles and Anderson, took similar positions as Robertson on this issue, Marshall and Manuel approached it from a radically different perspective. As stated earlier in the chapter, Marshall and Manuel believed the Constitution originated in the mind of God as a covenant between Him and the nation. When discussing the sources of the Constitution, Marshall and Manuel assigned to it the "divine origin of its inspiration"[147] along with the contributions of the Puritans. For these authors, the omission of religious language in the Constitution is irrelevant because the document is divinely inspired and "the greatest legal minds of two centuries have continued to marvel at it as being almost beyond the scope and dimension of human wisdom."[148]

Clearly then, the argument that the Bible exerted an overshadowing presence and influence in the founding documents has been viewed as unassailable by the proponents of CA. It is one of the most important arguments forwarded in support of the CA thesis. If it can indeed be demonstrated that the Bible was central to the founding of America, it seems to follow that the CA thesis must be taken seriously by the secular world. An opportunity would then exist to recover biblical principles in civic life, and thus return the nation to the Founders' intention for it.

A Final Unifying Theme of CA: Appeal to Return to Christian Roots

To close the treatment of commonly held historical, philosophical, and theological themes of the CA thesis, the chapter must address one final significant tenet. No survey of CA themes is complete without attending to the ubiquitous appeal for America to return to its Christian heritage in works that promote the thesis. In fact, all the writings of CA proponents drew the reader to same ends: an awakening to the reality that America has drifted from its founding identity as a Christian nation, and that the nation must recover this identity if it is to survive as the democratic republic intended from the beginning.

LaHaye did not wait until the end of his book to make the appeal to return. His book opened with a polemic against secularism in public education and how the contemporary generation "is being robbed of

147. Marshall and Manuel, *Light and Glory*, 343–44.
148. Ibid., 343.

its country's religious heritage."[149] As if he was at the head of an angry multitude, LaHaye challenged, "Whom do you blame? Don't blame the church; we still warn young people about the consequences of such activities. Don't blame parents! They don't want their children living like humanistic animals who have evolved from lower life forms. I blame the secular humanists, who have expelled traditional American moral values that were an integral part of our school curriculum for the first 150 years of our nation's history."[150] By casting the present-day perspective on history in ominous terms, LaHaye intended to create a stimulus for Christian action to reverse an insidious secular agenda and restore truth to American historical interpretation, especially among the young. He insisted that "Unless we return to traditional respect for the teaching of religion and morality, which was advocated by our Founding Fathers and which is essential to maintaining moral sanity in a democracy, this country will ultimately destroy itself from within."[151]

McDowell and Beliles cast a similarly grim vision of the current situation, but not quite as bluntly as LaHaye. These authors observed that many academics, liberals, and members of the elite media want America to be more like other nations which are secular to become a well-mannered member of the global community. They wrote, "There is a call for America to be like other nations. Some have said she should follow the directions of the United Nations or act like Europe, and in so doing we would then be civil, not stir up evil leaders, or cause other problems in the earth."[152] The consequences of this course of action are clear. Ignorance and tyranny are the result of abandoning the godly heritage built into the nation. The authors cited Benjamin Franklin in making this point: "Benjamin Franklin said that ignorance produces bondage: 'A nation of well informed men who have been taught to know and prize the rights which God has given them cannot be enslaved. It is in the region of ignorance that tyranny begins.'"[153] The answer for America, for McDowell and Beliles, is not to strive to be like other nations as ancient Israel did, but to

---

149. LaHaye, *Faith of Our Founding Fathers*, 1.
150. Ibid., 4.
151. Ibid., 10.
152. McDowell and Beliles, *American Dream*, 5.
153. Ibid., 34.

embrace and advance a thoroughly Christian worldview in the family, in education, and in government.

Falwell's appeal is based upon a realistic appraisal of the moral state of the country at the end of the twentieth century. Because of the national sins of abortion, homosexuality, pornography, humanism, and the collapse of the traditional family in society, America faced decline and ultimate destruction. He exhorted, "There is no excuse for what is happening in our country. We must, from the highest office in the land right down to the shoeshine boy in the airport, have a return to biblical basics. If the Congress of our United States will take its stand on that which is right and wrong, and if our President, our judiciary system, and our state and local leaders will take their stand on holy living, we can turn this country around."[154] For Falwell, the way to do this is painfully simple: "The time has come for America's Christians to confess the sins of our nation as well."[155] If the nation would but turn from its national sins, return to its Christian underpinnings, and once again acknowledge the God of the Bible in its civic life, America would be restored to greatness. Falwell explained the absolute need to return to God in these terms: "Only then will we become important to God, and only then will we once again know the great blessings of the Power that has made and preserved us a nation!"[156]

Barton's appeal was grounded in what he saw as the distortion of the First Amendment in recent years by the courts, as well as the robbing of religious freedom from the Christian population and the forsaking of original intent in the interpretation of the Constitution. After describing the slow but steady erosion of original intent in the First Amendment since 1947 in *America's Godly Heritage*, Barton pleaded with Christians to do more to get involved at every level to restore the biblical principles he maintained were at the founding. Barton entreated, "'Separation of church and state'—as we have it today—is not a Biblical teaching; it is not a teaching of the Founding Fathers; it is not a historical teaching; and it is not a teaching of law until recent years. The 3 percent has taken away our heritage, and we've lost sight of it. We have to get involved and take it back. A Godly heritage is the foundation of America; and the church must take right ground. We must recover the things that we've given up in recent

---

154. Falwell, *Listen, America!*, 18.
155. Ibid., 251.
156. Ibid., 50.

years. We must get involved!"[157] The responsibility for recovering biblical principles rests with the church. For Barton, only Christians, united in the purpose of restoring the original Christian intent of the Founders, will be able to reverse the tide of secularism.

The appeal to return from Marshall and Manuel is similar to Barton's in this regard. Only the church can check America's decline, because the church is to give voice to the will of God in society. Christians must fulfill the appeal of 2 Chr 7:14, and God will be faithful to keep His promise to restore the nation. They wrote, "For a whole nation to return to the Covenant Way seems impossible. But it is not impossible; it has been done before."[158] Thus, for Marshall and Manuel, Christians should not despair. The terms of God's covenant with America have not changed, so there is no complex formula to master in order to enjoy God's favor once again. The restoration of God comes to a nation just as it does to an individual, according to Marshall and Manuel. But it must start with Christ's people. They wrote, "we modern Christians *must* humble ourselves and renew the horizontal as well as the vertical aspect of our covenant with God. If we do this, He *will* hear, and forgive our sins, and heal our land."[159]

Much more space could be devoted to outlining further examples of the call by CA proponents to return to America's Christian past. This plea seemed to be the single most important motive for the writing of all the publications advocating for CA. To summarize, the most common features of the appeal to return are:

1. America is in a state of broad decline due to a drift toward secularism
2. This decline may be arrested only by a return to America's Christian roots
3. Christians must lead the nation back to these roots
4. While America's decline may be steep, it is not too late to mend the problems.

Action can still be taken to recover America's godly heritage.

---

157. Barton, *America's Godly Heritage*, 30; emphasis original.
158. Marshall and Manuel, *Light and Glory*, 355; emphasis original.
159. Ibid., 358.

CONCLUSION

This concludes the survey of the major historical, philosophical, and theological themes for the CA thesis. The fourteen themes treated in the above paragraphs represent those most widely advanced by CA writers in concluding that America is a Christian nation. To briefly review, the historical themes supporting the CA thesis were:

1. The Christian faith of the Founders.
2. The Christian character of the sources drawn from by the Founders.
3. The Christian character of colonial documents and early state constitutions.
4. The Christian character of early colleges.
5. The powerful Christian influence of the Great Awakening and radical Whig ideology on the revolutionary generation.

The philosophical themes reviewed were:

1. The original intent of the Founders may be accurately discerned by applying the same evangelical hermeneutical method as used when interpreting Scripture.
2. The original intent of the Founders was to build Christianity into the heart of the nation.
3. The role of the Enlightenment is not as significant as the role of Christianity in the founding.

The theological themes for the CA thesis included:

1. A providential view of history.
2. American exceptionalism as evidence of God's unique blessing on the nation.
3. America as God's chosen nation, a new Israel.
4. Liberty as a biblical notion finding its consummate application in the civic life of America.
5. The Bible as the primary source of the founding national documents.

Finally, the appeal for Christian Americans to lead the nation back to its Christian roots in order that God would be pleased to bless it and cause it to fulfill its purpose in the world was a theme appearing in all CA works. Clearly, the CA thesis should not be considered as a minimalistic argument, but one that has been well developed over the course of the past three decades.

3

Christian Contributions to American Notions of Freedom

A FAIR EVANGELICAL CRITIQUE of CA must give attention to the central role that Christianity has played in American history. To minimize or neglect that role is to do an injustice to the historical record and ignore the debt owed to Christianity by Americans of every generation. While Christianity is not the sole factor leading to the formation of the American character, the Christian faith has undoubtedly had a major impact on the ideas and principles which define it. This chapter will support Noll's version of a weak CA, which acknowledges the significant role that Christianity has played in American history from the first years of British colonization to the American founding.[1] It will seek to answer the question, how did Christianity's influence generally affect the American ideal of individual liberty? The answers to this question will hopefully provide an appropriate background to the critique of CA which will come in the next chapter, and help lend an accurate understanding of Christianity's role in the development of a key element of the American identity.

One of the most influential Christian theological systems bearing upon freedom in America is Puritanism. This system helped to define the contours of early English colonization, from politics, to economics, to church life. In fact, according to Noll, Puritanism was the main force shaping American life from 1630 to the Revolutionary period.[2] While it is far beyond the scope of this study to provide a thorough treatment of the influence of Puritan theology on American freedom, some introductory observations can be made that may help clarify the extent of that

1. See Noll, *One Nation*.
2. Ibid.

influence and help show the importance of Puritanism as a source for American revolutionary and founding thought.

The Puritan colonies of New England were among the first settlements in British North America.³ The settlement of the Massachusetts Bay Colony in 1630 took place during the period of great Puritan influence in England. The Puritans' establishment of New England in the early seventeenth century was a milestone in the history of England and America. A. Mervyn Davies observed, "Exactly a hundred years lie between the accession of Elizabeth I (1558) and the death of Oliver Cromwell, the lord protector [sic] (1658). These hundred years form the Puritan era in history of England. During it the foundations of the country's freedom and the foundations of its empire across the seas together were laid."⁴ The Puritan theological system which entailed the knitting together of all forms of human thought and practice under Reformed theology was revolutionary, especially in America. Its insistence on a pure church made up of regenerate and literate individual members formed the basis and justification for such a synthesis. Davies wrote, "The Puritan Revolution is a decisive event in the development of modern liberal democracy. For the English-speaking world it brought to a halt the universal trend toward absolute monarchy, and permitted Locke and Madison—not Hobbes and Bodin—to have the last word on what constituted political truth for the West."⁵

The primary influence in Puritan theology other than the Bible is John Calvin. David W. Hall wrote, "Western society owes many of its best political advances to Reformation theology, and the establishing of America during the early 1600s owes more to Calvinism than to other influences."⁶ The Christian theological system that Calvin labored to delineate in his *Institutes* is an apt summary of how Puritans thought about and lived their faith. Calvin's expressions of anthropology, hamartiology, Christology, and soteriology had the effect of lifting the individual out of the hopelessness of salvation by works and into the freedom of salvation

---

3. See chapter 1 for a brief treatment of the Puritans' motive for establishing the New England colonies, their basis for organizing and governing those colonies, and their conception of the relationship between religion and the state. See that chapter for a list of important sources on the Puritans of New England in the seventeenth century.

4. Davies, *Foundation*, 140.

5. Ibid., 154.

6. Hall, *Genevan Reformation*, 286.

by grace. For Calvin and the Puritans, man is neither ultimately bound by any law, nor any human authority, but is free because of the work of Christ. This idea, coupled with the dissemination of Reformation theology, would be significant for the colonization of New England. Hall wrote that "The liberation of religion from clerical domination in the sixteenth-century Reformation, aided by the democratization of literature by mass-publishing, spawned the real seeds of the New England settlement."[7]

For the Puritans, freedom accompanies gratitude and willing subservience to the God of salvation. Fear is replaced by love, and the impact of this dramatic shift in thought and practice affected Puritan civilization profoundly, and through it, the whole of the American colonial civilization. As Davies stated,

> The same man who bows his head the lowest before the inexorable decrees of God carries his head the highest. For Calvinism makes the ordinary man quite extraordinary in his courage, his independence of the world, his freedom from the things that bind and enslave human beings whose wills are not subservient to the divine Will. There is no one on earth he owns as master; and, as he is far "more fearful of displeasing God then all the world," he has what it takes to give him a sense of spiritual independence, which is the foundation of democracy.[8]

Still, even while the Puritan strain of Protestant theology contributed much to the idea of freedom, there were limits. The New England Puritans, as has been discussed in chapter 1, were not offering the individual members of each community unfettered intellectual freedom. They were also not advocating for a complete rejection of ecclesiastical authority. Perry Miller and Thomas Johnson stated that "Though Protestantism can be viewed as a 'liberation' of the common man, it was far from being a complete emancipation of the individual."[9] According to Miller and Johnson, it was not until the frontier mindset of the colonists set in during the early eighteenth century, a mindset which tended to "lessen the prestige of the cultured classes and to enhance the social power of those who wanted their religion in a more simple, downright and 'democratic' form, who cared nothing for the refinements and subtleties of historic theology."[10]

7. Ibid., 287.
8. Davies, *Foundation*, 74.
9. Miller and Johnson, *Puritans*, 16.
10. Ibid., 17.

But more democratic forms of Christianity than seventeenth-century Puritanism became inevitable in America, in part because the Puritans were strenuous in the contention that the Church does not stand as a mediator between God and man. This belief would ultimately help give American Christianity a more pietistic and less authoritarian flavor, especially during the Great Awakening. Miller and Johnson wrote that "as the Puritan doctrine that men were saved by the infusion of God's grace could lead to the Antinomianism of Mrs. Hutchinson, . . . , so the Puritan contention that regenerate men were illuminated with divine truth might lead to the belief that true religion did not need the assistance of learning, books, arguments, logical demonstrations, or classical languages."[11] This is what happened by the mid-eighteenth century. Noll wrote, "the Awakening marked a transition from clerical to lay religion, from the minister as an inherited authority figure to self-empowered mobilizer, from the definition of Christianity by doctrine to its definition by piety, and from a state church encompassing all of society to a gathered church made up only of the converted."[12] Thus, although the Puritans sought to maintain a degree of authoritarianism in religion and society in the seventeenth century, the Calvinist emphasis on individual freedom in Christ would be important in the development of distinctly American notions of freedom in the eighteenth.[13]

One final note is that seventeenth century Puritanism contributed largely to Americans' views of themselves as a people set apart by God. From the outset of Puritan settlement in America, the Puritans saw themselves as God's new chosen people, established in America to set a holy example to the world. George McKenna wrote, "The one constant running through all forms of this Protestantism is the belief that Americans are a people set apart, a people with a providential mission."[14] He quoted Samuel Danforth's 1670 sermon which compared the New England colonists with the Israelites fleeing from Egypt and entering the Promised Land. McKenna also showed that this view continued in the preaching during the American Revolution. He wrote, "Here, to take one example of many from that time, is Rev. Samuel Sherwood calling his country to

---

11. Ibid., 14–15.

12. Noll, *America's God*, 44.

13. See chapter 1 for a discussion on how the Puritan model of a state church was replaced by disestablishment of religion from the state by the late eighteenth century.

14. McKenna, *Puritan Origins*, 6.

arms against the British in 1776: 'Let your faith be strong in the divine promises. Although the daughter of Zion may be in a wilderness state, yet the Lord himself is her *Light*. The time is coming when Jehova [*sic*] will dry up the rivers of her persecuting enemies, and the *Ransomed of the Lord* shall *Come With Singing unto Zion, and Everlasting Joy.*"[15] This idea of divine exceptionalism would also be instrumental in helping to define the American identity.

While Puritanism was a regional political and social entity, as a theological entity it impacted all thirteen British colonies in some form. H. Richard Niebuhr wrote that the Puritan theological influence was felt everywhere in the American colonies. He stated,

> taken literally, the establishment of theocracy was not the hope of the Puritans only. It was no less the desire of Pilgrims and Plymouth, of Roger Williams and his assorted followers in Rhode Island, of the Quakers in the middle colonies, of German sectarians in Pennsylvania, of the Dutch Reformed in New York, the Scotch-Irish Presbyterians of a later immigration and of many a native movement. All of these had been deeply influenced, if not directly inspired, by the faith of the Protestant renewal with its fresh insistence on the present sovereignty and initiative of God. . . .[16]

The following statement made by Noll underscores Niebuhr's point: "Historians of early America, both of its religious and secular aspects, have agreed concerning the prominence of the Puritan strain in the nation's early history. The extent of this Puritan influence is indicated by the fact that approximately three-fourths of the colonists of the time of the Revolution were identified with denominations that had arisen from the Reformed, Puritan wing of European Protestantism: Congregationalism, Presbyterianism, Baptists, German and Dutch Reformed."[17] Hall observed that Presbyterianism in particular was on the rise in the American colonies in the early 1700s. He wrote, "Presbyterians were the most rapidly growing segment of American religion in the early eighteenth century; and in Pennsylvania, Virginia, and in both Carolinas, they were the largest distinctive ideological group."[18] Even though Anglicanism was dominant

---

15. Ibid., 7.
16. Niebuhr, *Kingdom of God*, 45.
17. Noll, *Christians in the American Revolution*, 29–30.
18. Hall, *Genevan Reformation*, 417.

in the South, according to Hall, "approximately two-thirds of the colonial population at the time of the Revolution was dominated by dissenting groups who retained little affection for Anglicanism or any other hierarchical structure."[19] Thus, Puritanism, alongside real Whig ideology, Enlightenment philosophy, English common law tradition, and classical antiquity, was a significant source for American revolutionary thought, and should not be overlooked.[20] Alden Vaughan wrote, "there is general agreement among students of our national character that deeply embedded in the assumptions and aspirations of today's Americans, for good or ill, lies a hefty portion of the Puritan tradition."[21]

COLONIAL DOCUMENTS AND SERMONS

One of the ways to observe how central Calvinist/Puritan theology would be to the development of American freedom is to read some of the documents and sermons of early colonial history. First, three colonial documents from New England will be treated: the *Fundamental Orders of Connecticut* (1639), the *Massachusetts Body of Liberties* (1641), and the *Frame of Government of Pennsylvania* (1682).

The *Fundamental Orders of Connecticut*, laid down by the townships of Windsor, Wethersfield, and Hartford, was meant to serve as a contract entered into by the men who comprised the settlement. It defined rules for how public officials were to be selected by men who owned property, lived in the townships, and who had taken an oath of loyalty to the colony. The preamble to the *Orders* stated,

> ... well knowing where a people are gathered together the Word of God requires that, to maintain the peace and union of such a people, there should be an orderly and decent government established according to God, to order and dispose of the affairs of the people at all seasons as occasion shall require; do therefore associate and conjoin ourselves to be as one public state or commonwealth; and do, for ourselves and our successors and such as shall be adjoined to us at any time hereafter, enter into combination and confederation together to maintain and preserve the liberty and purity of the gospel of our Lord Jesus Christ which we now profess, as also the

---

19. Ibid.
20. See Lutz, *American Constitutionalism*; and Bailyn, *Ideological Origins*.
21. Vaughan, *Puritan Tradition*, xi.

discipline of the churches which according to the truth of the said gospel is now practiced among us; . . ."[22]

In this document are found the theological principles of the authority of the Bible, the establishment of government with God as the basis, the covenant[23] entered into and agreed upon by equal members, and spiritual freedom and holiness that the gospel endows upon its followers through the discipline and teaching of the church. Thus, the *Orders* established these principles as the starting point for organizing themselves into a free political body of equal members.

The *Massachusetts Body of Liberties* similarly demonstrated the influence of Puritan theology on freedom. This document was designed to clearly define the liberties, not only of the voting population of the colony, but of every person living therein, including women and children. It even has a section devoted to the equitable and kind treatment of animals. A particularly salient feature of this document is that it laid down due process of law, so that for example, "no man's life shall be taken away; no man's honor or good name shall be stained; no man's person shall be arrested . . . unless it be by virtue or equity of some express law of the country warranting the same, established by a General Court and sufficiently published, or in case of the defect of a law in any particular case, by the Word of God; . . ."[24] It also defined the freedom of each member of the Commonwealth as being necessary to the Christian faith. "The free fruition of such liberties, immunities, and privileges as humanity, civility, and Christianity call for as due every man in his place and proportion without impeachment and infringement, has ever been and ever will be the tranquility and stability of churches and commonwealths; and the denial and deprival thereof, the disturbance if not the ruin of both."[25] Thus, any curtailment of the freedom of each person in Massachusetts threatened the very existence of the churches and the colony itself.

The final example is not taken from Puritan New England, but from Pennsylvania. Still, the *Frame of Government of Pennsylvania* is in accord with the above examples taken from the Puritans. The preamble to this document stated that the government was not to infringe upon the liberty

22. *Fundamental Orders of Connecticut*, 157.
23. See chapter 1 for a discussion of the covenant in Puritan society.
24. *Massachusetts Body of Liberties*, 163–64.
25. Ibid., 163.

of anyone who obeyed the law, but instead, was to deny it to lawbreakers. The Bible was taken to be the source of this idea. It stated,

> [Saint Paul] settles the divine right of government beyond exception, and that for two ends: first, to terrify evil doers; secondly, to cherish those that do well—which gives government a life beyond corruption and makes it as durable in the world as good men shall be. So that government seems to me a part of religion itself, anything sacred in its institution and end. For if it does not directly remove the cause it crushes the effects of evil and is as such (though a lower, yet) an emanation of the same divine power that is both author and object of pure religion.[26]

Although Pennsylvania was not established by Puritans, strictly speaking, the authority of Scripture and the idea that government possesses its direction and legitimacy from God, as well as the idea that government is not to tyrannize the law-abiding populace, fit well within the Puritan theological system.

The body of colonial Puritan sermons offers some insight into early views on liberty in addition to the colonial documents. John Winthrop, in a 1645 discourse on liberty, differentiated between "natural" and "civil" liberty, the former referring to "do what he list; it is a liberty to evil as well as to good."[27] This form, according to Winthrop, "makes men grow more evil, and in time to be worse than brute beasts: . . ."[28] In contrast to natural liberty, Winthrop said that civil liberty "is maintained and exercised in a way of subjection to authority; it is the same kind of liberty wherewith Christ has made us free."[29] Giving heed to one's natural liberties entails throwing off authority, but for Winthrop, the enjoyment of civil liberty is found in obedience to laws, because in these laws is found the individual and communal good. Commenting on Winthrop's speech, specifically the idea that liberty is enjoyed most under the rule of law, John Adair asserted that the American government owes a debt to Winthrop's view of liberty. He stated that "the reasoning behind the speech would serve as the charter for modern government in America" and "The American Constitution . . . is a legacy of this frame of mind."[30]

26. Penn, *Frame of Government*, 17.
27. Winthrop, "Speech on Liberty," 179.
28. Ibid.
29. Ibid.
30. Adair, *Founding Fathers*, 282–83.

John Cotton's (1584–1652) sermon, *An Exposition upon the 13th Chapter of the Revelation* (1639), stressed the reality of man's preponderance to use liberty as a furtherance to do evil. Rulers are no less susceptible to corruption in their administration of authority than anyone else, so they must be checked by a godly populace, according to Cotton. He said, concerning man's proclivity to abuse liberty, "There is a straine in a man's heart that will sometime or other runne out to excesse, unless the Lord restraine it. . . . It is necessary therefore, that all power that is on earth be limited, Church-power or other: . . ."[31] Furthermore, Cotton asserted, "A Prince himself cannot tell where hee will speak great things, then he will make and unmake, say and unsay, and undertake such things as are neither for his own honour, nor for the safety of the State. It is therefore fit for every man to be studious of the bounds which the Lord hath set: and for the People, in whom fundamentally all power lyes, to give as much power as God in his word gives to men: And it is meet that Magistrates in the Commonwealth, and so Officers in Churches should desire to know the utmost bounds of their own power, and it is safe for both: . . ."[32] Cotton here seemed to be stressing the need for some system of check and balance for those in authority. Since the fall of man touches everyone, including rulers in the church and the state, it is necessary for the people to limit the scope of a government's reach using the moral standard outlined in Scripture.

Jonathan Mayhew (1720–1766) preached *A Discourse concerning Unlimited Submission* on January 30, 1750. In it, he strongly critiqued the idea of divine right of kings, and asserted that it was the people's responsibility to throw off a tyrannical government. He said, "If we calmly consider the nature of the thing itself, nothing can well be imagined more directly contrary to common sense, than to suppose that *millions* of people should be subjected to the arbitrary, precarious pleasure of *one single man* . . . so that their estates, and every thing that is valuable in life, and even their lives also, shall be absolutely at his disposal."[33] Nothing in Scripture, and nothing in the common experience of man could ever warrant such an idea as divine right, according to Mayhew. All forms of tyranny are to be resisted by the people, and if the people refuse to resist tyranny, they are

---

31. Cotton, *13th Chapter of the Revelation*, 213.
32. Ibid.
33. Mayhew, *Unlimited Submission*, 277.

actually going against the will of God. He wrote, "For a nation thus abused to arise unanimously, and to resist their prince, even to the dethroning him, is not criminal; but a reasonable way of vindicating their liberties and just rights; it is making use of the means, and the only means, which God has put into their power, for mutual and self-defence. And it would be highly criminal in them, not to make use of this means.... And in such a case it would, of the two, be more rational to suppose, that they that did NOT *resist*, than that they who did, would *receive to themselves damnation.*"[34] For Mayhew, a tyrant was, by definition, an abuser of power, one whom Cotton would have censured as a ruler taking his liberty to excess, and one whom Winthrop would have chastised as exercising natural rather than civil liberty. Thus, far from being a legitimate ruler under which the people would enjoy liberty under laws established for their good, a tyrant is one who the people have a duty to overthrow in order to establish justice for themselves.

Thomas Buckingham taught similarly to Mayhew. In his 1729 sermon, *Moses and Aaron*, he advocated for a constitution that would clearly establish the boundaries for rulers. Consistent with the thought of Cotton, Buckingham sought to limit the freedom of rulers to rule arbitrarily. He wrote, "This is absolutely needful for the well Ordering and Governing of any People. It is not fit they should be left to do what is right in their own eyes; they need a rule to guide them and to bind them to their good Behaviour. Nor is it safe for Rulers to act Arbitrarily, and to make their Wills and Passions a Law to themselves and others. There should be some fixed Rules of Government, and these duely Published, that the subject might know what Terms he stands upon, and how to escape the lash of the Laws."[35] Harry Stout, commenting on Buckingham's sermon, wrote "When New Englanders eventually rose up against their sovereign, it was because he claimed powers that transgressed his constitutional limitations, trampling on the laws of men and the law of God."[36] It is important to note that Buckingham and Mayhew delivered their sermons decades before the controversies between the American colonies and Great Britain arose. Thus, the Puritan tradition of freedom would contribute significantly to later revolutionary thought.

34. Ibid., 280.
35. Buckingham, *Moses and Aaron*, 171.
36. Stout, *New England Soul*, 171–72.

RENAISSANCE EXPLORATION LED TO PROTESTANT COLONIZATION AND A NEW CONSCIOUSNESS

While considering Puritan theological influence on the colonies, it is important to remember that the narrative of English colonization (and the subsequent influence of Puritan theology on American colonial life) is part of the larger narrative of Renaissance exploration. The Puritan way of colonizing is part of a consistent series of historical events initiated by Reformation Christianity. Renaissance exploration was driven by a thirst for knowledge of the unknown along with opportunities to exploit whatever new wealth could be found. It was also part of a quest to expand the influence of the Church. Both Catholic and Protestant explorers and colonizers sought to reach heathen peoples with the gospel—some from pure motives, and some from impure. Still, as Montgomery asserted, "The deepest chord of the Renaissance was struck, not by the critic Valla, the sensuist Botticelli, the rationalist Pompanazzi, or even by the Promethean Leonardo da Vinci, but by the Moses and David of Michelangelo and the printed Greek New Testament of Erasmus. As 'Erasmus laid the egg that Luther hatched' (in the proper aphorism of the time), so the Renaissance laid the egg the Reformation hatched. And the quest for a new Eden which motivated the explorers of the 17th and 16th centuries was handed on as a legacy to the Protestant settlers who came to the American shores in the 17th century."[37] Thus, at least in part, Renaissance exploration was an attempt to rediscover the Christian faith in a new world untouched and unspoiled by human sin—what Montgomery called, "a new Eden." This is what motivated the Puritans to come to American shores—to establish a Christian commonwealth in the primeval wilderness, unhindered by latitudinarian resistance and official persecution in England. It is this Christian component of Renaissance exploration—the "quest for a new Eden"—that is passed on to the Puritans. They, in turn, would make their profound mark on colonial culture which helped shape the American political consciousness, one that distinguished itself sharply from that of the mother country during the Revolution.

This new consciousness, bequeathed to the Puritans by the Reformation, was a new emphasis on the potential of the individual. Page Smith identified several characteristics in his treatment of this new way of thinking, two of which will be addressed here. First, prior to the Reformation,

37. Montgomery, *Shaping*, 37.

people were not seen as individual persons, but as belonging to certain groups. He wrote that people belonged "to social groups and classes, to communes and communities—estates—by which they were defined in which set the boundaries of their worlds and establish their identities; they were clerks, aristocrats, priests, artisans, members of guilds, or burghs."[38] These social groups functioned as boundaries which provided for social stability and security. Each person knew his place. As Smith described, "These traditional orders did not so much submerge him as defined and protected him. Above all, they contained him."[39] Reformation theology, along with other influences, helped to transform this social structure, redefining it in terms of the value of the individual. The notion of the priesthood of the believer was essential to effecting this transformation. "Luther and Calvin, by postulating a single 'individual' soul responsible for itself, plucked a new human type out of this traditional 'order' and put him down naked, a re-formed individual in a re-formed world.... Thus there appeared modern man (or his essential integument), an introspective, aggressive individual who was able to function remarkably well outside these older structures that had defined people's roles and given them whatever power they possessed."[40]

The second characteristic identified by Smith is motivated by the first. With the new emphasis on individual potential in society, unbound by the confines of the "estate," untapped human vigor and initiative were unleashed into the world. One of the results of this unleashing of human initiative was the colonization of New England, but not merely that. It was the way in which New England was colonized that was unique. Describing the significance of the Mayflower Compact, Smith wrote, "In it the Pilgrims formed a 'civil body politic,' and promised to obey the laws their own government might pass. In short, the individual Pilgrim invented on the spot a new community, one that would be ruled by laws of its making."[41] This is in radical contrast to the way every other society in the West was structured at the time, as governments ruled by royal fiat.[42] Even though these characteristics were not necessarily limited to

38. Smith, ed., *Religious Origins*, 2.
39. Ibid.
40. Ibid.
41. Ibid., 3.

42. England's government was the noteworthy exception to this rule. Still, even England was ruled by a monarchy. The fact that the monarchy was limited by the Magna

the American colonies, it was in America that this new Reformation consciousness found the most fertile ground and thereby developed into the ideas that would help bring about the American Revolution.

It is helpful at this point to draw a contrast between the Protestant mode of colonization in the British colonies and that of Catholic Spain's mode of colonization in New Spain. This contrast presents in very clear terms how profoundly the Reformation consciousness mediated by the Puritans differentiated the premodern world of absolute rule with the modern world defined by individual liberty. Stark wrote, "As British colonists, North Americans inherited extensive freedom and a capitalist economy. In contrast, the Spanish colonists in Latin America inherited a repressive and unproductive feudalism."[43] The key to this difference was both political and religious. In the thirteen colonies, religious pluralism dominated the cultural scene, serving as an impetus for political freedom. In New Spain, the Catholic Church dominated religious life, in partnership with the Spanish Crown. In 1776 America, there were 3,226 congregations, representing sixteen Christian denominations (including Roman Catholic) as well as Judaism.[44] In New Spain, only one religion was permitted to flourish—Roman Catholicism. Stark's point was that New Spain's monolithic power structure, defined by the absolute unity of church and state controlling a feudal society, contributed to its failure to advance from the premodern to the modern world by instituting democracy. The United States ultimately would advance, as a result in part of the influence of seventeenth-century Protestantism.

ROGER WILLIAMS AND FREEDOM OF CONSCIENCE

A potential objection may be raised here regarding the relationship between Puritan theology and uninhibited religious freedom. This study has already shown in chapter 1 that the New England colonies did not consider negative religious freedom to be appropriate. The Puritans came to America to achieve freedom to worship God as they wanted, but were not willing to offer the same freedom to anyone in their jurisdiction. Still, it is important to bear in mind the influence of Roger Williams upon later

---

Carta starting in 1215 was little comfort to the Puritans who were fleeing the persecutions encouraged by James I and Charles I.

43. Stark, *Victory of Reason*, 197.
44. Ibid., 207–8.

generations of Americans, who himself held to Puritan theology. Davies saw Williams as the purest of the Puritans because he took Puritan theology to its logical conclusion, whereas those who banished him from Massachusetts were unwilling or unable to do so.

Davies wrote of Williams, that "in him were realized and brought to fulfillment all the liberal implications of Calvinism. If Calvin opened the door to liberty for Western man, Roger Williams was one Calvinist who went all the way through it. If Calvin planted seeds of democracy, Roger Williams nurtured them to their fullest harvest."[45] The ideas of the priesthood of the believer, the value of the individual, and that the state comes secondary to the society—each of these ideas demanded that every person have the freedom to worship in his preferred way. In Rhode Island, even Jews and Quakers were welcomed. It was not as if Williams lacked devotion to his own faith, or that he compromised his faith to welcome those who did not share it. Quite the contrary—Miller wrote that Williams "was not a rationalist and a utilitarian who gave up the effort to maintain an orthodoxy because he had no real concern about religious truth, but was the most passionately religious of men."[46] Davies wrote, "... though his sincere Calvinist soul was in complete disagreement with the Quakers, he would only argue with them, never persecute."[47]

Thus, the argument can be made that the fullest expressions of Puritan theology, as an outgrowth of Calvinism, actually demanded religious freedom. Furthermore, the fact that religious freedom could flourish in a New England colony is evidence of its necessity. Davies stated, "The idea of complete liberty for the individual conscience and complete equality in civil rights was more than unorthodox; it was revolutionary. No one then believed that a stable, successful community could possibly be built on such a shaky and anarchic base as that. This is why Rhode Island was one of the most crucial experiments ever undertaken in the organization of society."[48]

Interestingly enough, none other than Garry Wills would have to agree with Davies' argument. Wills is known for his argument that the positive role Christianity played in American history is largely over-

---

45. Davies, *Foundation*, 172.
46. Miller, *Roger Williams*, 2:255.
47. Davies, *Foundation*, 174.
48. Ibid., 173.

stated. Wills wrote concerning the passage of Jefferson's Virginia Statute for Religious Freedom, "Naturally, Jefferson did not know or admire the work of Williams but the success of his own bill depended on its congruence, in the eyes of those accepting it, with religious values Williams had championed. Williams believed, as surely as Locke and Jefferson, that the civil competence of the state did not reach to any person's private acts of belief...."[49] So while it is true that the Puritan colonies of New England, as a rule, did not offer religious freedom, there was a notable exception to that rule in Rhode Island. Rhode Island's model, not Massachusetts', would ultimately be the one followed when it came time to draft the Bill of Rights.

A consideration of some of Williams' own writings is appropriate here. Williams spent much of his life attempting to expose persecution emanating from Christians. In 1652, he wrote, "My end is to persuade God's Judah (especially) to wash their hands from blood, to cleanse their hearts and ways from such unchristian practices toward all that is man, capable of a religion and a conscience, but most of all toward Christ Jesus, who cries out (as He did to Saul) in the sufferings of the least of His servants: Old England, Old England, New England, New England, King, King, Parliaments, Parliaments, General Courts, General Courts, Presbyterians, Presbyterians, Independents, Independents, etc., why persecute you me?"[50]

In explaining the role of government, he differentiated between a civil and a spiritual arena and asserted that the government had not authority in the spiritual arena. In his *Bloody Tenent of Persecution*, written in 1644, Williams wrote, "Since all magistrates are God's ministers, essentially civil, bounded to a civil work, with civil weapons or instruments, and paid or rewarded with civil rewards. From all which, I say, ... [it] cannot truly be alleged by any for the power of the civil magistrate to be exercised in spiritual and soul matters...."[51] In his *Letter to the Town of Providence*, written in January, 1655, Williams likened the state to a ship, having on board people of many different faith systems. When it came to public prayers on board ship, the commander of the vessel ought not be concerned with how they were administered. Williams wrote, "none

---

49. Wills, *Under God*, 371.
50. Williams, *Bloody Tenent*, 66.
51. Ibid., 60.

of the papists, protestants, Jews, or Turks, be forced to come to the ship's prayers or worship, nor compelled from their own particular prayers or worship, if they practice any."[52] Still, the commander of the ship had a duty to establish order on board ship, but this responsibility did not pertain to spiritual matters. Williams stated, "I further add, that I never denied, that notwithstanding this liberty, the commander of the ship ought to command the ship's course, yea, and also command that justice, peace and sobriety, be kept and practiced, both among the seamen and all the passengers."[53]

Williams objected to the view that persecution was justified in New England because New England was the New Israel, and in ancient Israel, the purity of the faith was paramount. Williams sought to show that New England was not the New Israel, and that Old Testament Israel should not be used as a model for New England to follow in recommending the purity of the faith. Old Testament Israel serves as a type for the Christian church, according to Williams. Whereas Israel was the specially chosen land of promise for God's people, the church would have no physical boundaries. Williams stated that Canaan was "spied out and chosen by the Lord out of all the countries of the world to be the seat of His Church and people. But now there is no respect of earth, of places, or countries with the Lord. . . ."[54] Furthermore, Williams wrote, "While that national state of the Church of the Jews remained, the tribes were bound to go up to Jerusalem to worship. But now, in every nation, . . . he that fears God and works righteousness is accepted with Him."[55] Lastly, referring to Canaan, Williams wrote, "the Lord expressly calls it His own land ... a term proper unto spiritual Canaan. . . . But now the partition wall is broken down, and in respect of the Lord's special property to one country more than another, what difference between Asia and Africa, between Europe and America, between England and Turkey, London and Constantinople?"[56]

Thus, freedom of conscience was a key aspect of true Christianity. Williams wrote, "'tis impossible for any man or men to maintain their

---

52. Williams, *Town of Providence*, 225.
53. Ibid.
54. Williams, *Bloody Tenent*, 81.
55. Ibid., 81–82.
56. Ibid., 82.

Christ by the sword, and to worship a true Christ!"[57] Miller wrote that Williams "exerted little or no direct influence on theorists of the Revolution and the Constitution, who drew on quite different intellectual sources, yet as a figure and a reputation he was always there to remind Americans that no other conclusion than absolute religious freedom was feasible in this society."[58]

HEBREW METAPHYSIC

One final aspect of Puritan theology that made its mark on American freedom is the regular practice of applying Old Testament motifs to thought and practice. The Puritan colonists saw themselves in stark Old Testament terms. As seen previously, they considered themselves to be a New Israel, God's new chosen people who were inheriting a promised land in America. They were to be faithful to God in their lives and in their identity as the new Israel, and if they failed, God would deal with them as He dealt with Israel of old. Cotton preached a sermon in 1630 from 2 Sam 7:10[59] entitled "God's Promise to His Plantation." The sermon was to serve as a divine justification for leaving England and to provide encouragement to those who may have been flagging in their commitment to start a new life abroad. Cotton drew from numerous passages from the Old Testament which referred in some way to the Israelites taking possession of the land God had promised to Abraham in order to apply them to the colonists and their endeavor to start a colony in New England. Consider these statements of Cotton:

> The placing of a people in this or that country is from the appointment of the Lord....
>
> *Quest.* Wherein doth this work of God stand in appointing a place for a people?
>
> *Answ.* First, when God espies or discovers a land for a people, as in Ezek. 20:6: "He brought them into a land that He had espied for them." And, that is, when either He gives them to discover it themselves, or hears of it discovered by others, and fitting them.

---

57. Ibid., 234.
58. Miller, *Roger Williams*, 254.
59. "Moreover I will appoint a place for My people Israel, and I will plant them, that they may dwell in a place of their own, and move no more...."

> Second, after He hath espied it, when He carrieth them along to it, so that they plainly see a providence of God leading them from one country to another, as in Ex. 19:4: "You have seen how I have borne you as on eagles' wings, and brought unto Myself." So that though they met with many difficulties, yet He carried them high above them all, like and eagle, flying over seas and rocks, and all hindrances.
>
> Third, when He makes room for a people to dwell there, as in Ps. 80:9: "Thou preparedst room for them...."[60]

Referring to the consequences of being unfaithful to their covenant with God, recall the quote from Winthrop's sermon, "A Modell of Christian Charity" from earlier in the study. If the colonists forgot their covenant with God, then He would "surely break out in wrathe against us, be revenged of such a perjured people and make us knowe the price of the breache of such a Covenant."[61] The Puritans saw themselves and their efforts in powerful Old Testament terms, and drawing from the Hebrew metaphysic was an important influence on the American ideal of freedom.

Novak made this point forcefully in his work, *On Two Wings*. He identified four ways in which the Hebrew metaphysic, drawn upon so heavily by the Puritans, uniquely affected America. The idea that God created the world to have a purpose, that the world and His purposes were intelligible, that His creatures were created to live freely in relationship with Him, and that life's trials put that freedom to the test—these are the Hebrew perspectives that Novak stressed. He wrote, "Everything in the world is intelligible, and that to *inquire, invent,* and *discover* is an *impulse of faith* as well as of reason; that the *Creator endowed us with liberty and inviolable dignity*; while the Divine Judge shows concern for *the weak and the humble*; that life is a *time of duty and trial*; and that history is to be grasped as *the drama of human liberty*—all these are the background that makes sense of the Declaration of Independence."[62]

Furthermore, the Puritans drew heavily from the Old Testament in their administration of civil matters. John Cotton, in his "Abstract of the Laws of New England," called for all magistrates to be elected on the basis of the book of Exodus. Additionally, Hall observed that "Warrants

---

60. Cotton, "God's Promise," 1:107.
61. Winthrop, "A Modell of Christian Charity," 39.
62. Novak, *On Two Wings*, 12. Emphasis is in the original.

Christian Contributions to American Notions of Freedom 113

to call for the General Court were patterned after the practice in Joshua's time, and the powers of the governors were: (1) to provide for the good of the people (Num 11:14–16); (2) to organize appeals from lower courts (Deut 17:8–9); (3) to preserve religion (Exod 32:25–27); and (4) to oversee defense and 'with consent of the people to enterprise wars' (Prov 24:5)."[63] Each of these four powers can be found in the American government, respectively, in the Preamble to the Constitution, Article III of the Constitution, the First Amendment, and Article I of the Constitution.

To conclude, the Puritans' theology had a powerful effect in a number of general ways. This theology inherited mainly from Calvin can be seen in some of the earliest colonial documents which emphasize individual liberty. It helped motivate the Puritan colonists to settle in New England. It contributed to the formation of a new consciousness because of its emphasis on the individual. This new consciousness set the English colonies apart from the Spanish and French colonies in America. Roger Williams was shown to be perhaps the purest of the Puritans because his theology compelled him to offer complete religious liberty to everyone in his colony of Rhode Island. Finally, the Hebrew metaphysic, drawn on by the Puritans so heavily, would help to define and justify all that American freedom would come to mean by the time America declared its independence from Great Britain.

Advocates of CA in the strong sense have often made the point that America was intended from the beginning to be a Christian nation, that secular or Enlightenment ideas had very little to do with the formation of the American character. Thus, they have asserted that Americans should recover those biblical notions that made the country unique at the start. The next chapter will examine some of the reasons why these points are invalid. Still, it is necessary to ask the question, what role has Christianity played in the making of America? This chapter has shown, in general ways, how Christianity has helped shape the notion of American freedom. Much more could be said in that regard—this study has not sought to provide a comprehensive answer to that question. When approaching the question of America's origins, while it is important to avoid embracing a strong CA, acknowledging that Christianity is an important source for America's formation is imperative. As Noll has aptly stated, "It is clear that evangelicals make a mistake in claiming the founders as their

---

63. Hall, *Genevan Reformation*, 298.

own. It is not clear that they make a mistake in thinking that abandoning the founders' formula for the well-being of a republic would bring the American nation into serious peril."[64]

---

64. Noll, "Evangelicals," 156.

4

Critiquing the Christian America Thesis

THE PREVIOUS CHAPTERS HAVE provided the context for a critique of CA. The first chapter noted that the American Founders sought to enshrine religious liberty and not to establish a Christian nation. The second chapter outlined and described the predominant themes appearing in the writings of authors advocating that America was established as a Christian nation. The third chapter acknowledged Puritanism as a contributor to the idea of American freedom. The critique which follows is based upon the proposition that there is a Christian worldview orientation in America's revolution and founding, but America is not a Christian nation in any strong sense.

To review the thesis of the study, the historiographical construal of Christian America cannot be sustained because the ideas which formed the United States are mixed between secular and Christian sources. This chapter will also argue that America is not uniquely chosen by God for any special relationship with Him or for any divinely ordained purpose in the world. Rather than establishing America as a Christian nation, the Founders established it with religious freedom, a point made in chapter 1.

PHILOSOPHICAL CONSIDERATIONS: IMPRECISION IN DEFINING TERMS

Precision in language is essential in oral and written public discourse. Precise language presented in an argument provides clear definitions of terms to the parties involved. In any form of discourse, precise language eliminates ambiguity which frees the thinker to draw clear and justifiable conclusions. Imprecise language can include terms that carry more than one meaning and thus bring the possibility of confusion. Ironically, terms which are imprecisely defined are often assumed by their users to be clearly understood and agreed upon when, on reflection, they are not. M. Neil Browne and Stuart Keeley referred to this problem when they wrote, "The more abstract a word or phrase, the more likely it is to be susceptible to multiple interpretations and thus need clear definition by the author.... A term becomes more and more abstract as it refers less and less to particular, specific instances."[1]

The argument for CA often includes terms that carry more than one meaning and thus bring the possibility of confusion. Therefore, in this section, two terms used in defining or defending the CA thesis by its proponents will be examined. First, when the term "Christian nation" is used, confusion is possible because CA advocates did not always agree on a definition. Second, the term "Enlightenment" was ordinarily used by CA advocates referring to an inherently anti-Christian secular system of thought, which is an overly narrow application of the term. In these two cases, the failure of the CA writers to clearly understand, articulate, and apply crucial terms contributed to their being led to the flawed historiographical construal of America as a Christian nation.

Lack of Agreement in Defining the Meaning of a Christian Nation

D. Q. McInerney offered a simple procedure to avoiding ambiguity and defining terms in his book, *Being Logical*. He said that defining a term "relates a particular object (the object to be defined) to other objects and thereby give[s] it a precise 'location.'"[2] With this in mind, providing clear definitions involves two steps: "Step one: Place the term to be defined in its 'proximate genus.' Step two: Identify the term's 'specific difference.'"[3] There should be no trouble with ambiguity in defining "Christian nation," if McInerney's steps are followed. The "proximate genus" is "nation." The "specific difference" is "Christian." The nation is a Christian one. It is differentiated from other nations that are non-Christian. The term seems simple enough on the surface for all parties to agree on its essential meaning.

---

1. Browne and Keeley, *Asking the Right Questions*, 39–40.
2. McInerney, *Being Logical*, 37.
3. Ibid., 38.

Critiquing the Christian America Thesis 117

Unfortunately, things are not so simple. As was seen in chapter 2, the CA thesis is a multi-faceted view. That chapter outlined the CA thesis in terms of fourteen historical, philosophical, and theological themes. So, the task of defining "Christian nation" is not a simple one. Broadly speaking, there are indeed four ways in which CA advocates have defined America as a Christian nation:

1. It is a nation founded during a time of Protestant consensus
2. It was established on biblical principles
3. The Founders of the nation were Christians
4. The nation is a New Israel, exceptionally blessed with a special relationship with God and a special divine purpose in the world.

This section will describe how the various CA writers explained these ways of defining a Christian nation, and then will state how the term is made ambiguous by their failure to agree on important points.

First, the idea that America is a Christian nation because it was founded in an environment enjoying a Christian consensus seems to be common among CA authors. LaHaye aligned himself with Francis Schaeffer in affirming this notion. He connected the notion of a Christian cultural consensus in America with that of a constitutionally established Christian America. He wrote,

> I do not claim that this country was founded as a Christian nation, even though many of the original states were established as Christian colonies. As I shall demonstrate . . . , it was a nation so predominantly Christian that the culture evidenced what the late Dr. Francis Schaeffer called 'a Christian consensus.' This Christian consensus is easily verified by the fact that prior to 1789 (the year that eleven of the thirteen states ratified the Constitution) many of the states still had constitutional requirements that a man must be a Christian in order to hold public office.[4]

James Hutson also pointed to the Protestant consensus in eighteenth-century America to define and defend CA. Answering the critics Isaac Kramnick and R. Laurence Moore, Hutson cited a study by Patricia Bonomi and Peter Eisenstadt, claiming that between seventy-one and seventy-seven percent of Americans were churchgoers in 1776. This, he

---

4. LaHaye, *Faith of Our Founding Fathers*, 33–34.

wrote, would prove to be "a figure fatal to any claim about an unchristian nation."[5] Moreover, as observed in chapter 2 of this study, Hutson insisted that the Constitution itself reflects the consensus because the word "Lord" is used in Article 7 (as in "Year of Our Lord"). Further, according to Hutson, the Constitution implicitly affirms the sanctity of the Christian Sabbath in Article 1, Section 7 by assuming the President would not be available to sign any bill from Congress into law on that particular day. Hutson wrote, "This language does nothing less than write the Christian Sabbath into the Constitution by presuming that the president will not work on Sunday. Does this section make the United States a Christian nation? Many Americans in the early nineteenth century would have argued that it did...."[6]

DeMar also argued that America's past Christian consensus justifies one in classifying America as a Christian nation. First, DeMar clarified what he did not mean in using the term: "A belief in a Christian America does not mean that every American is now or ever was a Christian. Moreover, it does not mean that either the church or the State should force people to profess a belief in Christianity. Furthermore, a belief in a Christian America does not mean that non-Christians, and for that matter, dissenting Christians, cannot hold contrary opinions in a climate of a general Christian consensus."[7] Speaking of this consensus, DeMar stated that "A study of America's past will show that a majority of Americans shared a common faith and a common ethic. America's earliest Founders were self-professing Christians and their founding documents expressed a belief in a Christian worldview."[8] Furthermore, "History is clear: the Founding Fathers of the United States embraced Christianity as the unofficial yet universally acknowledged religion of the land."[9]

---

5. Hutson. *Forgotten Features*, 115.

6. Ibid., 114. Hutson's position here seems weak since he staked his argument upon an *ad populum* assertion to affirm America as a Christian nation.

7. DeMar, *America's Christian History*, 3.

8. Ibid., 5. DeMar pointed to John Winthrop's sermon "A Modell of Christian Charity" as evidence. The problem with this is that few argue against the fact that the Puritans were establishing a Christian commonwealth. The question is, was the *United States* formed as a Christian nation? DeMar, like many other CA advocates, did not differentiate between the motives of the Founders of the colonies, especially the New England colonies, and those of the Founders of the United States.

9. DeMar, *God and Government*, 169.

For LaHaye, Hutson, and DeMar, the U.S. government was established upon the foundation of an American society that demonstrated a general agreement on Christian theology and ethics. For this reason, according to them, America was founded as a Christian nation.

Second, the notion that America was founded on biblical principles is the most widely agreed upon definition among CA writers. McDowell explained what he meant in affirming CA by pointing to America's basis in the Bible: "A Christian nation is a nation that is founded upon Biblical principles, where Biblical truth and law are the standard for public life, law, and societal institutions. Defined this way, America certainly was a Christian nation, and in some sense still is...."[10] Eidsmoe put it this way: "every nation is founded on certain basic principles or values, and those values have their source in religious belief. If by the term Christian nation one means a nation that was founded on biblical values that were brought to the nation by mostly professing Christians, then in that sense the United States may truly be called a Christian nation."[11] Many others agreed with these assessments. Barton, Falwell, DeMar, and Beliles each insisted that since America was founded on biblical principles, this constitutes America as a Christian nation.

Still other writers affirmed that America is a Christian nation because its Founders were Christian. Because the Founders were Christian, it follows that the founding documents contain their Christian value system, according to these writers. CA advocates also asserted that their original intent for the nation was that it would maintain those values in perpetuity. Lillback and Newcombe, in their study of George Washington's faith, wrote, "What are the facts of history? And do they matter? The importance of this study is more than historical. Establishing that George Washington was a Christian helps to substantiate the critical role that Christians and Christian principles played in the founding of our nation.... We believe such a study would also empower, enable, and defend the presence of a strong Judeo-Christian worldview in the ongoing development of our state and national governments and courts."[12] Thus, according to Lillback and Newcombe, the fact of George Washington's Christian faith is itself an indelible stamp on the American identity.

10. McDowell, *Christian Nation*, 3–4.
11. Eidsmoe, "Operation Josiah," 103.
12. Lillback and Newcombe, *Sacred Fire*, 27.

Eidsmoe also looked to the Christian faith of the Founders as a basis for his understanding of CA, and their establishment of the Constitution on Christian principles. He understood the term "Christian" to mean, "a person whose basic doctrinal beliefs are in accord with those of Christianity but who may or may not personally trust in Christ for salvation" and also as "a person who rejects basic fundamental doctrines of the Christian faith, but who holds generally to Christian manners and morals and a basic Christian worldview."[13] For Eidsmoe, even if some of the Founders were not professing Christians, or even orthodox, as long as they held to a Christian way of life they may be called "Christian."

Another contention by many CA advocates is that America is God's chosen people, a New Israel. This view insists that America is central in salvation history because part of its ordained destiny is to shine the light of Christ into the world by the application of its power coupled with its fulfillment of the Christian mission.

Peter Marshall and David Manuel began their book, *The Light and the Glory* by explaining how they came to the conviction that God had a special plan and purpose for America, a plan made manifest to the earliest colonists. The main thesis of their book was that God's call on and plan for America was definite and unconditional, although it may not be as easily discernable now as in earlier and more faithful times.

Marshall and Manuel postulated that God's relationship with America was based upon a covenant not unlike that established between God and Old Testament Israel. This covenant would be one between the people and God and between the people themselves. While the people's faithfulness to the covenant would waver, God would never forget His own commitment to the covenant. Thus, three assertions were fundamental to the way Marshall and Manuel defined CA. The first is that *"God had put a specific 'call' on this country and the people who were to inhabit it. In the virgin wilderness of America, God was making His most significant attempt since ancient Israel."*[14] This call would be given to the earliest colonists as far back as Christopher Columbus who the authors attempted to show had a strong assurance of God's design for him and his mission. The second aspect of their definition is that *"this call was to be worked*

---

13. Eidsmoe, *Christianity and the Constitution*, 79.
14. Marshall and Manuel, *Light and the Glory*, 22; emphasis original.

out in terms of the settlers' covenant with God and with each other."[15] The covenant would not be formalized until the signing and ratification of the U.S. Constitution, which the authors not only asserted "was the culmination of nearly two hundred years of Puritan political thought" but also was divinely inspired.[16] Third, "*God did keep His end of the bargain . . ., and He did so on both an individual and a corporate basis.*"[17] This final point represents the key application and encouragement to Marshall and Manuel's audience: God's commitment to bless America as His special choice is not dependent upon the nation's faithfulness, but the nation's faithfulness is required if it is to recognize and benefit directly from that blessing. The authors stated, "When He enters a covenant, it is forever. The promises which He made to the early comers to His New Israel remain intact and unmodified, though now a far greater amendment of our lives is required in order to fulfill our end of the bargain."[18]

Like Marshall and Manuel, Beliles and McDowell approached CA with a high view of God's sovereignty. At the beginning of their book, *America's Providential History*, the authors defined history in terms of a strict view of God's sovereignty. They wrote, "Since God is the author of history and He is carrying out His plan in the earth through history, any view of the history of America, or any country, that ignores God is not true history."[19] For this reason, they began their history of the United States in the Garden of Eden in order to show where America fits into God's supreme plan for all nations. For Beliles and McDowell, America's founding belongs on center stage in the drama of salvation history.

LaHaye termed America a "miracle nation" and pointed to the "miracles" of Columbus' arrival, the success of colonial development, the revolt against Great Britain, the American victory in the Revolutionary War, the enduring existence of the new nation during the period under the Articles of Confederation, the formation of the Constitution, and America's twentieth century rise to superpower status.[20] The conclusion to all of this was: "What was the purpose of this 'miracle nation' that some call 'manifest

---

15. Ibid., 23; emphasis original.
16. Ibid., 343–44; emphasis original.
17. Ibid., 24; emphasis original.
18. Ibid., 355.
19. Beliles and McDowell, *America's Providential History*, vii.
20. LaHaye, *Faith of Our Founding Fathers*, 65.

destiny'? Many things, one of which would be that God would establish one nation that would do more to fulfill His basic objective for this age, to 'preach the gospel to the ends of the earth,' than any other nation in history."[21] For LaHaye, God clearly set America apart to fulfill the calling of Christ to the apostles.

There are two important points of disagreement between CA advocates on the meaning of "Christian America." First, while many believe that the Christian consensus is an important element that made America Christian at its founding, not all do. McDowell wrote, "Some might define a Christian nation as one where a majority of the citizens are Christian. While this could have been the situation in early America (a vast majority claimed to be Christian, though God knows the heart), this is not an appropriate measurement of what should constitute a Christian nation."[22] Beliles and McDowell developed this point further:

> What makes America a Christian nation? Many Christians erroneously believe it depends on whether or not our Founders were Christians. Others believe it depends on if a vast majority of Americans are Christians. The problem with these criteria is when one or more of our Founders are found not to be Christians; does that negate the rest? Who determines the arbitrary percentage of a population that must be Christian to qualify? 100%? 51%? What about when even our Christian Founding Fathers came short of God's glory and sinned against the Indians or in other ways? Does the fallibility of Christians in a Christian nation negate the claim? Of course not.[23]

These statements are in conflict with those made by LaHaye, Hutson, and DeMar, who affirmed the centrality of the Christian consensus. They also challenge the positions of Lillback, Eidsmoe, and Barton who insisted on the significance of the faith of the Founders to the American identity.

Second, and perhaps the most salient point of disagreement, is over the contention that America is God's chosen nation. For Marshall and Manuel, America lives in covenant with God as the New Israel. LaHaye, Falwell, Beliles, Anderson, and McDowell also stressed American chosenness, although not quite as strongly as Marshall and Manuel. LaHaye even seemed to contradict himself while attempting to define America as

---

21. Ibid.
22. McDowell, *Christian Nation*, 2–3.
23. Beliles and McDowell, *America's Providential History*, 185.

Christian. At first, he wrote, "I do not claim that this country was founded as a Christian nation, even though many of the original states were established as Christian colonies."[24] Later in the same book, he affirmed that America was a "miracle nation," singled out by God to fulfill the Great Commission. Thus, although LaHaye hesitated early in his work to pronounce that America originated as a Christian nation, he later seemed to fail to avoid coming to that exact conclusion. While other CA advocates affirmed American exceptionalism and chosenness to some extent, not all were comfortable with affirming that America is God's chosen nation. This idea is not found in the writings of Barton, Eidsmoe, or Amos, to name a few.

Adding to these difficulties, Noll, Hatch, and Marsden observed that the term "Christian nation" is inherently ambiguous. They noted that the term "Christian" is itself an abstract concept, one that is frequently diluted. According to these authors, to affirm something as Christian in the American contemporary culture is to say very little. Furthermore, if CA writers are going to stake so much on the notion that late eighteenth-century America enjoyed a Christian consensus, they are going to have to explain what made America distinct from any other Western nation in terms of biblical righteousness and justice. They wrote, "Almost everything in western culture from the late Roman Empire until about 1800 was 'Christian' in this [generic] sense. Yet it is clear that there are many such 'Christian cultural developments'—the Thirty Years War and persecution of the Jews and the Waldensians, for instance—of which we would not approve."[25] This led them to a second point, namely, that simply because a culture is Christian does not mean necessarily that all they do is consistent with Scripture.[26]

The term "Christian nation" is thus made ambiguous by CA authors' lack of agreement on a sound and accepted definition. Even more troubling is that the term "Christian" often fails to arrive at the standard

24. LaHaye, *Faith of our Founding Fathers*, 33.
25. Noll et al., *Search*, 30. The two-fold thesis of this work includes the notion that "Christian nation" is too ambiguous a term to be used as a meaningful classification. The authors wrote, "The argument of this book can be stated quite simply.... We feel ... that careful examination of Christian teaching on government, the state, and the nature of culture shows that the idea of a 'Christian nation' is a very ambiguous concept which is usually harmful to effective Christian action in society" (17).
26. Ibid.

exemplified by Christ, as Noll, Hatch, and Marsden have noted. These problems further weaken the CA thesis. The lack of a cohesive definition that is clearly articulated by the CA advocates creates confusion in the attempt to understand what a Christian nation actually entails. This problem appears to create a significant obstacle for CA advocates because if a concrete description of a Christian America cannot be provided and agreed upon, it can be exceedingly difficult to find one in history.

Enlightenment Philosophy As Inherently Anti-Christian

CA advocates who defined America as a "Christian nation" in ideological terms, rather than in terms of divine chosenness,[27] have portrayed the Enlightenment as singularly anti-Christian. This second definitional point obscures the significance and the meaning of Enlightenment philosophy's influence on the founding of the United States for advocates of CA. Since many of them viewed Enlightenment philosophy in fundamental anti-Christian terms, they rejected it as a significant source contributing to the American founding.

For many CA authors, secular thought amounted to that which is anti-Christian.[28] My contention here is that the term "secular" does not necessarily denote that which is anti-Christian. Ideas which are secular simply refer to those which do not have their source in Christian theology or the Bible. Enlightenment philosophy was secular, in that Enlightenment thinkers did not draw from religious sources, but rather, from reason and nature. Thus, while the sources for their conclusions were secular, they were not necessarily anti-Christian. This distinction in how the term "secular" is applied is important. If we are to understand Enlightenment philosophy and assess its impact on the American founding, the terms we use in discourse about it must be precise.

---

27. This statement refers to those CA writers who have based their definition of America as a Christian nation primarily on considerations other than the idea that America is divinely chosen by God as the new Israel. Writers such as Barton, Eidsmoe, Hutson, Lillback and Newcombe, and Amos fit into this category. These writers are to be sharply distinguished from advocates of the idea that America is God's New Israel, such as Marshall and Manuel.

28. Specific instances of this will be described later in this section. See Chapter 2 for an extended discussion on how CA authors have defined Enlightenment philosophy in particular anti-Christian terms.

Chapter 1 addressed the Enlightenment, especially as it occurred in England and in America.[29] May wrote, "Let us say that the Enlightenment consists of all those who believe two propositions: first, that the present age is more enlightened than the past; and second, that we understand nature in man best through the use of our natural faculties."[30] May was providing a broad summary of Enlightenment thought.[31] It is difficult to approach the Enlightenment as a unified system of beliefs or doctrines. Ahlstrom wrote to broadly classify the Enlightenment, that it "is thus not a doctrine, but a campaign for world renovation based on certain broad presuppositions which are informed above all by the achievements of the new science."[32] It seems that CA advocates who have addressed the Enlightenment as an anti-Christian philosophy have largely understood it as a monolithic set of ideas. It is this misunderstanding of the Enlightenment that has influenced their interpretation of its impact (or in their case, the lack thereof) on the American founding.

May divided Enlightenment thought into four categories. His first category, the "Moderate Enlightenment," "preached balance, order and religious compromise, and was dominant in England from the time of Newton and Locke until about the middle of the eighteenth century."[33] The Moderate Enlightenment issued the ideas classified by Russell as "liberalism." He stated, "Early liberalism was individualistic in intellectual matters, and also in economics, but was not emotionally or ethically self-assertive. This form of liberalism dominated the English eighteenth century, the Founders of the American Constitution, and the French encyclopédists."[34] Much of this thought was compatible with Christianity,

---

29. Chapter 1 provided a broad overview of Enlightenment philosophy as it appeared in England and America in the eighteenth century. See Ahlstrom, *Religious History*, Heimert, *Religion and the American Mind*, Holmes, *Founding Fathers*, Lambert, *Place of Religion*, May, *Enlightenment*, Noll, *History of Christianity*, Noll, *America's God*, and Ericson, *American Freedom* for works on how Enlightenment thought manifested itself in America from the colonial to the constitutional period.

30. May, *Enlightenment*, xiv.

31. This study is treating "Enlightenment" in philosophical terms, not historical. In other words, "Enlightenment" is understood here both as a method of understanding the world and as an ideological framework, unless otherwise specified. It is not being used to refer to an historical period, e.g. from the seventeenth to the nineteenth century.

32. Ahlstrom, *Religious History*, 352.

33. May, *Enlightenment*, xvi.

34. Russell, *History of Western Philosophy*, 599.

even though it came from secular sources. The Moderate Enlightenment provides a case in point that some ideas can be secular, but not necessarily anti-Christian.

Still, May's second category, the "skeptical Enlightenment"[35] was largely critical of the church and church authority. Here, "secular" thought became anti-Christian in certain respects which will be addressed later. But May stated that this thought arose out of Britain and France, and was most influential in the second half of the eighteenth century. According to May, "Its dogmas were usually elliptically stated and often mere negations, but if it was pursued systematically it issued either in the systematic epistemological skepticism of Hume or the systematic materialism of Holbach."[36]

Voltaire was also a spokesman for this system of thought. Will and Ariel Durant recorded a poem written by Voltaire in 1756 after the Lisbon earthquake which killed thousands of people, many of them as they were attending mass.[37] Voltaire's anger at the church's theodicy is clear in the lines of the poem, as he questioned the very idea of the justice of God. He wrote,

> Say you, "This follows from eternal laws
> Binding the choice of God both free and good"?
> Will you, before this mass of victims, say,
> "God is revenged, their death repays their crimes"?[38]

Voltaire's poem underscores the importance of the skeptical Enlightenment's critique of the authority of the church and its traditionally accepted pronouncements on world events. For Voltaire, the spokesmen for Christianity did not value reason, but rather, superstition.

The third category, the "Revolutionary Enlightenment,"[39] was most influential in revolutionary France at the end of the eighteenth century, but it also had an American manifestation in Thomas Paine. According to May, this philosophy was known by "the belief and the possibility of constructing a new heaven and earth out of the destruction of the old."[40]

35. May, *Enlightenment*, xvi.
36. Ibid.
37. Durant and Durant, *Story of Civilization*, 9:721.
38. Voltaire, "On the Lisbon Disaster," 9:721.
39. May, *Enlightenment*, xvi.
40. Ibid.

May's fourth category, the "Didactic Enlightenment," moderated some of the thought of the skeptical and Revolutionary Enlightenment while still attempting "to save from what it saw as the debacle of the Enlightenment the intelligible universe, clear and certain moral judgments, and progress."[41] May was referring primarily to the Scottish Enlightenment that included the common sense realism of Thomas Reid.

Richard Tarnas noted that it was not until the nineteenth century that Enlightenment philosophy presented a systematic challenge to Christian theology. It seems easier to broadly classify secular thought coming from the nineteenth century in anti-Christian terms than that from the eighteenth. Tarnas wrote, "It would be the nineteenth century that would bring the Enlightenment's secular progression to its logical conclusion as Comte, Mill, Feuerbach, Marx, Haeckel, Spencer, Huxley, and, in a somewhat different spirit, Nietzsche all sounded the death knell of traditional religion."[42]

LaHaye defined eighteenth century Enlightenment thought in anti-Christian terms. As he did so, he was vigorous in his rebuke of contemporary historians who have, in his view, distorted the historical record by tarnishing the Christian image of the Founders by linking them with Enlightenment philosophy. He said, "In recent years, it has become popular for secular humanists, atheists, and other 'free thinkers' to claim that the Fathers of our country were not Christians or religious people after all, but at most deists, atheists, or secularists. Some even go so far as to suggest that several were more addicted to French Enlightenment philosophy than they were to Christianity."[43] LaHaye seemed to suggest that to be influenced by the Enlightenment, one would have to be a deist, atheist, or a secularist, and "addicted" to French Enlightenment thought. He did not seem to be open to the possibility that some eighteenth century Enlightenment thought, such as that of the Moderate Enlightenment, may be compatible with Christianity on certain issues.

Amos was the most forceful on this point. He wrote that, "When Americans today think that all the Founders were deists who consciously rejected the Bible and Christian principles, they are basing their opinions

---

41. Ibid.
42. Tarnas, *Passion of the Western Mind*, 310.
43. LaHaye, *Faith of our Founding Fathers*, 30.

on a myth."[44] He went further in his critique, writing "By the alchemy of history and the wave of the historian's pen, Biblical and Christian ideas are changed into Enlightenment paganism. This makes it impossible for a Christian who takes Romans 1 and 2 seriously not to be called a child of the Enlightenment. And it causes the Christianity of early America to be described in such a way that no Christian influence on the founding could be possible."[45] In addition to these statements, Amos asked, "Can the ideas embodied in the Declaration of Independence be traced to the church and the Bible? Or must they be traced to deism, the Enlightenment, the Renaissance, and ultimately to pagan Rome and Greece? Are early American notions about law, rights, liberty, and resisting tyrants anti-Biblical at the core? In short, is it true that the Bible and Christianity had little or nothing to do with developing the great legal and political ideas of western liberty and constitutionalism?"[46] For Amos, the ideas that brought into existence America's founding documents had to be either rooted in Christian theology or in anti-theistic secularism, or "Enlightenment paganism," as he styled it. As with LaHaye, Amos did not seem to be open to any compatibility between secular and Christian ideas.

As seen in chapter 2, Barton compared the American founding and system of government with that of the French, Russian, and Italian governmental systems. His point was to contrast the American founding, rooted in biblical Christianity, with those that were founded based on secular (and anti-Christian) ideas. The intended lesson was that a government formed on biblical principles will be stable, virtuous, and prosperous, while those which are not will be marred by instability and constant revolution. The problem with Barton's view is that it seemed to ignore the fact that the government formed by America's Founders—the same one supposedly formed on the basis of Christianity—almost did not survive its first century. The American Civil War tore the nation apart and was the costliest war in American history. Over 600,000 Americans died as a result of the war. The states of the South were ravaged by the impact of the war. Their economies were ruined for nearly a century. Furthermore, it is essential to remember that the dissolution of the Union occurred in large measure over the issue of slavery as a point of morality. This is essential to

---

44. Amos, *Defending*, 11.
45. Ibid., 20.
46. Ibid., 25.

bear in mind when considering Barton's viewpoint, and his emphasis on the significance of Christian principles in the founding and endurance of the United States.[47]

In contrast to the CA view as articulated by LaHaye, Amos, and Barton, the fact remains that several theorists from the Enlightenment period did offer secular views that were compatible with Christianity. Two thinkers will be considered here: Isaac Newton and John Locke, both English theists.

Newton's research was guided by certain rules that were based on inductive reasoning rather than religious authority. Newton took the scientific method to be reliable and sufficient to judge all future hypotheses that might arise to contradict preliminary ones. For example, his fourth rule of reasoning in philosophy (science) was *"we are to look upon propositions inferred by general induction from phenomena as accurately or very nearly true, notwithstanding any contrary hypotheses that may be imagined, till such time as other phenomena occur, by which they may either be made more accurate, or liable to exceptions."*[48] Newton did appeal to divine revelation at times in his writings, such as in his *Observations Upon the Prophecies of Daniel and the Apocalypse of St. John*, but in the *Mathematical Principles*, he stressed that human reason is sufficient to find truth.

This did not mean that Newton failed to affirm the supremacy of the personal God who is the Creator of the cosmos. In Book III of his *Mathematical Principles*, Newton praised not only the existence of God, but the eternity, perfection, dominion, personhood, omnipotence, omniscience, wisdom, and truth of God. He wrote, "And from his true dominion it follows that the true God is a living, intelligent, and powerful Being; and, from his other perfections, that he is supreme, or most perfect. He is eternal and infinite, omnipotent and omniscient; that is, his duration reaches from eternity to eternity; his presence from infinity to infinity; he governs all things, and knows all things that are or can be done."[49] Thus, Newton's belief in the sufficiency of human reason and use of the inductive method in his research was not inconsistent with his explicitly stated theistic convictions.

---

47. See Freehling, *Road to Disunion*, vol. 1, Stampp, *America in 1857*, and Weigley, *Great Civil War*.

48. Newton, *Mathematical Principles*, 271; emphasis original.

49. Ibid., 370.

Locke, one of the most important philosophers of the Enlightenment period, was a moderate on issues concerning the role of reason and revelation in determining truth. His *Essay Concerning Human Understanding* attempted, among other things, to demonstrate the relationship between reason and divine revelation. Human reason, unassisted by revelation, is sufficient to discover truth, according to Locke. For example, the existence of God is knowable by human reason alone. Locke wrote concerning this, "from the consideration of ourselves, and what we infallibly find in our own constitutions, our reason leads us to the knowledge of this certain and evident truth,—*That there is an eternal, most powerful, and most knowable Being....*"[50] Furthermore, while Locke acknowledged the Source and authority of divine revelation, reason is a more certain guide into matters of truth. Locke stated, "For whatsoever truth we come to the clear discovery of, from the knowledge and contemplation of our own ideas, will always be certainer to us than those which are conveyed to us by *traditional revelation*. For the knowledge we have that this revelation came at first from God can never be so sure as the knowledge we have from the clear and distinct perception of the agreement or disagreement of our own ideas...."[51] So although Locke did not place special revelation above human reason, he still held to the authority of special revelation. For this reason, Locke was not anti-Christian, even though his epistemology placed more trust in human reason.

This brief look at Newton and Locke is sufficient to show that Enlightenment philosophy of the seventeenth and eighteenth centuries should not necessarily be classified as anti-Christian. Still, it would be inappropriate to say that anti-Christian secular thought was absent in the eighteenth century, even in England. A brief consideration of eighteenth century Enlightenment thought that is not compatible with Christianity will illustrate the transition from the moderate to the skeptical Enlightenment.

David Hume's (1711-1776) work, *An Enquiry Concerning Human Understanding*, sought to show, among other things, the limitations of cause and effect reasoning. He divided all objects of human reasoning into two kinds, *a priori* and *a posteriori* propositions. *A priori* propositions he called "relations of ideas" and *a posteriori* propositions he called "mat-

---

50. Locke, *Human Understanding*, IV.X.6; emphasis original.
51. Ibid., IV.XVIII.6; emphasis original.

ters of fact."[52] Relations of ideas are mathematical and are not discovered through the use of evidences. Matters of fact depend on evidence to be understood, and this is where the operation of cause and effect becomes meaningful. For Hume, one cannot observe every cause and every effect *ad infinitum*. Similarly, one cannot observe future causes and effects to predict how things will happen later. One can only determine that causes determine effects by actually experiencing them. Thus, Hume wrote, "That no man, having seen only one body move after being impelled by another, could infer that every other body will move after a like impulse. All inferences from experience, therefore, are the facts of custom, not of reasoning. Custom, then, is the great god of human life. It is that principle alone which renders our experience useful to us, and makes us expect, for the future, a similar train of events with those which have appeared in the past."[53]

Because of this, he was distrustful of religious authority and theological dogmas. How could anyone know, for example, that God works miracles in the world? All theological dogmas are matters of fact, discernable only by evidences and experiences. Since it was really only custom to draw conclusions from cause and effect relations, it would be unreasonable to conclude that God works miracles. It would be more probable, according to Hume, that reports of miracles were fraudulent, given that men lie, than that the report was true. On the reliability of miracles, Hume wrote, "When anyone tells me, that he saw a dead man restored to life, I immediately consider with myself, whether it be more probable, that this person should either deceive or be deceived, or that the fact, which he relates, should really have happened. I weigh the one miracle against the other; and according to the superiority, which I discover, I pronounce my decision, and always reject the greater miracle."[54]

François Marie Arouet (1694–1778), or Voltaire as he was known from 1718, was another Enlightenment period thinker many of whose ideas were anti-Christian. His influence was felt mostly in Europe. He was not as radical as other thinkers, but his ideas were more critical of Christianity than most in England or in America. In assessing his influence, the Durants wrote, "We shall say nothing about him that has not

---

52. Hume, *Concerning Human Understanding*, IV.I.20–21.
53. Ibid., V.I.36.
54. Ibid., X.I.91.

been said a hundred times before; and he said nothing about Christianity that had not been said before. It is only that when he said it the words passed like a flame through Europe, and became a force molding his time, and ours."[55]

Voltaire wrote widely on a diverse range of topics. Voltaire said that anything that affirmed God as eternal and supreme was not faith but reason. According to Voltaire, "Faith consists in believing, not what seems true, but what seems false to our understanding."[56] Like Hume, he was skeptical of the truth of miracles. He wrote, "Let there be an eclipse of the sun during a full moon, let a dead man walk five miles carrying his head in his arms, and we'll call that a miracle."[57] On religion, Voltaire thought that the best religion would be the one that was most reasonable, that appealed to the best in nature—"Wouldn't it be the simplest one? Wouldn't it be the one that taught a good deal of morality and very little dogma? The one that tended to make men just, without making them absurd? The one that wouldn't command belief in impossible, contradictory things insulting to the Divinity and pernicious to mankind, and wouldn't dare to threaten with eternal punishment anyone who has common sense?"[58]

Finally, Voltaire defined a theist as one who is reasonable in his belief in God. In other words, the theist believes in the God revealed to him by what he observes in nature, rather than depending upon the authority of that which is billed to be of supernatural origin. He described the theist as one who is "firmly convinced of the existence of a supreme Being, as good as it is powerful, which has created all the extended, vegetating, feeling, and reflecting beings; which perpetuates their species, which punishes crimes without cruelty, and rewards virtuous actions with kindness.... To do good—that is his worship; to submit to God—that is his doctrine."[59] Voltaire's rejection of the supernatural is thus at odds with Christianity on a significant point.

Still, even in Voltaire's writings, not everything was incompatible with Christian teaching. He was bitterly opposed to any religion which subjected its adherents to fear of persecution. He was vociferous in his

---

55. Durant and Durant, *Age of Voltaire*, 715.
56. Voltaire, *Philosophical Dictionary*, 275.
57. Ibid., 392.
58. Ibid., 445.
59. Ibid., 479.

defense of toleration. He equated the Golden Rule with the law of nature, and persecution with the law of the jungle: "*do unto others as you would have done unto yourself*, now, following this principle, there is no way a man may say to another, *believe that which I believe and you cannot believe, or you'll die.* . . . The right to persecute is therefore absurd and barbaric; it is the law of the jungle. Nay, it is yet worse, for wild animals kill only to eat, whereas we have exterminated one another over parcel of words."[60] He also mocked those who would excommunicate scientists who discovered truths that would prove universally beneficial to humanity just because their discoveries seemed to go against accepted theological teaching. He said, "It is time for men who were so enlightened to stop being slaves of the blind. I laugh every time I see an academy of science forced to defer to the decision of the congregation of the Holy Office."[61]

This brief survey of some Enlightenment thinkers is offered to show that what is termed "Enlightenment philosophy" is not necessarily anti-Christian, nor is it one particular set of beliefs and ideas. On certain points, it certainly does deviate from Christian orthodoxy. But at other points, it is not entirely incompatible with it. CA authors such as LaHaye and Amos have been narrow in their understanding and application of the term "Enlightenment." Although there were anti-Christian elements in some eighteenth century thought, some CA authors have associated Enlightenment philosophy too closely with anti-Christian thought. This narrow understanding and application of Enlightenment thought has led many CA authors to flawed conclusions about the influence that eighteenth-century thinkers had on the American founding.

HISTORICAL CONSIDERATIONS

Although the United States was founded in an era of a Protestant consensus, that consensus has largely broken down. Robert Handy wrote that for "the first quarter of its existence the United States was virtually monolithic in its Protestant orientation and character."[62] It has been replaced by a broad plurality of religious beliefs which now permeates the American society.[63]

---

60. Voltaire, *Treatise on Tolerance*, 28; emphasis original.
61. Voltaire, *Political Writings*, 147.
62. Handy, *Protestant Quest*, v.
63. For works on the significance of Christianity in early America, see Bercovitch, *Puritan Origins*; Bonomi, *Cope of Heaven*; Brauer, *Religion and the American Revolution*;

Diana Eck, in her study of religious pluralism in America, wrote, "The United States has become the most religiously diverse nation on earth."[64] This shift from a Protestant consensus in the eighteenth and nineteenth centuries to religious pluralism in the twentieth and twenty-first centuries underscores the scope and significance of religious freedom established in the First Amendment.[65]

A treatment of religious pluralism seems pertinent to a critique of CA. The reason for this is that the American Founders intended for a plurality of religions to exist in America. The basis for this assertion is found in the text of the First Amendment: "Congress shall make no law respecting an establishment of religion, or prohibiting the free exercise thereof; . . ."[66] The First Amendment accomplished two things: first, it prevented the legal establishment of a particular religion. Second, it guaranteed that everyone would have the freedom to hold the faith system of their choosing by ensuring "the free exercise" of religion.

This point is made plainer upon consideration of the drafts and proposals of the establishment clause of the First Amendment, which were debated from June to September of 1789 in the House of Representatives and the Senate. Disestablishment of religion was always accompanied by the affirmation of freedom of conscience in each draft. Gaustad collected the House and Senate proposals of the language for the First Amendment. Four drafts were proposed in the House and five in the Senate. By September 25, 1789, the existing language was accepted by the House and Senate, and the amendment was ratified on December 15, 1791.

Noll, *Christians in the American Revolution*; Noll, *Old Religion*; Noll, *Work We Have To Do*; Heimert, *Religion and the American Mind*; Sassi, *Republic of Righteousness*. See Handy, *Christian America*; Handy, *Protestant Quest*; Ahlstrom, *Religious History*; Marty, *Righteous Empire*; Noll, *History of Christianity*; Herberg, *Protestant—Catholic—Jew*; and Way, "Death of the Christian Nation," 509–29, for treatments of the breakdown of the Protestant consensus in the nineteenth and early twentieth centuries. For treatments of the state of religious pluralism in contemporary American society, see Allitt, *Religion in America*; Carroll et al., *Religion in America*; Eck, *New Religious America*; Marty, *Religion and Republic*; Silk, *Spiritual Politics*; Thiemann, *Religion in Public Life*; and Wuthnow, *Restructuring of American Religion*.

64. Eck, *New Religious America*, 4.

65. See chapter 1 for the study's treatment of how American notions of the relationship between religion and the state evolved from the Puritan model of the Christian commonwealth to that of disestablishment of religion and the establishment of religious freedom in the First Amendment.

66. U.S. Const., amend. I.

A. House of Representatives

1.) June 7 [1789]. Initial proposals of James Madison. "*The Civil Rights of none shall be abridged on account of religious belief or worship*, nor shall any national religion be established, *nor shall the full and equal rights of conscience be in any manner, nor on any pretext infringed.*"...

2) July 28. House Select Committee. "No religion shall be established by law, *nor shall the equal rights of conscience be infringed.*"

3) August 15. Full day of debate with many alterations and additions, with some question, still, whether any such amendment was necessary. Following the suggestion of his own state's ratifying convention, Samuel Livermore of New Hampshire proposed: "Congress shall make no laws touching religion, *or infringing the rights of conscience.*"

4) August 20. Fisher Ames (Massachusetts) moved that the following language be adopted by the House, and it was agreed: "Congress shall make no law establishing religion, *or to prevent the free exercise thereof, or to infringe the rights of conscience.*"

[This House version sent to the Senate]

B. Senate

1) September 3. Several versions passed or rejected in quick succession.

Rejected: "*Congress shall not make any law infringing the rights of conscience*, or establishing any religious sect or society."

Also rejected: "Congress shall make no law establishing any particular denomination of religion in preference to another, *or prohibiting the free exercise thereof, nor shall the rights of conscience be infringed.*"

Initially rejected, but later passed: "Congress shall make no law establishing one religious society in preference to others, *or to infringe on the rights of conscience.*"

Passed at the end of the day: "Congress shall make no law establishing religion, *or prohibiting the free exercise thereof.*"

2) September 9. "Congress shall make no law establishing articles of faith or a mode of worship, *or prohibiting the free exercise of religion.*"

[This Senate version was sent back to the House.]⁶⁷

Thus, from the beginning of Congressional debate on the language of the First Amendment, these two pillars of religious freedom always stood together. Full freedom of conscience ultimately leads to religious pluralism, and from the earliest drafts of the First Amendment, this was the Founders' clear intent.

Martin Marty offered a helpful definition of religious pluralism and what it entails. He described it as an environment where "no religion was to have a monopoly or a privileged position and none should be a basis for second-class status for others. Dialogue mean[s] that people could have exposure to each other across the lines of differing faiths without attempting to convert in every encounter, without being a threat, and with the hope that new understanding would result. The goal would be a richer co-participation in 'the city of man,' the republic, or the human family."⁶⁸ Diana Eck further developed this definition. She wrote, "[Pluralism] does not displace or eliminate deep religious commitments or secular commitments for that matter. It is, rather, the encounter of commitments. . . . I would argue that pluralism is engagement with, not abdication of, differences in particularities."⁶⁹ Thus, for these writers, a religiously pluralistic society encourages the acknowledgement of distinctions between faith commitments, discourages those faith groups to compromise on their value systems, and promotes dialogue and mutual understanding between them in spite of their differences. It is in this kind of environment that a plurality of religions can flourish, and each faith group has equal opportunity to influence the society. This kind of environment was intended by the language in the First Amendment, namely, that the "the free exercise" of religion would be guaranteed.

Contrary to the view of religious pluralism described by Marty and Eck, many CA writers have taken it to be a development spurred by anti-Christian secularism and moral relativism.⁷⁰ Francis Schaeffer,

---

67. Gaustad, *Faith of the Founders*, 157–58. Emphases on affirmations of religious freedom added.

68. Marty, *Righteous Empire*, 254.

69. Eck, *New Religious America*, 71.

70. In the interest of space, only one example has been provided to show how CA authors associated religious pluralism with secular humanism. See also Hart, *Faith and Freedom*; Whitehead, *Second American Revolution*; LaHaye, *Faith of Our Founding Fathers*; Kennedy and Newcombe, *What If?*; McDowell, *Christian Nation*; Barton, *Original Intent*; Barton, *Myth of Separation*; and Barton, *American Government* for other examples.

in his work *A Christian Manifesto*, attempted to differentiate between a fair religious pluralism where all faith commitments are on equal footing and a pluralism that degenerates into moral relativism. He wrote that in contemporary times, pluralism has lost its earlier meaning of "a general religious freedom from the control of the state for all religion."[71] Today the term "is used to mean that all types of situations are spread out before us, and that it really is up to each individual to grab one or the other on the way past, according to the whim of personal preference. What you take is only a matter of personal choice, with one choice as valid as another. Pluralism has come to mean that everything is acceptable."[72] For Schaeffer, religious pluralism in society is a fine thing—all faith systems may compete through persuasion and all have equal opportunities to grow in influence. But in contemporary times, according to Schaeffer, the term "pluralism" has become a cover for moral relativism.

The CA perspective on religious pluralism is motivated by a desire to show that the United States was founded to be Christian. People would be free to worship as they chose, but Christianity would be the faith system that enjoyed predominance. According to CA authors, America has lost this Christian distinctive over the past several decades because of anti-Christian secularism and moral relativism, but it must be recovered.[73] The paragraphs below will maintain that religious pluralism in American society does not *necessarily* need to be associated with anti-Christian secularism or moral relativism. A brief historical account of the demise of the Protestant consensus and the rise of religious pluralism will be provided in order to justify this assertion. Also, this section will argue that a societal environment encouraging free religious choice is the inevitable outcome of the religious liberty guaranteed by the First Amendment.

Demise of the Protestant Consensus and Rise of Religious Pluralism

The history of the demise of the Protestant consensus and rise of religious pluralism can be divided into two periods. The first period, accounting for the demise of the Protestant consensus, was gradual, taking place roughly from the Civil War (1861–1865) to the Depression of the 1930s. The second period, accounting for the rise of religious pluralism in American so-

---

71. Schaeffer, *Complete Works*, 5:440.
72. Ibid.
73. Chapter 2 discusses these themes in detail.

ciety, was rapid, taking place during the tumultuous decades of the 1960s and 70s. An examination of these developments will help to show that they can be explained by a variety of historical trends, rather than merely a cultural shift away from Christianity and toward moral relativism.

Several factors from the 1860s to the 1930s coalesced to undermine Protestant dominance in American society. Each of these factors caused divisions in Protestant churches which would prove impossible to mend, resulting in the loss of the predominant Protestant influence in the culture. Robert Handy listed six contributing factors to this loss:

1. The movement of African-Americans away from white churches after the Civil War.
2. The rise of the influence of liberal Protestant theology.
3. Immigration of Jews and south and east Europeans to America during the latter nineteenth and early twentieth centuries.
4. General disillusionment after World War I.
5. The modernist/fundamentalist controversies of the 1920s.
6. The onset of economic depression in the 1930s.[74]

African-Americans had often been viewed by whites, in both North and South, as inferior. Handy wrote, "With all too few exceptions, whites in the South and North believed in the inferiority of blacks and resisted any ideas of social equality.... The separate black churches had been originally founded because of the unwillingness of whites to accept black worshipers as equals."[75] This perspective had not changed after the North's victory over the Confederacy and the abolition of slavery in 1865. African-American Christians thus moved out of the traditional Protestant denominations and formed their own after the war. Segregation of the races was thus at the heart of this particular division within Protestantism, according to Handy. Noll argued the same point. He wrote, "After the Civil War, the black churches rapidly became the center for black culture generally as well as for black religious life. The failure of political Reconstruction—with the end to the protection that had been provided by Union troops, the beginning of violent repression associated with the Ku Klux Klan, and the enactment of Jim Crow laws enforcing a demeaning segregation—meant

---

74. See Handy, *Christian America*, 60–184.
75. Ibid., 61.

that freed slaves were stripped of control of every institution except the church. In the North, where the legal situation was better, racial prejudice was nevertheless almost as widespread."[76]

The influence of liberal Protestant theology also caused significant internal divisions in the Protestant denominations. Theological controversies would have repercussions in the churches lasting well into the twentieth century. Patrick Allitt observed,

> In the late nineteenth century, intellectual disputes contributed to more Protestant fragmentation. Religious scholars, as they began the historical-critical study of the ancient world, came to regard the Hebrew Bible (the Old Testament) as one of many collections of religious writings from the ancient Near East.... Charles Lyell's discoveries in geology and Charles Darwin's theory of evolution also transformed scholars' understanding of the nature of the earth and of life itself, casting doubt on whether the beginning of the Book of Genesis described actual historical events.[77]

Thus, theological liberals and conservatives within Protestantism drew their battle lines over the nature, authority, uniqueness, and veracity of the Bible.

Immigration after the Civil War reached new peaks as immigrants began pouring in from places other than the British Isles and Germany, places from where most immigrants traditionally came prior to 1860. To be sure, immigrants from Britain and Germany still arrived, but with them came people from Scandinavia, Italy, Poland, Austria, Russia, Greece, and the Balkans. Will Herberg stated,

> In fifteen of the thirty-five years from 1865 to 1900 the annual influx went beyond 400,000 [immigrants], with some 800,000 entering in 1882 alone. Through the first decade and a half of the new century up to the outbreak of World War I, all previous levels were surpassed: in three of the fifteen years the figure reached a million; in 1907 it topped 1,250,000.... Virtually every European linguistic dialect and ethnic strain was now to be found within the confines of the continental United States, together with many more from Africa, Asia Minor, and the Far East.[78]

---

76. Noll, *History of Christianity*, 341–42.
77. Allitt, *Religion in America*, 7.
78. Herberg, *Protestant—Catholic—Jew*, 7–8.

Among these new arrivals were Protestants in large numbers, but also Roman Catholics, Eastern Orthodox Christians, Jews, and secularists.

At the close of World War I, many American Protestants had set their hope on American moral leadership in the world, informed largely by the idealism of Woodrow Wilson. H. W. Brands wrote, "The president asserted the United States had negotiated the peace in the same way it had fought the war, as the disinterested champion of right. And America must remain the champion of right."[79] The League of Nations, established after the signing of the Treaty of Versailles in 1919 was to be the international body ensuring peace, stability, and justice in the world. American leadership was essential to the success of the League, and American Protestants were hopeful for the prospects of Christian morality in international affairs. By 1920, the Senate had rejected both the Treaty and the League, beginning an era of American isolationism which would last till the outbreak of World War II. According to Handy, "In the sharply changed atmosphere, the idealistic interpretation of the war fell under increasing criticism as its professed goals seemed to remain unfulfilled and its cost and brutality appeared to growing numbers to have been in vain. The sense of disillusionment deepened as world reaction to the global struggle began to be heard, much of it unflattering to the West and to Christendom."[80]

The decade of the 1920s would present a host of challenges to Protestant consensus from many quarters. The failure of Protestants to address each challenge decisively and with a unified voice contributed to the further decline in Protestant influence. Sydney Ahlstrom wrote, "Protestant America, consequently, did not really face its first great moment of truth until it marched onto the moral and religious battlefields of the twenties, the tumultuous decade of prohibition, immigration, evolution, jazz, the KKK, short skirts, the movies, Al Smith, and the Crash. Here, indeed, was the antipodes of the Great Awakening."[81] For example, the Scopes Trial of 1925 revealed what to many was the naiveté and obscurantism of fundamentalist Protestantism. Marsden wrote, "Although the outcome of the trial was indecisive and the [anti-evolution] law stood, the rural setting and the press's caricatures of fundamentalists as rubes and hicks discredited fundamentalism and made it difficult to pursue further the serious

---

79. Brands, *Woodrow Wilson*, 119.
80. Handy, *Christian America*, 165.
81. Ahlstrom, *Religious History*, 8.

Critiquing the Christian America Thesis   141

aspects of the movement."[82] Furthermore, Marsden stated, "Before 1925 the movement had commanded much respect, though not outstanding support, but after the summer of 1925 the voices of ridicule were raised so loudly that many moderate Protestant conservatives quietly dropped support of the cause rather than be embarrassed by association."[83] By the 1930s, Protestantism's predominance in American society had effectively come to an end. Handy wrote, "It was on a Protestantism weakened by the spiritual decline of the twenties that the weight of the economic depression fell, slashing budgets, reducing memberships, halting benevolent and missionary enterprises, dismissing ministers, closing churches.... Though many only later became aware of it, during the depression period the 'Protestant era' in American history came to a close."[84] Ahlstrom similarly concluded that, "In retrospect, it becomes clear that the decade of the twenties marked a crucial transition in American religious history."[85]

To summarize the section thus far, several factors converged to undermine the Protestant consensus that had dominated American culture in the late eighteenth and early nineteenth centuries. While some of these factors arose from anti-Christian secularism, others were not based upon any critique of Christianity.

Following the waning of Protestant dominance in the 1930s Protestantism was further weakened as a moral and theological force in the culture during the 1960s and 70s. According to Ahlstrom, these decades witnessed the convergence of major challenges to Protestant notions of religion, nationhood, and morality. During the 1960s, a combination of foreign and domestic crises dominated the lives of the majority of Americans: the Vietnam War and the Civil Rights Movement being the most important. Related to these crises was a general failure of confidence on the part of the general population in ideas which, in previous generations, were never questioned, such as moral values, patriotism, and respect

---

82. Marsden, *Understanding Fundamentalism*, 60.

83. Marsden, *Fundamentalism and American Culture*, 191. Marsden noted later in his work that fundamentalism would actually experience resurgence outside of mainstream Protestant circles in the 1930s. He wrote, "In general, although the rest of American Protestantism floundered in the 1930s, fundamentalist groups, or those at least with fundamentalist sympathies, increased" (194). Still, even Marsden did not deny that the overall influence of Protestantism was on the decline by the 1930s.

84. Handy, *Christian America*, 179, 184.

85. Ahlstrom, *Religious History*, 917.

for authority. Ahlstrom wrote, "The idea of America as a Chosen Nation and a beacon to the world was expiring. The people had by no means become less religious, and their sense of moral urgency was, if anything, heightened. Yet unmistakably at the heart of the prevailing anxiety was the need for reexamining fundamental conceptions of religion, ethics, and nationhood."[86] More specifically, Ahlstrom observed five catalysts for such radical and swift changes in the culture:

1. "Rampant, unregulated urban and industrial growth," leading to intense problems of social justice, particularly among non-whites.
2. "Technological developments in agriculture and industry" joined with the liberalizing effect of Vatican II among both Roman Catholics and Protestants, the election in 1960 of the first Roman Catholic president, and the undermining of the influence of Protestantism in the public square by the decisions of the Supreme Court.
3. "Widely publicized advancement of science."
4. The humanitarian crises created by Nazism and the spread of Stalinism as well as the threat of nuclear war.
5. President Johnson's escalation of the Vietnam War."[87]

All contributed to the dilution of societal obsequiousness to traditional Protestant authority.

Along with these challenges, religious pluralism, in terms of a wide range of distinct faith systems, arose in earnest during the 1960s. The Immigration and Nationality Act of 1965 changed the immigration policies of the United States that had been in force since the Immigration Act of 1924. During that forty-one year period, strict quotas limited the number of non-white (and non-Christian) immigrants arriving in the United States. The 1965 act, signed into law by President Lyndon Johnson, opened the United States to immigrants from these countries, and with them, their diverse faith systems. Jennifer Ludden assessed the act as a major shift in the ethnic makeup of the United States. She wrote, "The current system of legal immigration dates to 1965. It marked a radical

---

86. Ibid., 967.
87. Ibid., 1091–93.

break with previous policy and has led to profound demographic changes in America."[88]

Eck wrote, assessing the pluralistic society in America, "There is no going back. As we say in Montana, the horses are already out of the barn. Our new religious diversity is not just an idea but a reality, built into our neighborhoods all over America. Religious pluralism is squarely and forever on the American agenda."[89] The reason for this is that "a new post-1965 immigration was bringing immigrants to America from all over the world. Never again would an analysis of America's religious life look so simple. The post-1965 immigrants have brought with them their many religious traditions—Hindu, Sikh, Muslim, Buddhist, Jain, and Zoroastrian. . . . Now the 'Protestant, Catholic, Jewish' image of America has been amplified to include many other voices, and a new era of America's religious pluralism has begun."[90] Eck stressed that the Protestant dominance of American cultural life has come to a definite end.

Still, it is important to note that, according to R. Stephen Warner, the religious pluralism that has come to dominate since 1965 does not merely mean that non-Christian religions have grown in presence and influence. Warner stated that, although non-Christian religions have grown impressively, non-Protestant, non-white Christians have accounted for much of the post-1965 arrivals to American shores. He wrote, "What many people have not heard, however, and need to hear, is that the great majority of newcomers are Christian. . . . This means that the new immigrants represent not the de-Christianization of American society but the de-Europeanization of American Christianity."[91] Christians arriving to America from Latin America, Asia, the Middle East, Africa, and eastern Europe have added to the many non-Christian immigrants to bolster the religious pluralism that defines contemporary society.

Another significant aspect of the post-1965 immigration waves is the fact that, while immigrants' ethnic identities historically have been expected to change into an American identity, their religions have not been expected to conform to an American religion, since there is none. This fact was observed by Herberg in the 1950s, prior to the start of the

88. Ludden, "1965 Immigration Law."
89. Eck, *New Religious America*, 46.
90. Ibid., 63.
91. Warner, "Coming to America," 20.

new immigration policies of the 1960s. His observation proved to be quite correct, both for the previous waves of immigrants from Protestant, Catholic, Orthodox, and Jewish traditions, but also for the later waves of immigrants from non-Christian traditions. Herberg wrote, "The newcomer is expected to change many things about him as he becomes American—nationality, language, culture. One thing, however, he is *not* expected to change—and that is his religion."[92]

It was not only the fact that non-Europeans were bringing their religions with them to America that contributed to the rise of religious pluralism in the 1960s and 70s. It was also the fact that native-born Americans of European stock were adopting many Eastern faith systems themselves. This was due partly to a rejection of traditional religious forms in America, and also to the relative ease of initiation to certain Eastern religious practices, like Transcendental Meditation. Celebrities such as the Beatles, Jane Fonda, and Mia Farrow sought inner peace and enlightenment at the feet of Maharishi Mahesh Yogi, the Indian avatar of Transcendental Meditation.[93] This kind of publicity was positive and compelling to many Americans. Allitt remarked that "By the mid-1970s a wide array of Asian religions was available to the American consumer. Harvey Cox, the liberal Protestant theologian and Harvard professor who had celebrated the 'secular city' ten years earlier, surveyed his hometown of Cambridge, Massachusetts, and found more than forty Asian religions represented there, including TM, Zen and Tibetan Buddhism, Sufi dancing, Ananda Marga, Hare Krishna, Divine Light, Sikhs, Sri Chinmoy, and an array of Yoga and Tai Chi centers."[94]

Robert Bellah, in a 1967 essay entitled "Civil Religion in America," attempted to assess the significance of the waning of Protestant predominance and the beginning of the new pluralism. His point was that America's religious identity was progressing from that defined by a Protestant form of Christianity to a more common, neutral, civil religion. Bellah defined this civil religion as being distinguished from Christianity, although there were elements in it which were generally compatible with it. He wrote, "Although matters of personal religious belief, worship, and association are considered to be strictly private affairs, there are, at the same time,

---

92. Herberg, *Protestant—Catholic—Jew*, 23. Emphasis is in the original.
93. Allitt, *Religion in America*, 140.
94. Ibid., 141.

certain common elements of religious orientation that the great majority of Americans share.... This public religious dimension is expressed in a set of beliefs, symbols, and rituals that I am calling the American civil religion."[95] Bellah asserted that these beliefs, while basically theistic and compatible with Christianity, might draw from other religious traditions as well. It was even conceivable to him that the American civil religion might develop into an atheistic form. His point was that, "There is no formal creed in the civil religion" and that "It is useless to speculate on the form such a civil religion might take, though it obviously would draw on religious traditions beyond the sphere of Biblical religion alone."[96] So, beginning in the 1960s, this notion of a generally held cultural appreciation of a transcendence which undergirded the national identity, as opposed to a specific national adherence to orthodox Christian teaching, seemed to be more appropriate given the historical development of the culture over several decades as well as the contemporary climate of the times.

Religious Pluralism and Religious Freedom

The point of tracing the demise of the Protestant consensus and rise of religious pluralism in America is to underscore the significance of negative religious liberty as a central element in the American way of life. Positive and negative religious liberty were defined in chapter 1. To review, positive religious liberty offers freedom of conscience within a particular group. Dissenters within this group are free to leave the group. This was the model established in the New England colonies, excepting Rhode Island. Negative religious liberty offers freedom of conscience to anyone. Each individual is free to pursue his own faith system without interference from the state. This model was established in Rhode Island, and later, in the First Amendment.

Recall also from the first chapter, that the founding generation did not intend to establish Christianity as the defining element in America's identity. The Puritan settlers of the seventeenth century did intend this, but the generation which declared independence from the British did not. They intended to establish America as a nation with negative religious freedom—unhindered freedom of conscience for every individual. The First Amendment would guarantee that the government would not at-

95. Bellah, "Civil Religion in America," 5–6.
96. Ibid., 17.

tempt to establish a particular religion for Americans, but would create an environment in which each faith system would have equal opportunity to attract and sustain membership as well as impact the culture surrounding them with its own ethical and theological value system. When it came to religious choice, the government would leave it to the personal preferences of the citizens, rather than to its endorsement or legal establishment.

This seems to be the view held by most contemporary American Christians. Christian Smith, in his 1995–1997 survey of evangelical Christians on their views of religious pluralism and religious freedom, found that they are as ready to engage with other faith systems in dialogue and understanding as ever. The first wave of research involved 130 active members in Protestant churches from six locations in America who were personally interviewed in two-hour sessions. Sixty-five were white evangelicals, twenty-seven were conservative African-American Christians, and the others were from mainline Protestant denominations. The research also included a 1996 telephone survey of 2,591 American Protestants, and a final wave of two-hour interviews with another 187 evangelical Christians from twenty-three states. Smith found that most evangelical Christians, rather than seeking to exclude other faith systems in the marketplace of ideas, were enthusiastic about dialogue, and valued religious freedom in society above any form of Christian dominance. Smith asked, "Do evangelicals really want cultural uniformity grounded in their own worldview?"[97] Resoundingly, the answer to this question was, no. Smith found that "For every one evangelical opposed to pluralism, there were about *five* other evangelicals who voiced a strong commitment to freedom of choice and toleration of diversity."[98] Furthermore, Smith wrote, "All of these evangelicals expressed one way or another the need for Christians to accept the plurality of America's different peoples, lifestyles, and religions."[99] Finally, "if a most consistent theme among evangelicals on the question of other religions can be identified, it is the imperative of religious freedom in toleration. For most evangelicals we interviewed, when all was said and done, religious liberty was the touchstone of their

---

97. Smith, *Christian America?*, 61.
98. Ibid., 64; emphasis original.
99. Ibid., 68.

thinking on the matter. For this reason, few of them sounded like intolerant bigots, though critics sometimes described them that way."[100]

It would seem that those advocates of CA who associated religious pluralism with anti-Christian secularism and relativism, or even denied that the Founders intended liberty for worshippers of all religions and not just Christian denominations, are well outside the mainstream of American evangelical thinking.[101] His findings also argue for the success of the idea of religious freedom in America.

The passing of the Protestant era and the rise of religious pluralism in America is the inevitable outcome of negative religious liberty. The notion that each religion would have to compete with other religions on equal terms for adherents and cultural influence is a notion that began in the eighteenth century with the First Great Awakening and the preaching of the itinerants like George Whitefield.[102] The religious pluralism seen in today's culture is the continuation, indeed the fulfillment, of that notion rooted in the Awakening. Stephen Waldman, noting the reality of today's religious pluralism and tying it to the Founders' intentions, wrote,

> Today America is home to more Hindus than Unitarians, more Muslims than Congregationalists, and more Buddhists than Jews. In fact, there are more than twelve million non-Christians in America—about four times the entire population of the colonies when the Constitution was ratified. Immigration combined with continuous splintering of existing denominations to create a breathtaking diversity of sects. These "facts on the ground" reinforce the Founders' pluralistic impulse and forever shut the door on the possibility that America could be, in any official sense, deemed a Protestant, or even a Christian, nation.[103]

Marty critiqued the CA association of religious pluralism with anti-Christian secularism and relativism. He differentiated between what he called

---

100. Ibid., 80.

101. "The Founders, however, not only chose not to establish federally any particular denomination of Christianity, they further never intended the First Amendment to become a vehicle to promote a pluralism of other religions" (Barton, *Original Intent*, 31); emphasis original.

102. See Moynahan, *Faith*; and Noll, *Old Religion*. See also Chapter 1 of this study for a treatment of the First Great Awakening and its impact on colonial American religious culture.

103. Waldman, *Founding Faith*, 190.

political and public theological assumptions.[104] In his estimation, CA advocates have abandoned public theology in favor of political theology. In other words, Marty asserted that advocates of CA would seek strictly to limit free religious choice to the bounds of Christian denominations.

First, Marty classified public theology in terms of both Bellah's civil religion and Eck's definition of pluralism. He wrote, "A public theology, as numbers of us have set out to define it, allows for the integrity of movements that are not conservative Protestant, Christian, or Jewish-Christian at all. God can work his 'order' through the godless, in secular-pluralism."[105] Public theology acknowledges the reality of religious pluralism, values it as a benefit to culture, and understands that God's sovereignty both over and within culture is not compromised in the least.

By contrast, the political theology espoused by CA advocates, "is born of separatists who do not regard nonfundamentalists with any positive ecumenical feelings. The fundamentalist political scope may recognize Catholics and Jews or 'traditional theists' as belonging to the civil order, but then insists nontheists are outsiders, to be tolerated at best."[106] Thus for Marty, CA advocates call for a return to Christian roots risks excluding non-Christians from a meaningful contribution to the civic life of the nation.[107]

Pierard's critique addressed the association of religious pluralism with anti-Christian secularism by CA advocates such as Whitehead.[108] Specifically, he pointed to the use by CA advocates of the term "secular humanism" to describe the contemporary society in which religious pluralism thrives. Pierard wrote, "To be sure, secular humanism is an elusive concept, a scare word that means different things to different people.... But evangelicals who use it to designate 'the enemy' want nothing to do with a pluralistic system that they feel is a smokescreen obscuring the hegemony exercised by an alien, godless ideology."[109] Pierard argued against the view held and described earlier in this chapter by Schaeffer and other CA advocates.

104. Marty, *Religion and Republic*, 295.
105. Ibid.
106. Ibid.
107. See Chapter 2 for a discussion on how CA authors exhort American Christians to retrieve the nation's Christian heritage.
108. See Whitehead, *Second American Revolution*.
109. Pierard, "Standing," 371.

Rather than seeking to cast religious pluralism in anti-Christian and moral relativist terms and make "a return to biblical basics,"[110] Pierard stated that the way to combat anti-Christian secularism in the culture is to emphasize religious freedom. He acknowledged that CA advocates have a point in protesting religious discrimination in the public square in the name of religious pluralism and separation of church and state. But according to Pierard, secular humanism's "hold should be eliminated through disestablishment . . . Neutrality must not be allowed to degenerate into an establishment of secularism or a device to foster irreligion."[111]

Eck made this point by observing that those holding to CA are not only in the unenviable position of neglecting the religious pluralism that defines contemporary American society. They also are at risk of undermining religious freedom. Eck wrote,

> Today, the invocation of a Christian America takes on a new set of tensions as our population of Muslim, Hindu, Sikh, and Buddhist neighbors grows. The ideal of a Christian America stands in contradiction to the spirit, if not the latter, of America's foundational principle of religious freedom. As long as religious diversity meant Methodists, Congregationalists, Southern Baptists, and Catholics, or as long as it meant, at the most, Christians and Jews, the issues were not so troubling and attention not so palpable. Today however, America is in the process of coming to terms with this deep contradiction, this very complex form of hypocrisy.[112]

To review, many CA authors justify the CA thesis by asserting that America was founded within a culture of Protestant consensus. The fact of religious pluralism is emblematic of America's cultural drift away from Christianity and toward moral relativism. The First Amendment, however, guarantees that America would not only disestablish religion, but also that the peoples' free choice of religion would not be hindered. This is clear not only from the text of the First Amendment, but also from the Congressional debates on the language of the First Amendment in 1791. Individual freedom of religious choice always stood with disestablishment. During the course of the nineteenth and twentieth centuries, the Protestant predominance of the culture gave way to religious pluralism on account of a variety of explanations, not merely a drift toward moral

---

110. Falwell, *Listen, America!*, 18.
111. Pierard, "Standing," 371–72.
112. Eck, *New Religious America*, 46.

relativism. The religious pluralism witnessed by contemporary society was the inevitable result and intent of the First Amendment.

THEOLOGICAL CONSIDERATIONS

So far, this study has examined the assertion that America is, by design, a Christian nation from philosophical and historical bases. It lacks sufficient grounds both in logical reasoning and historical fact. Terms that seem to be central to the argument for CA are not clearly defined by its proponents. Furthermore, the historical record seems to show that religious pluralism was the intent of the First Amendment, and this intent became reality as a result of the breakdown of the Protestant consensus. Still, as seen in chapter 2, the CA thesis includes two prominent theological contentions—that the Bible was the primary authority undergirding the founding documents and that American exceptionalism is evidence of God's unique calling on America. Both of these contentions have been ardently defended by advocates of CA. Authors such as Kennedy and Newcombe, Amos, Eidsmoe, Beliles and Anderson, DeMar, Hutson, Robertson, and Marshall and Manuel all defended the first assertion. LaHaye, McDowell and Beliles, Falwell, Marshall and Manuel each explicitly defended the second, while others did so implicitly. This section will offer a critique of both of these contentions.

Christian Theology Not the Primary Authority for America's Founding

Chapter 2 provided a treatment of how CA advocates justified the claim that the Bible and Christian theology form the primary authority for America's founding documents. Works by Amos, Eidsmoe, and Beliles and Anderson were cited in the attempt to show that a key theme in the CA thesis is that the ideas expressed in the founding documents are primarily based in Christian theology. For example, Amos insisted that of all the ideas expressed in the Declaration, if they did not originate directly from Scripture, they at least came from the Christian intellectual tradition. They claimed that ideas which seemed to originate from the Enlightenment, such as a term like "Nature and Nature's God," were actually borrowed from the Christian tradition. Amos wrote, "My theme is simple. The Declaration of Independence was not the bastard offspring of anti-Christian deism or Enlightenment rationalism. The ideas in the

Declaration are Christian despite the fact that some of the men who wrote them down were not. Those ideas are not opposed to the teachings of the Bible or of mainstream Christianity."[113] Thus, the CA contention is that America's heritage is singularly Christian, owing little or nothing to secular sources. The following paragraphs will argue against this contention.

Lutz's table categorizing the Founders' sources in their writings has had a profound effect on writers such as Barton and Eidsmoe. The conclusion they drew from this data was that the Bible is clearly the most prominent source consulted by the Founders in their writings, in comparison with other intellectual categories of sources like the Enlightenment and radical Whiggism. If this is true, then it is clear that the founding documents lean most heavily on the Bible, and thus America's founding is Christian at its core. Barton, commenting on Lutz's table and quoting a *Newsweek* article by Kenneth Woodward and David Gates, wrote, "... some have even conceded that 'historians are discovering that the Bible, perhaps even more than the Constitution, is our Founding document.'"[114] Lutz's table, from his work *The Origins of American Constitutionalism*, is reproduced here:

Distribution of Citations[115]

Category	1760s	1770s	1780s	1790s	1800–05	% of total
Bible	24%	44%	34%	29%	38%	34%
Enlightenment	32 (21)	18 (11)	24 (23)	21 (20)	18 (17)	22 (19)
Whig	10 (21)	20 (27)	19 (20)	17 (18)	15 (16)	18 (21)
Common-Law	12	4	9	14	20	11
Classical	8	11	10	11	2	9
Other	14	3	4	8	7	6
	100%	100%	100%	100%	100%	100%
	n = 216	n = 544	n = 1,306	n = 674	n = 414	N = 3,154

113. Amos, *Defending*, 20. In rebuttal to Amos' point, "not opposed" is not equal to "originated from."

114. Woodward and Gates, "How the Bible Made America," 44.

115. Lutz, *Origins of American Constitutionalism*, 141. Permission to reprint the chart granted with kind permission by Louisiana State University Press. The percentages appearing in parentheses represent the values when Locke is shifted from an Enlightenment source to a Whig source.

Lutz stated that about three-fourths of the biblical citations came from reprinted sermons. The writings of Paul were the most frequently cited, followed by Peter's writings, the gospel of John, Deuteronomy, Isaiah, Genesis, Exodus, and Leviticus.[116] To clarify the point, Lutz wrote, "If we ask which book was the most frequently cited in that [public political] literature, the answer is, the Bible."[117]

On the surface, the CA argument seems compelling. But Barton's conclusion, that the Bible is more America's founding document than the Constitution, seems to be a leap. All that might be said from this data is what Lutz affirmed in the above quoted statement. Lutz said that if one limits the question of influential prominence to a single book, then the Bible prevails.

Two further issues undermine the CA argument here. First, Lutz's table shows that the Bible consists of only about one-third of all citations in the public political literature of the 1760s to the first decade of the 1800s. The rest come from five other intellectual categories. Second, Lutz did not specify the context of the biblical citations, specifically, which of those were used authoritatively and which were used illustratively. To be sure, this was not the point of Lutz's survey. But because of this, it does not seem possible to draw the conclusion, based on Lutz's data, that the Bible is the primary intellectual source for the American Revolution and founding.

In assessing the importance of sources undergirding the ideas of America's founding documents, one must also keep in mind that disparate groups of sources merged to form an integrated whole during the revolutionary period. Bernard Bailyn identified these major groups of sources, and asserted that one particular group of writings brought unity from disparity. He wrote, "... ultimately this profusion of authorities is reducible to a few, distinct groups of sources and intellectual traditions dominated and harmonized into a single whole by the influence of one peculiar strain of thought, one distinctive tradition."[118]

According to Bailyn, five groups of sources formed the basis for American revolutionary thought. These were classical antiquity, the Enlightenment, English common law, the Puritan theological tradition,

---

116. Ibid.
117. Ibid.
118. Bailyn, *Ideological Origins*, 23.

and the radical Whig ideology of the Commonwealth period in England's history.[119] The single source which brought unity out of disparity, according to Bailyn, was the body of writings from the Commonwealth period. Bailyn wrote,

> What brought these disparate strands of thought together, what dominated the colonists' miscellaneous learning and shaped it into a coherent whole, was the influence of still another group of writers, a group whose thought overlapped with that of those already mentioned but which was yet distinct in its essential characteristics and unique in its determinative power. The ultimate origins of this distinctive ideological strain lay in the radical social and political thought of the English Civil War and of the Commonwealth period; but its permanent form had been acquired at the turn of the seventeenth century and in the early eighteenth century, in the writings of a group of prolific opposition theorists, "country" politicians and publicists.[120]

Thus, the writings of the Commonwealthmen, such as Milton, Algernon Sidney, Locke, Molesworth, Lord Somers, and Benjamin Hoadley, harmonized the ideas arising from sacred and Christian sources.[121] Pauline Maier concurred with Bailyn's assessment. She stated, "I share with him [Bailyn], above all, a conviction that the set of ideas brought together in the 'Real Whig' tradition of seventeenth- and eighteenth-century England are of central importance in explaining the American Revolution; that, in fact, the revolutionary movement takes on consistency and form only against the background of English revolutionary tradition."[122]

Of the Commonwealthmen, the writings of Trenchard and Gordon were most influential in bringing unity to the groups of sources of revolutionary thought. Bailyn stated: "To the colonists the most important of these publicists and intellectual middlemen were those spokesman for extreme libertarianism, John Trenchard (1662–1723) and Thomas Gordon (d. 1750)."[123]

---

119. Ibid., 23–34.

120. Ibid., 34.

121. See Chapter 1 for an introduction to the real Whig writings of the Commonwealth period.

122. Maier, *From Resistance to Revolution*, xx.

123. Bailyn, *Ideological Origins*, 35. See chapter 1 for an introduction to Trenchard and Gordon and their body of writings collected in *Cato's Letters*.

One of the aspects of the *Letters* is that Trenchard and Gordon did not regularly draw from Scripture or Christian tradition to justify their ideas on political and religious liberty. Rather, they drew from history, common experience, and reason and used these as bases for their ideas. This is a significant point, given the importance of the writings of the Commonwealth tradition to American revolutionary thought in general, and the writings of Trenchard and Gordon in particular. It is also important to note that these writers' ideas, though they are secular, are not anti-Christian. This provides further rebuttal to those CA writers who too closely associated secular with anti-Christian thought.[124]

There are several examples from the *Letters* that expressed the secular origin of Trenchard and Gordon's ideas which will be cited in the following paragraphs. The purpose here is to show that Trenchard and Gordon relied upon history, common experience, and reason rather than on divine revelation as justification for their ideas. Again, this goes to show that America's heritage is not singularly Christian, but owes to important secular sources.

In Letter No. 15, dated February 4, 1720, Trenchard and Gordon made the point that common wisdom and liberty arose from the individual freedoms of thought and speech. They stressed that these freedoms are the inherent rights of everyone:

> Without freedom of thought, there can be no such thing as wisdom; and no such thing as publick liberty, without freedom of speech: Which is the right of every man, as far as by it he does not hurt and control the right of another; and this is the only check which it ought to suffer, the only bounds which it ought to know. . . . This sacred privilege is so essential to free government, that the security of property; and the freedom of speech, always go together; and in those wretched countries where a man cannot call his tongue his own, he can scarce call any thing else his own.[125]

To justify this assertion, the authors pointed to several historical examples, both positive and negative. They cited recent history, such as the negative example set by Charles I in denying freedom of speech. They cited ancient history, as in the positive example set by the republican Romans Horatius, Valerius, and Cincinnatus who upheld freedom of speech. Other virtu-

---

124. See the section on Enlightenment philosophy earlier in this chapter.
125. Trenchard and Gordon, "No. 15," 110.

ous examples mentioned by Trenchard and Gordon in this letter were the Roman Emperors Titus, Nerva, Trajan, and Marcus Aurelius, whose collective rule they described as "righteous administration."[126] They contrasted these rulers with Sejanus, Tigellinus, Pallas, and Cleander, who were wicked bureaucrats and advisors to Emperors Tiberius, Nero, Claudius, and Commodus respectively.[127]

The letter is fraught with historical references, each one serving as proof that individual liberty is the key to the success of any government. Most of the references were from ancient Rome, and Tacitus was quoted liberally. For example, they wrote, "freedom of speech is the great bulwark of liberty; they prosper and die together: And it is the terror of traitors and oppressors, and a barrier against them. It produces excellent writers, and encourages men of fine genius. Tacitus tells us, that the Roman commonwealth bred great and numerous authors, who writ with equal boldness and eloquence: But when it was enslaved, those great wits were no more."[128] During the years of the Roman Republic, freedom of speech was commonly enjoyed, but this freedom ceased to be under the wicked emperors of later years. In Letter No. 18, they wrote, "Let us therefore grow wise by the misfortunes of others: Let us make use of the Roman language, as a vehicle of good sense, and useful instruction; and not use it like pedants, priests, and pedagogues. Let their virtues and their vices, and the punishment of them too, be an example to us; and so prevent our miseries from being an example to other nations: …"[129] For Trenchard and Gordon, history provided a sure set of examples, negative and positive, for any civilization to follow in regards to the state of individual liberty. Moreover, the future would look to the example set in their own country and historical setting. They urged their readers to value individual freedoms in order to present a positive example to future generations.

Just as history provided a powerful justification for their views on liberty, the common experience of man did so as well. In Letter No. 25, the authors looked to contemporary examples in the Spanish colonies in America, in the Ottoman Empire, and in Morocco, all of which were examples of suppression of liberty. It is almost as if they were attempting to

126. Ibid., 112.
127. Ibid., 112n8.
128. Ibid., 114.
129. Trenchard and Gordon, "No. 18," 131.

bring shock value to their audience as they described the tyrannies of these foreign potentates. They wrote, "Let us look round this great world, and behold what an immense majority of the whole race of men crouch under the yoke of a few tyrants, naturally as low as the meanest of themselves, and, by being tyrants, worse than the worst; ..."[130] The example of the king of Morocco was grim: "Old Muley, the Lord's anointed of Morocco [Ismail, Sultan of Morocco from 1672-1727], who it seems is still alive, is thought to have butchered forty thousand of his subjects with his own hands. Such a father is he of his people! And yet his right to shed human blood being a genuine characteristick [sic] of the church of Morocco, as by law established, people are greedy to die by his hand; which, they are taught to imagine, dispatches them forthwith to paradise:..."[131]

In addition to history and experience, Trenchard and Gordon based their views on reason and nature, two powerful authorities in 1720s England and 1770s America. When it came to the rights of men, Trenchard and Gordon affirmed that nature was their source and that it had bestowed on them equally and without regard to social or economic status. In Letter No. 45, they wrote, "Nature is a kind and benevolent parent; she constitutes no particular favourites with endowments and privileges above the rest; but for the most part sends all her offspring into the world furnished with the elements of understanding and strength, to provide for themselves."[132] Equality is thus the natural and happy state of man. Inequality and tyranny are unnatural. In particularly stark terms, they wrote, "Whoever pretends to be naturally superior to other men, claims from nature which she never gave to any man.... Death and diseases are the portion of kings as well as of clowns; and the corpse of a monarch is no more exempted from stench and putrefaction, than the corpse of a slave."[133]

In answer to those who would affirm the divine right of kings, and would deny that men are equal and are endowed by God with inherent rights, Trenchard and Gordon said that Scripture was not the basis of government, but man himself. In Letter No. 60, they wrote, "There is no government now on earth, which owes its formation or beginning to the

---

130. Trenchard and Gordon, "No. 25," 179.
131. Ibid., 183.
132. Trenchard and Gordon, "No. 45," 306.
133. Ibid., 308.

immediate revelation of God, or can derive its existence from such a revelation: ... Government therefore can have no power, but such as men can give, and such as they actually did give, or permit for their own sakes: nor can any government be in fact framed but by consent, if not of every subject, yet of as many as can compel the rest; ..."[134] This position is similar to that taken by Locke in his rebuttal to Sir Robert Filmer (1588–1653), who defended the notion of the divine right of kings in his work, *Patriarcha*. Letter No. 60 seems to have drawn liberally from the writings of Locke, for it appears to assume the reliability of notions such as man in the state of nature, the social contract, and the principle of government by consent of the governed.[135] It is to a brief examination of Locke and the basis for his ideas the study now turns.

CA advocates such as Amos and Eidsmoe claimed Locke as one of their own, an evangelical Christian. CA detractors, such as Isaac Kramnick and R. Laurence Moore and Carl Becker cast Locke in thoroughly secular (but not anti-Christian) terms.[136] It is almost as if the debate over whether or not America is a Christian nation is encapsulated in the debate over whether or not Locke belongs with the evangelical Christians or the secularists. Two things, however, are clear about Locke: first, his influence in American revolutionary thought is preeminent, and second, the basis for his thought was not revelation, but reason.

One objection that has been made in reference to this assertion, particularly by Amos, is that Locke was thoroughly drawing from the Christian tradition. On the relationship between reason and revelation, namely that reason is a more certain guide to truth than revelation, Locke was specifically within the Thomistic tradition. Frederick Copleston wrote, "... Locke's distinction between the light of nature and revelation recalls Aquinas' distinction between the natural law, known by reason, and the divine positive law; ..."[137] According to the objection, even though Locke did not cite biblical chapter and verse in his *Second Treatise* to ground his views in Christianity, his views were still consistent with Christian tradition. The problem is that if one intends to make the claim that the Bible is the preeminent authority justifying American revolutionary and

134. Trenchard and Gordon, "No. 60," 413–14.

135. Ibid., 413–17.

136. See Kramnick and Moore, *Godless Constitution*; and Becker, *Declaration of Independence*.

137. Copleston, *History of Philosophy*, 127.

founding ideas, then it would seem crucial to the claim that a first rate thinker such as Locke would have directly cited it, at least occasionally, as an authority. He did not, either in the *Second Treatise* or in the *Essay* as his basis for authority.

Another problem that is easy to overlook is that Locke was a Western thinker, writing in the seventeenth century. Christian thought was the framework in which all thought, sacred and secular, was developed. It is not appropriate to say that every idea arising out of the Enlightenment of the seventeenth and eighteenth centuries strictly conformed to Christian theology, merely because it arose out of an intellectual environment dominated by Christianity. If it were, then one would be forced to affirm that other strains of philosophical and theological thought were "Christian" because they arose out of a Christian intellectual framework. Take Hume's skepticism as an example. It is not possible to honestly assess Humean skepticism as "Christian," even though Hume's ideas were conceived within a culture of Western Christian consensus.

The ideas put forth by Trenchard and Gordon and Locke are secular because they did not originate in the Bible, nor did they claim Christian doctrine as their primary authority. As will be argued in the following paragraphs, Locke's political ideas, which were so influential to American revolutionary thought, were secular as those also of Trenchard and Gordon. Trenchard and Gordon did not depend on divine revelation or on Christian doctrine as their authority. Neither did Locke.

Locke expressed his political philosophy in his *Two Treatises Concerning Civil Government*. His *Second Treatise* was most relevant and influential to American revolutionary thought. He was careful to define his terms so as not to leave his readers confused by ambiguous terms and concepts. He defined political power, freedom, the state of Nature, and the social compact among other things in the first seven chapters. Nowhere did he base his definitions in Scripture, either explicitly or implicitly. He based political power in the "public good."[138] He based his definition of freedom in nature and reason, stating that "there being nothing more evident than that creatures of the same species in rank, promiscuously born to all the same advantages of Nature, and the use of the same faculties, should also be equal one amongst another,

---

138. Locke, *Concerning Civil Government*, I.3.

without subordination or subjection, ..."[139] The state of Nature, that condition which all men find themselves in prior to the establishment of governments, Locke defined on the basis of reason. He wrote, "The state of Nature has a law of Nature to govern it, which obliges everyone, and reason, which is that law, teaches all mankind who will but consult it, that being all equal and independent, no one ought to harm another in his life, health, liberty or possessions; ..."[140]

Similarly, Locke based his understanding of the social compact in the law of Nature. The law of Nature, which teaches that all men are equal, also teaches that no political society can protect life and property without the authority given to it by private and free men. Thus Locke wrote, "all private judgment of every particular member being excluded, the community comes to be umpire, and by understanding in different rules and men authorized by the community for their execution, decides all the differences that may happen between any members of that society concerning any matter of right, and punishes those offenses which any member hath committed against the society with such penalties as the law has established; whereby it is easy to discern who are, and are not, in political society together."[141]

Locke did not cite Genesis authoritatively to justify his ideas on the earliest societies. He cited history and reason as his justification. He noted that the reason it is difficult to theorize about the earliest societies is that governments generally do not keep historical records until they have reached a state of stability and strength. He wrote, "Government is everywhere antecedent to records, and letters seldom come in amongst a people till a long continuation of civil society has, by other more necessary arts, provided for their safety, ease, and plenty."[142] There is no reference in Locke's writing to the Bible as an authority in understanding the nature of the social compact. Locke did refer to the Bible in some instances, but these were to use the Bible as illustrative, rather than authoritative, material. For example, in explaining the fact that kings have historically been generals in wartime, but in peacetime customarily lay down their wartime power, he used ancient Israel as an example. He stated, "in Israel itself, the

139. Ibid., II.4.
140. Ibid., II.6.
141. Ibid., VII.87.
142. Ibid., VIII.101.

chief business of their judges and first Kings seems to have been to be captains and war and leaders of their armies which... appears plainly in the story of Jephtha."[143] Locke placed this Old Testament example alongside the example of native Americans. Thus, Locke used biblical and non-biblical history as an illustration to make the point that kings are limited in their power. He wrote, "we see that the kings of the Indians in America, ... whilst the inhabitants were too few for the country, and want of people and money gave men no temptation to enlarge their possessions of land or contest for wider extent of ground, are little more than generals of their armies; and though they command absolutely in war, yet at home, and in time of peace, they exercise very little dominion, and have but a very moderate sovereignty...."[144] Locke no more cited Genesis as an authority than he cited the experience of native Americans as an authority.

Locke did not appeal to Scripture to substantiate the revolutionary concept that men had the right to overturn their government when it no longer served to protect their rights. He appealed to the state of Nature. Locke gave five reasons why governments are dissolved:

1. When a monarch elevates his will above the laws established by the legislative body.
2. When a monarch prevents the legislative body from meeting.
3. When a monarch interferes with the elective process.
4. When the government is overthrown by a foreign power in wartime.
5. "When he who has the supreme executive power neglects and abandons that charge, so that the laws already made can no longer be put in execution; this is demonstratively to reduce all to anarchy, and so effectively to dissolve the government."[145]

At any of these times, the people must provide for themselves a new government to take the place of the old? Why? Is it because Scripture or Christian doctrine demands it? Locke wrote, "... the people are at liberty to provide for themselves by erecting a new legislative differing from the other by the change of persons, or form, or both, as they shall find it most

---

143. Ibid., VIII.109.
144. Ibid., VIII.108.
145. Ibid., XIX.219.

for their safety and good."[146] The common good, that is, the state of Nature wherein equality is guaranteed under the law and no man can set himself up as a tyrant over his fellows, is the basis for this act.

The point of citing the writings of Trenchard and Gordon and Locke is to argue that, contrary to Barton's statement, the Bible is not the founding document of America. It is not the sole authority, nor even the most important authority, for revolutionary or founding ideas. This is not to say that the Bible had no influence in the founding. But to make the claim that the American public political literature and its founding documents are informed preeminently by the Bible is to miss entirely the secular ideas which informed these important writers. Protestant theology was a source to revolutionary and founding thought. It was not the primary source. The ideas that defined the American revolutionary and founding periods were not singularly Christian. They arose from a mixture of Protestant and secular sources.

American Exceptionalism

Reviewing from the second chapter's discussion on the CA emphasis on American exceptionalism: McDowell and Beliles wrote, "America is different than any nation in history.... America is the most free and prosperous nation to have ever existed. America is exceptional."[147] Falwell wrote, "... America has reached the pinnacle of greatness unlike any nation in human history...."[148] Marshall and Manuel lamented, "*America, America*—until about fifteen years ago, the name by itself would evoke a feeling of warmth.... In general, we were the most steadying influence on an uneasy globe."[149] Concerning the American Constitution, Hart asserted, "... the U.S. Constitution has worked because there has been a sacred aura surrounding the document; it has been something more than a legal contract; it was a covenant, an oath before God."[150] Beliles and Anderson took a similar position, stating, "America's Constitution, like the Corinthian church the apostle Paul was referring to, was in many ways

---

146. Ibid., XIX.220.
147. McDowell and Beliles, *American Dream*, 3.
148. Falwell, *Listen, America!*, 29.
149. Marshall and Manuel, *Light and Glory*, 13.
150. Ibid.

'written not with ink, but with the Spirit of the living God.'"[151] LaHaye referred to America as a "miracle nation" with the divinely ordained destiny of leading the nations to faith in Christ. He wrote, "And now at the time of the world's greatest population and the world's greatest technological explosion, it is no accident that millions of Christians are willing to send billions of dollars with their sons and daughters to proclaim God's message of love to the ends of the earth. Perhaps that is the main purpose for the existence of this miracle nation."[152]

These statements cast America in exceptional terms based upon divine chosenness. In other words, as seen in Chapter 2 and in the statements above, American exceptionalism is defined by the fact that America, as God's chosen nation, has been blessed by God to an extent unknown in history. The evidence for this blessing is seen in the fact that no other nation has reached the heights of power comparable to America's. No other nation in history has been the force of stability in the world as America has been. The U.S. Constitution is all but sacred, serving as the written basis for a special relationship with God. Finally, no other nation but America has had either the sense of divine mission to evangelize the world, or the will and the resources to do so.

Richard Land wrote, "American exceptionalism is the understanding that America is a unique nation with a unique sense of purpose that started with the nation's settlement and has since morphed through various meanings, all of them centered on the observation that America is distinct from other countries in the world...."[153] Land was willing to grant that America was uniquely blessed in terms of standard of living, being insulated by two oceans, natural resources, the circumstances surrounding America's founding, and the freedoms Americans enjoy.[154] He was not willing to admit that these blessings were evidence of a special relationship between God and America. He wrote, "I do not believe that America is God's chosen nation.... We are not God's gift to the world."[155] Richard Hughes wrote, "It is one thing to claim that America is exceptional in its

---

151. Beliles and Anderson, *Contending*, 3.
152. LaHaye, *Faith of our Founding Fathers*, 65–66.
153. Land, *Divided States of America*, 189.
154. Ibid., 192.
155. Ibid.

own eyes. It is something else to claim that America is exceptional because God chose America and its people for a special mission in the world."[156]

If, by the term "American exceptionalism," one is referring to a general historical trend that has manifested itself in America's uniquely strong and influential position in the world relative to other nations, then it is possible to affirm such a notion. Land's articulation of American exceptionalism seems to be substantiated by history. If however, by "American exceptionalism," one is referring to divine chosenness, then the idea is fraught with theological and historical problems. First, this notion lacks biblical support. Second, history has not shown that America is the only nation ever to have cast itself as God's chosen. History has also not shown that America is exceptionally blessed by God in terms of power and influence—that no other nation has reached the heights of blessing that America has reached. Has God blessed the Anglo-American nations in special ways? Has America in particular been used in remarkable ways in history to spread the ideas of liberty to the world and to share her bounty with people everywhere? Yes, indeed. But since Old Testament times, God has not singled out particular nations for a special relationship with Him.[157] The United States is not divinely chosen; it is not exceptional in this strict sense of the term. One cannot rely on this notion to make the point that America is a Christian nation.

American exceptionalism, when defined as divine chosenness, is inconsistent with the Christian mission to carry the gospel to the nations because it lacks biblical support. Genesis 12 records the promise of God to Abraham that He will make from him a great nation. The books of Exodus and Deuteronomy discuss how God took Israel for Himself as His chosen people. But God's special choice of Israel was inimitable. Hughes wrote of Roger Williams's critique of the Puritans' claim of divine chosenness: "God chose only one people, Williams thundered, and those were the Jews. There has never been another."[158] Hughes quoted Williams: "As he put it, 'The State of the Land of Israel, the Kings and people thereof

---

156. Hughes, *Myths America Lives By*, 19.

157. See Land, *Divided States of America*; Hughes, *Myths America Lives By*; Boyd, *Myth of a Christian Nation*; Noll et al., *Search*; Noll, *One Nation*; and Brown, *Protest of a Troubled Protestant*.

158. Hughes, *Myths America Lives By*, 32.

in Peace & War, is proved figurative and ceremonial, and no pattern nor precedent for any Kingdom or civil state in the world to follow."[159]

Since the first advent of Christ, no nation can claim that it is the chosen of God, at least by appealing to the Bible. Peter wrote concerning the church in 1 Pet 2:9, "But you are a chosen race, a royal priesthood, a holy nation, a people for God's own possession, so that you may proclaim the excellencies of Him who has called you out of darkness into His marvelous light." God's chosen people exists today as the church, not as any particular ethnic group or political entity. Greg Boyd wrote, "While God is by no means through with Israel, he is no longer using them or any other nation to grow his kingdom on the earth. The kingdom is now growing through Jesus Christ who lives in and through his corporate body. In this sense, Jesus and the church constitute a new Israel."[160] Noll, Hatch, and Marsden wrote, "Is it, after all, ever proper to speak of a Christian nation after the coming of Christ? From Scripture we know that Old Testament Israel enjoyed a special status as a nation under God. . . . But regardless of how a Christian feels about the modern Jewish nation, is it proper ever to look upon the American nation as the special agent of God in the world?"[161] According to Noll, "the Bible is very clear about the status of nations. Only one nation in the history of the world has enjoyed divine favor, in its status as a nation, and that was Old Testament Israel. Standard Christian teaching holds, moreover, that Old Testament Israel enjoyed its special status as 'chosen nation' in order to prepare the entire world for the reception of God's saving grace. After the full revelation of God's glory in Christ, 'God's country' was made up of believers 'from every tribe and tongue and people and nation' (Rev 5:9)."[162]

Harold O. J. Brown observed from Scripture that no people ever became God's chosen through their own choice. God chose Israel on His terms. Brown wrote, "This is an important distinction. In biblical terms, a people cannot become God's people by deciding to serve him: it becomes his people because he calls it forth. God called Israel out of Egypt (Hosea 11:1)."[163] Brown's statement is also consistent with Deut 7:7, in which God

---

159. Williams, "Bloody Tenent," 153.
160. Boyd, *Myth of a Christian Nation*, 152.
161. Noll et al., *Search*, 20–21.
162. Noll, *One Nation*, 8.
163. Brown, *Protest of a Troubled Protestant*, 80.

explained to Israel that His divine choice was not based on any merit found in the nation, but on His love for it.[164] Furthermore, Brown took a similar position as Noll in saying, "In the biblical sense, the Christian nation is not a nation at all, but the church—that is the community which corresponds today to ancient Israel. The New Israel is spiritual."[165] Brown asserted that "The concept of 'a Christian America' is in the first place not biblical, in the second place hardly likely to be attained, and in the third place, if it were attained, it would probably go a good deal farther than most of its sentimental advocates wish."[166] This third point of Brown's may already have become a reality. The politicization and subsequent success of evangelicals in the public square has served to dilute its biblical distinctive.[167]

Appropriating the status of having been chosen by God is not unique to America. Noll wrote, "Americans are not alone in the world in their belief that God has singled out their nation for special divine prerogatives. The kinds of claims that are made about America's special relationship with God have also been made at various times in recent centuries by the Dutch, by Germans, by Russians, and by citizens of other European countries."[168] Anthony Smith traced the history of nationalistic views of chosenness in Europe and America. His research demonstrated that a host of nations, dating as far distant in time as the fourth century after Christ, considered themselves to be the exceptional choice of God.

These nations each held a common belief structure. Smith described it: ". . . what were the objects of the sense of the sacred? In the first place, the community itself, the chosen people, the elect nation of believers and the families. Secondly, the holy land in which the people dwell, with its memories, heroic exploits, monuments, and the resting places of ancestors. Then there was the great and glorious past, our past, the golden age of the people, before the present sad decline. And finally there was the

---

164. "It was not because you were more in number than any other people that the LORD set his love on you and chose you, for you were the fewest of all peoples" Deut 7:7 ESV.

165. Ibid., 83.

166. Ibid.

167. See Feinberg, ed., *Foundations of Evangelical Theology*; Noll, "Evangelicals"; Bruce, *New Christian Right*; Boyd, *Myth of a Christian Nation*; Cromartie, ed., *No Longer Exiles*; Martin, *With God on Our Side*; and Toulouse, *God in Public*.

168. Noll, *One Nation*, 189.

sacrifice of all those who had fallen."[169] One can clearly see each of these elements in the CA thesis. The fact is, as much as many CA authors considered America's Christian mission and identity as distinct and unique, this very notion is repeated in many other nations.

Smith observed the notion of exceptionalism and nationalistic chosenness in many nations in Europe and America. A selection of only five will suffice here to make the point that America has not been alone. The fourth-century kingdom of Armenia, the Boers, Russia, France, and Great Britain have been among those believing themselves to be uniquely chosen by God.

The fact that the idea of chosenness is not unique is important to the critique of the idea of America as divinely chosen in two ways. First, according to Scripture, God's setting apart of one nation has only occurred in the case of ancient Israel. Any other claim on divine chosenness is contrary to Scripture, and therefore, wrong. If other nations have been wrong in claiming divine chosenness, then America is wrong as well.

Second, the fact that many nations have believed themselves to be divinely chosen is no proof that they actually were. Similarly, the fact that many Americans in history and in contemporary times have believed America is God's chosen people will not suffice as evidence. Greg Boyd stated, "Unlike Israel, we have no biblical or empirical reason to believe God ever intended to be king over America in any unique sense. True, some of those who were part of the original European conquest of this continent claimed this, but why believe they were right?"[170] America cannot claim to be exceptional based on divine chosenness with any truer basis than other nations who have done similarly. The CA argument from exceptionalism and divine chosenness is thus weakened considerably here.

As stated previously, the belief in national chosenness goes back a long way in history. Smith noted that Armenia's church traces its roots to the Apostle Thaddeus and that its king, Tiridates, was converted to Christianity in 301. This event occurred eleven years prior to the conversion of Constantine, who legalized Christianity in the Roman Empire. For this reason, fourth-century Armenia may deserve the title of "first Christian nation." Although Tiridates was probably converted later than

---

169. Smith, *Chosen Peoples*, vii.
170. Boyd, *Myth of a Christian Nation*, 148.

Constantine, Smith observed, "this belief in chronological primacy has been a source of national pride and comfort and darker times, especially when Armenians felt deserted and alone."[171] Furthermore, the kingdom of Armenia during this time believed that it was in a covenant with God. This covenant called them to faithfulness to Christ and to convert the heathen nations surrounding them. Smith wrote, "possession of the holy covenant also entailed a mission: to preserve the true faith and convert the heathen, notably in Caucasian Iberia and Albania in the north, and subsequently to influence their doctrines, even after the separation of their churches from the Armenian Church."[172]

The kingdom of Armenia appears to show that the idea of nationalistic chosenness is very old. The Boers of southern Africa show that this sense has taken place among nations far removed from the European and American continents. Similar to the Puritans who fled England to come to America, the Boers (who were of Dutch descent) felt oppressed by the British who were colonizing southern Africa in the middle of the 1800s. From 1834 to 1838, the Boers fled north of British Cape Colony to establish their own colonies free from British interference. Their journey is known as the Great Trek, and those who took part in it were known as the *voortrekkers*. Like the Puritans of the seventeenth century, the Boers compared themselves to the Israelites being led out into the wilderness to escape the oppression of Pharaoh. Smith wrote, "Just as the Lord had saved the Israelites from Pharaoh's hosts, and from Midianites and Amalekites, and caused them to cross the Jordan, so had he miraculously delivered the Boer *voortrekkers* from danger and defeat at the hands of the British imperialists, and the Ndebele and Zulu warriors."[173]

Russia and France present interesting examples of nations which viewed themselves as God's chosen. Many CA writers point to these nations, particularly France, as being representative of the kind of antitheistic secularism threatening to infect American contemporary culture. Russia in the fifteenth century viewed itself as the Third Rome because of the union between the crown and the Russian Orthodox Church. The belief was that God had first singled out Rome, then Constantinople, and after punishing these empires for apostasy, had chosen Russia. According

---

171. Smith, *Chosen Peoples*, 69.
172. Ibid., 71.
173. Ibid., 78.

to Smith, Russians after the fall of Constantinople and the Byzantine Empire in 1453 believed, "If Byzantium could not be recaptured and the heretic Holy Roman Empire was unacceptable, could not the Orthodox Russian state of Muscovy, the largest surviving Orthodox state, assume the imperial mantle?"[174] France, even though it had seen shocking forms of apostasy during the 1790s, considered itself in the nineteenth and early twentieth centuries to be exceptional. Earlier varieties of nationalistic chosenness in France, especially during the medieval period to the seventeenth century, had been based in Catholic Christianity. Still, Smith wrote that "After the Revolution, the traditional religious forms of nationhood and election lost much of their meaning, along with the monarchy that they underpinned, but they were replaced by the ideology and religion of *la Grande Nation*, the sacred communion of the people in arms."[175]

These examples are meant to show that, far from being alone in claiming a unique Christian identity and destiny, American considerations of itself have been in line with a long European tradition of viewing itself in divinely exceptional terms. To restate the objections, first, the Bible affirms that only one ethnic and political entity, Old Testament Israel, has ever enjoyed divinely exceptional status. Second, the mere claim of divine exceptionalism, absent from revelatory justification, is no guarantee of the reality of divine exceptionalism.

While the above examples are compelling, perhaps the greatest historical example opposing American exceptionalism is found in the British Empire spanning the nineteenth and early twentieth centuries. The British Empire shows that, relative to its historical setting, America is not uniquely blessed by God in terms of power or evangelistic reach. This assertion challenges the CA argument that America is unmatched by any other nation in terms of world power because of its special standing with God. At its peak, the British Empire was the largest empire in the world's history. One quarter of the world's land surface was controlled by Britain, and one quarter of the world's population were British subjects. In comparing the British to the Roman Empire, James Morris estimated that at Rome's height 120 million subjects paid allegiance to the emperor and two and a half million square miles of territory were guarded by the Roman army. At the height of British supremacy in 1914, the Empire con-

---

174. Ibid., 101.
175. Ibid., 114.

sisted of 372 million subjects and eleven million square miles.[176] More importantly, during the approximately hundred year period between Trafalgar and World War I, the British navy was unmatched by any navy in the world, literally dominating the trade routes of every ocean. Morris said, "In theory no other state could ship an army across the seas without British consent, and in practice the merchant shipping of the rest of the world was largely dependent upon British cables and coaling stations. The presence of the sea, at once insulating the Mother Country and linking it with the Empire, gave the British an imperial confidence. 'I do not say the French cannot come,' as Admiral St. Vincent had once remarked; 'I only say they cannot come by sea.'"[177]

The nineteenth century was defined by the Pax Britannica, because the peace and prosperity of the world was ensured by British economic and naval power. Robert Massie said that when the wars with Napoleon concluded in 1815, "Britain became the arbiter of affairs beyond the seas. Britons landed on the shores of every ocean. They explored the continents; mountains, rivers, lakes, and waterfalls were named for British explorers. Railroads were laid, cities sprang up, governments were created, endorsed, or overthrown; by 1897 a multitude of kings, maharajahs, nawabs, nizams, khedives, emirs, pashas, beys, and other chieftains set on thrones only at London's discretion."[178] London was the financial capital of the world and the British pound was the dominant currency. Britain led the world into the industrial age because of its ample deposits of coal. Morris stated, "The British stood at the threshold of a colossal boom [at Queen Victoria's accession in 1837], for they possessed a virtual monopoly of the techniques of steam, which was presently to prove itself the basic energy of the age."[179]

Not only did Britain occupy the preeminent position of world power from the Napoleonic Wars to World War I, the British considered themselves to be chosen by God to use their power to advance Christianity in the world. Morris wrote that "The Victorians were *believers*. They believed in their Christian Master, in their providential destiny, in their servants of steam and steel, in themselves and their systems, and not least in their

176. Morris, *Pax Britannica*, 42.
177. Ibid., 46.
178. Massie, *Dreadnought*, xx.
179. Morris, *Heaven's Command*, 22.

Empire."[180] British missionaries poured into Africa, India, China, Australia, and New Zealand. Morris reported, "By 1850 the Christian missionaries could claim to have converted 20,000 Indians, at least 10,000 Africans, almost all the Maoris of New Zealand and virtually the entire population of Fiji."[181] For the British during Victoria's long reign (1837–1901), imperialist fervor was both a matter of national pride and a fulfillment of a biblical mandate to make the nations Christian. The Empire itself was viewed as an extension of Christ's kingdom. Morris described the way the British viewed the empire as "not simply humanitarianism, not Burke's sense of trusteeship, but a Christian militancy, a ruling faith, whose Defender on earth was the Queen herself, and whose supreme commander needed no identification. Every aspect of Empire was an aspect of Christ . . ."[182]

These examples from history substantiate the fact that while America has developed into a powerful, prosperous, technologically advanced, evangelistically minded, and influential nation, this is not to say that God has never blessed any other nation in the same, and arguably sometimes greater, ways. America at the beginning of the twenty-first century is the world's only superpower, but the British Empire was the world's predominant power during the nineteenth and early twentieth centuries. The twentieth century witnessed a Pax Americana, but the nineteenth witnessed a Pax Britannica. The idea of divine exceptionalism applied to America is thus not a sufficient justification for the CA thesis. American exceptionalism, if defined as God's special setting apart of America for unique blessing and standing in the world, betrays a lack of appreciation both of history's lessons and the application of theology to them.

CONCLUSION

This critique has attempted to show that logical reasoning, history, and theology cannot bear out the notion that America is uniquely Christian, or that America was singled out by God and exalted over other nations. Generally speaking, Protestant theology was a source in the founding. American society did experience a Protestant consensus in the first century or so of its existence. The United States has enjoyed singular opportunities for world leadership and expansion of the gospel in its history.

---

180. Ibid., 318; emphasis original.
181. Ibid.
182. Ibid., 319.

These assertions make up a weak version of the CA thesis, and one may affirm them with care. Still, evangelical Christians can recognize that the Protestant consensus in America is gone and religious pluralism is the current sociological reality. They can seek to honestly assess not only the history of their own nation, but also the history of the ideas that have formed it—sacred and secular ideas. Finally, evangelicals must strive to apply Christian doctrine appropriately to the study of history, and align their understanding of how God reveals Himself to nations with what the Bible, particularly the New Testament, teaches.

America's history points to a mixture of sacred and secular ideas. The nation is defined more realistically by religious freedom rather than a Christian identity. God is transcendent over and above history and Creation, but is also immanent, working in the culture no matter how it denies Him. Evangelical Christians will do well to be focused on living the truth of Christ, fulfilling what it means to be salt and light. They can approach those who do not share their faith commitment in peace and respect, knowing that the culture will be conformed to Christ when religious freedom is enjoyed equally by all. They will then avoid being distracted from that legitimate calling by seeking to equate the kingdom of God with the kingdom of men.

5

Closing Arguments and Areas for Further Study

This chapter will offer an assessment of the Christian America thesis.[1] It concludes that America is not a Christian nation in the strong sense, but its uniqueness is partly found in the fact that it is a nation built on the foundation of religious liberty. It will present closing arguments drawing from the content presented in the first four chapters. At the conclusion of the chapter, some areas for further study will be identified. The study has presented evidence that seems sufficient to sustain the argument that the notion of America as a Christian nation in the strong sense is an unsustainable position on several grounds. Rather, the history of the American founding is a mix between secular and Christian elements. Evangelicals can and should emphasize that rather than being founded as a Christian nation, America was founded as a nation with religious liberty.

There are a number of reasons why a critique of the assumptions undergirding the Christian America notion is important from an evangelical perspective. To begin any work of this sort, the question asked by Noll, Marsden, and Hatch is eminently appropriate: "What is the point, some may ask, in subjecting our ideas about the past to religious scrutiny? Even if it turns out that the common picture of an American Christian past is inaccurate, what difference does it make?"[2] Simply put, the mission of Christ's church in the world is at stake. The church is to fulfill the greatest commandment (Matt 22:36–40) as well as the Great Commission (Matt 28:18–20). Noll, Marsden, and Hatch affirmed that "a

---

1. This chapter has also appeared in edited form in the *Global Journal of Classical Theology*. See Wilsey, "Historiographical Construal." It is reprinted here with permission from the editors.

2. Noll et al., *Search*, 21.

true picture of America's past will make Christians today better equipped to speak the gospel in evangelism and to put it to work in social concern."[3] Conversely, if Christians embrace an inaccurate perspective on the history of America, and ascribe to it an undeserved and unsubstantiated status, their mission to love God and love others through worship of Him and evangelism and social effort will fall far short. For example, Boyd saw a crude politicization of the kingdom of God within the historiographical construal of Christian America. Boyd observed that non-Christians around the world who are exposed to America as a Christian nation recoil from Christianity because they often view the faith system in purely political terms. He wrote,

> ...because this myth links the kingdom of God with certain political stances within American politics, it has greatly compromised the holy beauty of the kingdom of God to non-Christians. This myth harms the church's primary mission.... Because the myth that America is a Christian nation has led many to associate America with Christ, many now hear the good news of Jesus only as American news, capitalistic news, imperialistic news, exploitative news, antigay news, or Republican news. And whether justified or not, many people want nothing to do with any of it.[4]

Also, an evangelical critique is needed because CA is simply not true to the historical record, and affirming the notion further isolates evangelicals from culture. Jon Meacham stated, "the right's contention that we are a 'Christian nation' that has fallen from pure origins and can achieve redemption by some kind of return to Christian values is based on wishful thinking, not convincing historical argument."[5] Furthermore, Noll, Marsden, and Hatch stressed that "a view of American history which gives it a falsely Christian character is a hindrance, first, because it distorts the nature of the past. Positive Christian action does not grow out of distortion or half-truths. Such errors lead rather to false militance, to unrealistic standards for American public life today, and to romanticized visions about the heights from which we have fallen."[6] Embracing CA, though fraught with the good intentions of reestablishing "traditional moral values" in a culture that has largely abandoned them, involves cherry picking

3. Ibid.
4. Boyd, *Myth of a Christian Nation*, 13.
5. Meacham, *American Gospel*, 18.
6. Noll et al., *Search*, 22–23.

from the historical record. How can evangelicals be taken seriously in the culture if they are not scrupulous in their study of history?

Finally, the notion of a Christian America potentially undermines one of the Constitution's most valued and cherished principles, that of religious liberty. Pierard feared that the evangelicals who embrace CA are in danger of locking those with different religious faiths out of the culture. He referred to the fact that America has changed in the last century, transforming from a culture with a common Protestant consensus to one that is greatly diverse in its religious life. This transformation, as Pierard observed, has made "the principles that originally guaranteed liberty to Christians of every denominational persuasion equally operative in our highly pluralistic age."[7] Moreover, he stated that the "campaign to bring America 'back to God' will, if successful, mean the imposition of their [evangelicals'] deeply felt religious values upon the nation at large . . . ."[8] A denial of religious liberty to followers of all faiths would be a betrayal of what is widely agreed upon as among the main intentions of the Founders.

CONTEXTUAL SYNOPSIS

From 1630 to 1789, the American conception of religion's role in the state shifted dramatically. The New England colonies were founded during a period of Western history when it was taken for granted that the church and state should be unified. Religion and the state were viewed as partners, and this partnership had historically been viewed by Westerners as indispensable in securing order in society and providing the nation with an identity rooted in a Christian metanarrative. Gaustad drew a contrast between the attitude of that time and our own when he wrote, "We of today ask where the state left off and the church began; they of yesterday can only shake their heads in wonderment at so meaningless a question."[9]

Still, during this period which witnessed the development of the thirteen British North American colonies, the Revolutionary War which separated those colonies from Britain, and the establishment of the fledgling United States of America, a fundamental shift had taken place. The New England colonies had been established as Christian colonies.

---

7. Pierard, "Standing," 370.
8. Ibid., 368.
9. Gaustad, *Faith of the Founders*, 12.

Closing Arguments and Areas for Further Study 175

They viewed themselves in covenantal terms, both with God and with each other. Furthermore, they understood their journey from England to America in strongly biblical terms. John Winthrop urged his fellow colonists, that

> Wee shall finde that the God of Israell is among us, when ten of us shall be able to resist a thousand of our enemies, when hee shall make us a prayse and glory, that men shall say of succeeding plantacians: the lord make it like that of New England: for wee must Consider that wee shall be as a Citty upon a Hill, the eies of all people are upon us; soe that if wee shall deale falsely with our god in this worke wee have undertaken and soe cause him to withdrawe his present help from us, wee shall shame the faces of many of gods worthy servants, and cause theire prayers to be turned into Cursses upon us till wee be consumed out of the good land whither wee are goeing: . . ."[10]

By the time the Constitution was being drafted in the summer of 1787, these Puritan notions of chosenness and covenant were not part of the American value system. The fifty-five delegates to the Constitutional Convention had no intention of modeling the new nation on the Puritan model. The historical bond between church and state, the attitude that their partnership was indispensable to the health of the nation, had disappeared. What had replaced this idea was that of the freedom of the individual to decide how he would relate to his God, or even choose not to relate. John Noonan wrote that James Madison, one of the principal authors of the First Amendment, had practical and theological reasons for holding to religious liberty. He observed that, for Madison, "The right to determine this duty [the duty to be religious] in conscience belongs to each person and is 'unalienable' for two reasons: first, the exercise of the right must depend on evidence, and each person will determine what evidence is sufficient for conviction; and second, the duty, as it runs to the Creator, can never be relaxed by any human being."[11] Furthermore, according to Noonan, for Madison, "To rely on governmental support 'is a contradiction to the Christian Religion itself for every page of it disavows a dependence on the powers of the world.'"[12] Not only were these important considerations, but Madison also sought to limit the dominance

---

10. Winthrop, "Christian Charity," 40.
11. Noonan, *Lustre of Our Country*, 72.
12. Ibid.

of one religious sect over others by encouraging freedom of conscience. No one religion ought to have dominant influence, just as no one political faction should monopolize public opinion. Madison said, "Extend the sphere, and you take in a greater variety of parties and interests; you make it less probable that a majority of the whole will have a common motive to invade the rights of other citizens; or if such a common motive exists, it will be more difficult for all who feel it to discover their own strength, and to act in unison with each other."[13]

Lambert posited three dynamics of change to account for this shift, which occurred between the founding of the Massachusetts Bay Colony in 1630 and the enactment of the U.S. Constitution in 1789: the Great Awakening, the Enlightenment, and radical Whig ideology. The Great Awakening made it possible for individuals to choose how they would worship God by decentralizing religious authority. The Enlightenment brought a new emphasis on human reason as an epistemological authority, alongside, and even superior to, divine revelation. Radical Whig ideology, articulated by the Commonwealth men of seventeenth- and early eighteenth-century England and undergirded by Locke's political philosophy, stressed complete political and religious freedom for the individual, and would provide the intellectual fuel for the American Revolution. Lambert summarized the effect of the shift saying, "religious freedom in the 'City upon a Hill' meant freedom from error with church and state, though separate working together to support and protect the one true faith. Those who believed differently were free to go elsewhere and sometimes compelled to do so. The Founding Fathers had a radically different conception of religious freedom. Influenced by the Enlightenment, they had great confidence in the individual's ability to understand the world and its most fundamental laws through the exercise of his or her reason."[14] The relevance of this shift to the central argument of the study is simple: America was founded on the basis of religious freedom, not on the basis of the Christian religion.

Throughout the writings of many of the most prominent CA writers, most notably Peter Marshall, Pat Robertson, Jerry Falwell, Tim LaHaye, David Barton, Gary DeMar, John Eidsmoe, Mark Beliles, Stephen

---

13. Hamilton, Madison, and Jay, *Federalist*, no. 10, 52.
14. Lambert, *Place of Religion*, 3.

McDowell, Gary Amos, and Benjamin Hart, numerous common themes emerged. These included, historically:

1. The Christian faith of the Founders.
2. The Christian character of the sources drawn from by the Founders
3. The Christian character of colonial documents and early state constitutions
4. The Christian character of early colleges
5. The powerful Christian influence of the Great Awakening and radical Whig ideology on the revolutionary generation.

The philosophical themes included:

1. The original intent of the Founders may be accurately discerned by applying the same evangelical hermeneutical method as used when interpreting Scripture
2. The original intent of the Founders was to build Christianity into the heart of the nation
3. The role of the Enlightenment is not as significant as the role of Christianity in the founding.

Some of the common theological themes for the CA thesis were:

1. A providential view of history
2. American exceptionalism as evidence of God's unique blessing on the nation
3. America as God's chosen nation, a new Israel
4. Liberty as a biblical notion finding its consummate application in the civic life of America
5. The Bible as the primary source of the founding national documents.

Also, the appeal to Christian Americans to lead the nation back to its Christian roots in order that God causes it to fulfill its purpose in the world was common. McDowell wrote, "America became the most free and prosperous nation in history due to our Christian foundation. We are still the most free and prosperous nation in the world, but we have been living off of the capital or fruit of Christianity for some time. We cannot continue to do so, but must reestablish Christian principles as the foundation of the nation if we hope to remain free and prosperous."[15] Falwell wrote,

> America must not turn away from the God who established her and who blessed her. It is time for Americans to come back to the faith of our fathers, to the Bible of our fathers, and to the biblical principles that our fathers used as a premise for this nation's establishment. We must come back lovingly but firmly, and establish as our priorities once again those priorities that are God's priorities. Only then will we become important to God, and only then will we once again know the great blessings of the Power that has made and preserved us a nation![16]

This appeal to return to America's Christian roots was especially important in CA writings. The appeal underscores the fact that the CA thesis is ultimately perceived as theological. It is this theological basis that provides the CA thesis with its resiliency, its urgency, and its attractiveness to evangelical Christians from a wide range of denominational traditions.

It is important in any treatment of CA to acknowledge the contribution that Christianity played in the formation of the ideas leading up to the American Revolution and founding. It is not the contention of this study that Christianity had nothing to do with the American national founding. Such an assertion is unhistorical. Still, America's foundation owes debts to both Christian and secular sources. Thus, it argues not for a strong view of CA, but a weak view. As Noll wrote in his differentiation of the two views, "in the case of United States, certain features of the national history stand out as exemplary, from the angle of Christian interpretation. At their best, the nation's traditions of democratic liberty fit well with biblical teachings on the dignity of all people under God. . . . And many people from other lands still look to America, and with considerable justice, as a promised land of economic, political, and religious freedom."[17] In addition to these considerations, it is important to acknowledge the distinctly Christian sources that contributed to the revolutionary and constitutional thought that ultimately brought the United States into existence.

15. McDowell, *Christian Nation*, 40.
16. Falwell, *Listen, America!*, 50.
17. Noll, *One Nation*, 10.

When speaking of the Christian contribution to the emergence of the American nation, Puritanism must be emphasized as being among the most important Christian theological influences. According to Noll, Puritanism was the main theological force shaping American life from 1630 to the Revolutionary period.[18] Thus, Puritanism would be the most important theological source contributing to revolutionary thought. Far from being a local phenomenon limited to New England, Puritan theology would exert its influence throughout the colonies. Noll stated, "Historians of early America, both of its religious and secular aspects, have agreed concerning the prominence of the Puritan strain in the nation's early history. The extent of this Puritan influence is indicated by the fact that approximately three-fourths of the colonists of the time of the Revolution were identified with denominations that had arisen from the Reformed, Puritan wing of European Protestantism: Congregationalism, Presbyterianism, Baptists, German and Dutch Reformed."[19]

Puritan theology bequeathed a distinct value to the individual, something that was truly revolutionary. Rather than being divided into social or economic groups, the Puritans stressed that each individual was valuable to God, each person had full access to God through Christ. Because of this freedom, individual potential was unleashed upon the world. Suddenly, individuals had a reason to be productive, to contribute to society. God had placed a calling upon each life. Politically, this idea would translate into the notion of government by consent. Describing the significance of the Mayflower Compact, Smith wrote, "In it the Pilgrims formed a 'civil body politic,' and promised to obey the laws their own government might pass. In short, the individual Pilgrim invented on the spot a new community, one that would be ruled by laws of its making."[20]

Because of this emphasis on liberty, Puritan theology logically entailed religious freedom. To be sure, uninhibited religious freedom was not given in the New England colonies—except Rhode Island. Roger Williams, Founder of the Rhode Island colony and a Puritan, opposed persecution of all forms. William's eighth point in his "Bloody Tenent of Persecution" of 1644 was, "God requireth not a uniformity of religion to be enacted and enforced in any civil state; which enforced uniformity (sooner or later)

---

18. Ibid, 22.
19. Noll, *Christians in the American Revolution*, 29–30.
20. Smith, *Religious Origins*, 3.

is the great occasion of civil war, ravishing of conscience, persecution of Christ Jesus in his servants, and of the hypocrisy and destruction of millions of souls."[21] The 1663 charter of Rhode Island declared,

> ... That our loyall will and pleasure is, that noe person within the said colonye, at any tyme hereafter shall be any wise molested, punished, disquieted or called in question for any differences in opinion in matters of religion and doe not actually disturb the civill peace of sayd colony, but that all and every person and persons may from tyme to tyme and at all tymes hereafter freely and fullye enjoye his and their own judgements and consciences in matters of religious concernments, they behaving themselves peaceably and quietly, and not using this libertie to lycentiousness and profanenesse, nor to the civill injurye or outward disturbance of other.[22]

Thus, Williams took the Puritan emphasis on the value of the individual before God to its logical conclusion. If the individual in covenant with the community and with God is given primary importance in Puritan theology, then it must follow that the individual should enjoy the freedom to worship as he chooses.

These are a few of the salient points regarding the role of Puritan theology in American notions of freedom. They help show that Puritan theology is a source contributing to the American identity. Thus, Noll's encouragement to evangelicals to adopt a weak version of CA, one that acknowledges the existing Christian heritage without affirming that America is a Christian nation, is helpful.

OVERALL ASSESSMENT OF CA

Religious liberty is one of the prime contributions the American Constitution has made to humankind's benefit. It was a revolutionary idea, one that had never been tried on a scale as large as that of the United States. Bearing in mind the centrality of religious liberty to the American identity, a philosophical, historical, and theological critique of CA from an evangelical perspective seems fitting.

CA authors have been unable to avoid ambiguity in their use of important terms comprising their arguments. Their ambiguity necessarily led these authors to the wrong conclusion, namely, that America is a

---

21. Williams, "Bloody Tenent," 88.
22. *Charter of Rhode Island*, 88.

Christian nation. In the case of the term, "Christian nation," there were four basic ways in which CA authors classified it:

1. It is a nation with a Christian consensus
2. It was established on biblical principles
3. The Founders of the nation were Christians
4. The nation is a New Israel, exceptionally blessed with a special relationship with God and a special divine purpose in the world.

While the most agreement among the authors was centered upon the idea that America was founded on biblical principles, there was some significant disagreement between them, accounting for the ambiguity of the term. Several of the authors insisted that the Christian consensus of the eighteenth century was the key to defining the term. Others were equally insistent that this facet was immaterial. The most salient point of disagreement however, was found between those holding to one or a combination of the first three propositions, and those holding to a strong form of the fourth proposition. Marshall and Manuel were direct in their assertions that America is the New Israel. While others were willing to agree on American exceptionalism in general, few others were willing to go as far as Marshall and Manuel. This lack of uniformity in the understanding of what "Christian nation" ought to mean led to great difficulty in the ability to demonstrate it as a historical or contemporary reality.

CA authors' use of the term "Enlightenment" was also problematic. Amos and Hart were among those who explicitly equated the Enlightenment with a form of secularism that is strictly opposed to Christian theism. Unfortunately for these authors, to classify the Enlightenment in these terms is not accurate. The Enlightenment was not one thing, but a multi-faceted intellectual movement that must be understood in context. May divided the Enlightenment into four categories: the "Moderate (it might be called Rational) Enlightenment," the "skeptical Enlightenment," the "Revolutionary Enlightenment," and the "Didactic Enlightenment."[23] It was the Moderate Enlightenment that was the most influential to the founding generation. According to May, it "preached balance, order and religious compromise, and was dominant in England from the time of Newton and Locke until about the middle of the eighteenth

---

23. May, *Enlightenment*, xvi.

century [1688–1787]."[24] Russell classified this as philosophical liberalism. He wrote, "Early liberalism was individualistic in intellectual matters, and also in economics, but was not emotionally or ethically self-assertive. This form of liberalism dominated the English eighteenth century, the Founders of the American Constitution, and the French encyclopédists."[25] Newton and Locke were shown to be theists who affirmed supremacy of God and the authority of revelation, even though their ideas and methods were rooted in secular thought. Hume and Voltaire were shown to represent a secularism that in many ways was incompatible with Christianity. All this is to show that the Enlightenment is not so simply defined. The term, when not precisely and accurately defined, becomes a loaded term meant to evoke a strong emotional response rather than a clear and objective approach to its assessment on the reader's part.

When taken together, these terms as they are used by CA authors seem to be important to the conclusion that America is a Christian nation. But since the terms were either not precisely defined and agreed upon, or were misunderstood and misapplied by those who advocated for CA, the conclusion cannot be logically sustained.

The historical critique of CA was centered upon two distinct, yet closely related, realities: the demise of the Protestant consensus in American society and the growth of religious pluralism. One of the important assertions of CA authors was that America is a Christian nation because it was founded in an atmosphere of Protestant consensus. There were very few non-Christians living in the United States in the 1770s and 80s. The predominant worldview held by Americans at that time was a Christian worldview. Therefore, for many CA authors, America's founding is Christian. The problem with this assertion is that it does not account for the high value the Founders placed on religious liberty. Religious pluralism was the intention of the Founders, because they sought to guarantee not only the disestablishment of religion, but also its "free exercise"[26] in the First Amendment.

Proponents of CA are right in asserting that a Protestant consensus dominated American culture at the end of the eighteenth century. This consensus would endure into the twentieth century. Still, it has been

---

24. Ibid.
25. Russell, *History of Western Philosophy*, 599.
26. U.S. Const., amend. I.

shown that despite this Christian consensus, the Founders who drafted the First Amendment valued religious liberty over any form of legal establishment of Christianity. Furthermore, due to a combination of influences which divided the Protestant churches, that consensus would eventually break down. These influences included the segregation of white and black Christians after the Civil War, immigration of Jews, Catholics, and Orthodox Christians, the spread of liberal Protestant theology, general disillusionment after World War I in America, the modernist-fundamentalist controversy of the 1920s, and the economic depression of the 1930s. Each of these factors served to cause Protestant churches to lose cohesion and influence in the culture.

Nearly concurrent with the demise of the Protestant consensus arose a fundamental change in U.S. immigration policy in 1965 with the passage of the Immigration and Nationality Act during the Johnson Administration. Effectively overturning previous policy discriminating against people from eastern hemisphere nations, the 1965 act threw the doors open to people claiming different religious outlooks from the Protestant-Catholic-Jew paradigm described by Herberg in 1955. Eck wrote that, "Today our cultural differences are magnified with the new immigration. It's not just Swedes and Italians, Lutherans and Catholics, but Russian and Iranian Jews, Pakistani and Bengali Muslims, Trinidadi and Gujarati Hindus, Punjabi Sikhs, and Sinhi Jains."[27] She pointed out further that while the national motto, *E Pluribus Unum*, has historically had a political meaning, since the late nineteenth century it has taken a cultural and religious meaning as well. "With the booming immigration of the late nineteenth and early twentieth centuries, the motto took on a cultural dimension—from many peoples or nationalities, one people."[28]

Religious pluralism has existed in America since the thirteen colonies were first settled. Because of the impact of the Awakenings of the eighteenth and nineteenth centuries, pluralism spread to embrace more and more Christian traditions. By the twentieth century, pluralism had extended beyond Christian traditions and had come to include a significant Jewish population. Still, up until the early 1960s, America could still be defined in terms of a Judeo-Christian melting pot. After 1965, however,

---

27. Eck, *New Religious America*, 29.
28. Ibid.

this description would prove to be far too narrow. Full religious pluralism has taken shape over the past few decades. As Waldman pointed out,

> Today America is home to more Hindus than Unitarians, more Muslims than Congregationalists, and more Buddhists than Jews. In fact, there are more than twelve million non-Christians in America—about four times the entire population of the colonies when the Constitution was ratified. Immigration combined with continuous splintering of existing denominations to create a breathtaking diversity of sects. These 'facts on the ground' reinforce the Founders' pluralistic impulse and forever shut the door on the possibility that America could be, in any official sense, deemed a Protestant, or even a Christian, nation.[29]

Waldman's statement further emphasizes the significance of religious liberty in America. The First Amendment entails full religious freedom and therefore, true religious pluralism. Maier stated, "in the cause of religious freedom, [the Founders] were willing to contemplate even the remote possibility that someday a Muslim might hold public office."[30]

The theological critique centered around two assertions commonly made by CA authors, namely, that the Bible is the primary (if not the sole) authoritative source for the ideas which culminated in the founding documents, and that America is exceptional as a nation because of its singular Christian heritage (at least) or its status as God's chosen nation (at most).

To counter the argument that the Bible or Christian theology is at the core of America's founding two points were made. First, the idea that the Bible is the primary source is put forth by Barton, Eidsmoe and others. Their main source for this contention was Lutz's survey of the public writings of the Founders from the 1760s to 1805. The Bible was demonstrated by Lutz to have accounted for about a third of the citations used in those writings, alongside other sources belonging to the Enlightenment, radical Whig ideology, common law tradition, classical antiquity, and others. Barton, responding to Lutz's survey, quoted a *Newsweek* article by Kenneth Woodward and David Gates, wrote, "... some have even conceded that 'historians are discovering that the Bible, perhaps even more than the Constitution, is our Founding document.'"[31]

29. Waldman, *Founding Faith*, 190.
30. Pauline Maier, email message to the author, January 11, 2009.
31. Woodward and Gates, "How the Bible," 44.

The problem with drawing this conclusion from Lutz's data is that, while it is true that the Bible is the single most cited source in eighteenth-century writings, this does not in itself demonstrate that it is the primary source for America's founding concepts. For example, while Lutz did state where the many citations from the Bible came from, it was not his purpose to give the context in which they were quoted. Lutz did not specify whether the biblical texts were being authoritatively or illustratively at any point. Second, while about a third of the citations are taken from the Bible, two thirds are taken from other sources, most of them secular. Added together, two thirds of the citations found in eighteenth-century writings are taken from Enlightenment, radical Whig, common law, and classical sources.

To further emphasize this point, it was noted that Bailyn and Maier wrote that the Whig sources, especially those of Trenchard and Gordon, were instrumental in bringing unity to the disparity of the sources. Puritanism, common law tradition, the Enlightenment, and classical antiquity were all sources for revolutionary thought. Still, the writings that brought these different sources into a unified whole were those of the radical Whig ideological tradition, and particularly those of Trenchard and Gordon.

The CA authors had little to say about Whig influence in general and Trenchard and Gordon in particular. According to Bailyn, however, their importance should not be underestimated. He wrote, "The ultimate origins of this distinctive ideological strain lay in the radical social and political thought of the English Civil War and of the Commonwealth period; ..."[32] Trenchard and Gordon, in their series of letters compiled under the title *Cato's Letters*, did not appeal to Scripture upon which to base their revolutionary ideas. They primarily appealed to reason, history, and experience.

Locke was classified by Lutz as being among the leading three sources outside the Bible, with most of his influence being felt in the 1760s and 70s. Locke appealed to Scripture often in his *Second Treatise*, but his appeals were always made illustratively, not authoritatively. This makes sense, especially after having seen in his *Essay Concerning Human Understanding* that he placed reason above divine revelation as epistemological authority. His political philosophy expressed in the *Second Treatise*

---

32. Bailyn, *Ideological Origins*, 23.

is consistent with his epistemology. Rather than appealing to revelation to base his ideas on individual liberty, social compact, government by consent, the people's power to overthrow tyrannical government, and other views, he appealed regularly to reason. Thus, Locke's views, while usually compatible with Scripture, did not have Scripture as their source.

Regarding the idea of American exceptionalism, the notion itself cannot be sustained either by appealing to history or to theology, as long as "exceptionalism" is synonymous with "divine chosenness." This particular notion is unbiblical, owing to the fact that only one nation in history has ever really been blessed exceptionally on the basis of its having been chosen by God—ancient Israel. Noll stated, "After the full revelation of God's glory in Christ, 'God's country' was made up of believers 'from every tribe and tongue and people and nation' (Rev 5:9)."[33] Furthermore, Noll wrote, "a providential interpretation of history that features a special divine covenant with the United States leads to very awkward conclusions."[34]

Not only is the idea of American exceptionalism unbiblical, it is unsubstantiated by history. Simply put, America is not exceptional. Other nations have viewed themselves as the New Israel. Smith's study of the idea of national chosenness among European nations showed that it is almost as old as the history of Christendom itself. Fourth-century Armenians, fifteenth-century Russians, nineteenth-century French, and the Boers of southern Africa each saw themselves in similar ways as the Puritans of New England. Also, the overshadowing presence of the British Empire in the history of the world helps to show that America has not been the only nation to enjoy predominance. No other nation except Britain had been as powerful or as blessed as it was at its peak, and no other nation deserved to be called exceptional. No other nation had such a sense of divine destiny that it had been chosen by God to evangelize the heathen nations wherever it colonized. Not since the Roman Empire had the world witnessed such predominance, militarily, economically, and diplomatically. The very songs sang by the British in the nineteenth and early twentieth centuries are pregnant with the sense of chosenness, divine favor—exceptionalism.

The fact of the British imperial presence in the world from the battle of Trafalgar in 1805 to the outbreak of World War I in 1914, specifically

33. Noll, *One Nation*, 8.
34. Ibid., 9.

the Pax Britannica which ensured British expansion to every corner of the world, serves to undermine the assertion that there has been no other nation as blessed as the United States. The British could, and did, make the same claims to exceptionalism at the peak of their world prestige as proponents of CA do in reference to the United States. The fact that Scripture points only to Old Testament Israel as enjoying divine exceptionalism is evidence against the idea that America is exceptional. Furthermore, the fact that so many European nations have claimed the same exceptionalism as America was no proof that they were, in fact, exceptional. In the same way, the fact that many Americans have believed in their own exceptionalism cannot suffice as evidence. America cannot claim to be exceptional on any more reliable basis than other nations that have made the same claim.

Therefore, the critique of a strong view of Christian America is twofold. First, the central constitutional tenet of religious liberty is at the heart of the creation of the American republic. This is evident in the language of the First Amendment, as well as in the history of the development of the ideas that contributed to American revolutionary and founding ideas. Second, the notion of Christian America in the strong sense cannot be substantiated logically, historically, or theologically. In sum, the United States was founded as a nation with religious liberty, not with a Christian identity.

ISSUES FOR FURTHER STUDY

Any study of American origins is going to be expansive in its scope. The CA thesis is no exception. As was shown in chapter 2, the belief that America is a Christian nation is based on a host of propositions. All of these propositions demand attention, and each one could be studied at length individually. This study is emphatically not the final word on CA. It set out to provide a fair and broad critique of the idea. Still, there are many other avenues for studying it.

For example, the question of how expansive was the impact of Puritan theology on American revolutionary and founding ideas needs more attention than this study intended to give. Chapter 3 presented a broad treatment of Puritan contributions to freedom. Still, what is needed is a more comprehensive treatment of Christianity as a source for the American founding by authors from the evangelical theological tradition. This treatment would demand a balanced assessment of the role of Christianity as a source alongside that of secular sources. It would need to avoid ambiguity in terms, and the use of loaded language. It would need to consult the historical record free from an agenda influenced by political or social ambitions for evangelicalism. For example, what are the specific applications of Christianity on founding ideas?

Noll is one of the foremost evangelical scholars critiquing CA.[35] There are several other scholars who identify with evangelicalism[36] who have treated CA, either to critique the idea or to offer insight into the Christian contribution to the American founding. There are also more than a few non-evangelicals who have written on CA.[37] While each of these writers has offered valuable insights, there remains to be seen an evangelical treatment of American origins that successfully examines and assesses sacred and secular sources with an eye toward objectivity. Noll has offered an invaluable help in differentiating between a strong and weak CA, asserting that strong CA cries out for critique, while weak CA might be an acceptable position. Defining the precise contours of a weak CA seems necessary.

Moyer addressed a hermeneutical issue that needs further study in his well-researched study surveying CA writings.[38] He called the CA hermeneutic the "Logos paradigm." "For the evangelical, Biblical revelation is ascertained by discerning the intended meaning of Scripture in its originating context.... There is not much of a leap to apply these same methods to interpreting the 'sacred' documents of American history,"[39] wrote Moyer. He asserted that what is gained in the use of this method of interpretation, both in the study of Scripture and in the study of the founding documents, is authority: "... original intent is tied to the idea

---

35. See Noll, "American History," 114:515–18; *Christians in the American Revolution*; "Evangelicals," 137–58. *One Nation*; "Bible in Revolutionary America"; *Bible in American Law*; and *Work We Have To Do* for a sampling of Noll's work in critiquing CA and accounting for the role of Christianity in the Revolutionary and founding period. See also Noll et al., *Search*.

36. Richard Pierard, Gregory Boyd, Martin Marty, Nathan Hatch, George Marsden, Stephen Nichols, John W. Montgomery, and Michael Novak are a few examples.

37. Garry Wills, Jon Meacham, Stephen Waldman, Isaac Kramnick, and R. Laurence Moore are a few examples.

38. See chapter 2.

39. Moyer, "Battle for the City," 302.

of authority."⁴⁰ Is this a valid methodology in historical, constitutional, and legal interpretation? An evangelical exposition and critique of this method of historical interpretation would be most helpful in defining what is meant by the idea of "original intent" and by assessing it.⁴¹

Another area that ought to be studied further is the issue of liberty. Specifically, is there a connection between spiritual liberty and political liberty? Many CA authors insist that there is, and they attempt to demonstrate the connection mainly by pointing to colonial sermons preached during the revolutionary period. Barry Alan Shain's study seemed to support this methodology. He wrote, "Spiritual liberty was Revolutionary-era Americans' most fundamental understanding of liberty—so much so that it set the standard by which other forms of liberty were judged."⁴² The history of the development of liberty as an idea is intricate, and demands great care on the part of the researcher.⁴³ An evangelical attempt at a comprehensive treatment of Christianity's role in the development of the idea is also greatly needed.

Any new study on CA from an evangelical perspective must include a serious treatment of the writings of the Commonwealth men of England. An assessment of Trenchard and Gordon, Sidney, Molesworth, and others needs to be presented in terms of their contribution to the American Revolution and drafting of the Constitution. The existing CA writings have little to say on radical Whig ideology. Noll, Marsden and Hatch, as well as Bonomi, and others, have noted that much biblical language had been appropriated by colonial preachers to justify Whig assertions. Noll, Marsden, and Hatch stated, "It was easy to slip back and forth between the Christian and the patriotic meanings of terms like *liberty*, which makes it difficult to see where Christian Whigs were bringing Scripture to bear on politics, or where politics had robbed words of their Christian content while retaining their religious force."⁴⁴ Bonomi added, "an ideology of dissent that linked religious with civil tyranny created a common

---

40. Ibid., 304.

41. See Levy, *Original Intent*, for an excellent treatment by a non-evangelical on this subject. He argued that original intent cannot be discerned, and it is futile to seek to attempt to interpret the law in the basis of it.

42. Shain, *Myth of American Individualism*, 193.

43. See Sandoz, ed., *Roots of Liberty*, for a collection of essays tracing the origins of liberty as a legal concept, particularly in England.

44. Noll et al., *Search*, 82; emphasis original.

ground upon which were rationalists and evangelicals alike could join to justify their opposition to England."[45] So, the question that should be addressed is, to what extent did colonial preachers borrow from biblical language to justify the Revolution? If the extent is indeed great, what does that mean in terms of how much Christianity influenced revolutionary and founding ideas? Is it possible to discern the religious beliefs of the Commonwealth men? Did their religious beliefs impact their notions of freedom? And in terms of the relevance of the personal beliefs of important figures in British and American political and intellectual history—are those religious beliefs relevant to the study of the origins of the American nation and to original intent?

CONCLUSION

Religious liberty is a fragile privilege. Evangelicals would do better to focus on this precious gift as one of the central aspects of our identity as Christian Americans. They will win the culture because of religious liberty. Recall the statement made by Noll, Marsden, and Hatch: "a true picture of America's past will make Christians today better equipped to speak the gospel in evangelism and to put it to work in social concern."[46] The Founders built religious liberty into the fabric of the American identity, freeing the church to fulfill its purposes as the body of Christ. The church, because of religious pluralism in America, can take comfort in the fact that the nations are actually coming here and it can spread the gospel message in many respects without having to leave American shores. The church can also remember that all faith systems represented in America are indebted to religious liberty. It follows that they are equally indebted to the Christian faith for helping to ensure their equal standing in the marketplace of ideas.

---

45. Bonomi, *Cope of Heaven*, 208.
46. Noll et al., *Search*, 21.

Bibliography

Adair, John. *Founding Fathers: The Puritans in England and America*. London: Dent and Sons, 1982.
Adler, Mortimer J. *We Hold These Truths: Understanding the Ideas and Ideals of the Constitution*. New York: Collier, 1987.
Adler, Mortimer J., and Charles Lincoln Van Doren, editors. *1493-1754: Discovering a New World*. Annals of America 1. Chicago: Encyclopedia Britannica, 1968.
Ahlstrom, Sydney E. *A Religious History of the American People*. New Haven: Yale University Press, 1972.
Alley, Robert S., editor. *James Madison on Religious Liberty*. Amherst, NY: Prometheus, 1985.
Allitt, Patrick. *Religion in America Since 1945: A History*. Columbia Histories of Modern American Life. New York: Columbia University Press, 2003.
Amos, Gary T. *Defending the Declaration: How the Bible and Christianity Influenced the Writing of the Declaration of Independence*. Charlottesville, VA: Providence Foundation, 1989.
"Apology for 'Christian Nation.'" *Christian Century* 109 (December 16, 1992) 1160.
Bacon, Francis. *Novum Organum: Aphorisms Concerning the Interpretation of Nature and the Kingdom of Man*. The Great Books of the Western World 30. Chicago: Encyclopedia Britannica, 1952.
Bailyn, Bernard, editor. *The Ideological Origins of the American Revolution*. Enlarged ed. Cambridge, MA: Belknap, 1992.
———, editor. *The Debate on the Constitution: Federalist and Antifederalist Speeches, Articles, and Letters During the Struggle Over Ratification*. Part 1, *Debates in the Press and in Private Correspondence: September 17, 1787—January 12, 1788; Debates in the State Ratifying Conventions: Pennsylvania, November 20—December 15, 1787; Connecticut, January 3-9, 1788; Massachusetts, January 9 February 7, 1788*. The Library of America 62. New York: Penguin, 1993.
———, editor. *The Debate on the Constitution: Federalist and Antifederalist Speeches, Articles, and Letters During the Struggle Over Ratification*. Part 2, *Debates in the Press and in Private Correspondence: January 14—August 9, 1788; Debates in the State Ratifying Conventions: South Carolina, May 12-24, 1788; Virginia, June 2 -27, 1788; New York, June 17—July 26, 1788; North Carolina, July 21—August 4, 1788*. The Library of America 63. New York: Penguin, 1993.
Balmer, Randall. *Mine Eyes Have Seen The Glory: A Journey into the Evangelical Subculture in America*. New York: Oxford University Press, 1989.
Barton, David. *America's Godly Heritage*. Aledo, TX: WallBuilders, 1993.
———. *The Foundations of American Government*. Aledo, TX: WallBuilders, 1993.

———. *Keys to Good Government According to the Founding Fathers*. Aledo, TX: WallBuilders, 1994.

———. *The Myth of Separation*. Aledo, TX: WallBuilders, 1992.

———. *Original Intent: The Courts, the Constitution, and Religion*. Aledo, TX: WallBuilders, 1996.

Bebbington, D. W. *Evangelicals in Modern Britain: A History from the 1730s to the 1980s*. London: Unwin Hyman, 1989.

———. *Patterns in History: A Christian Perspective on Historical Thought*. Vancouver: Regent College, 1990.

Becker, Carl. *The Declaration of Independence: A Study in the History of Political Ideas*. New York: Knopf, 1942.

Beliles, Mark A., and Douglas S. Anderson. *Contending for the Constitution*. Charlottesville, VA: Providence Foundation, 2005.

Beliles, Mark A., and Stephen K. McDowell. *America's Providential History*. Charlottesville, VA: Providence Foundation, 1991.

Bellah, Robert N. *The Broken Covenant: American Civil Religion in a Time of Trial*. Weil Lectures. New York: Seabury, 1975.

———. "Civil Religion in America." In *Religion in America*, edited by William G. McLoughlin and Robert N. Bellah, 3–23. Boston: Beacon, 1968.

———. "The Kingdom of God in America: Language of Faith, Language of Nation, Language of Empire." In *Religion and the Public Good: A Bicentennial Forum*. Macon, GA: Mercer University Press, 1988.

Bellah, Robert N., and Phillip E. Hammond. *Varieties of Civil Religion*. San Francisco: Harper & Row, 1980.

Bercovitch, Sacvan. *The Puritan Origins of the American Self*. New Haven: Yale University Press, 1975.

Bewkes, Eugene, Howard B. Jefferson, Herman A. Brautigam, Eugene T. Adams, and J. Calvin Keene. *The Western Heritage of Faith and Reason*. New York: Harper & Row, 1963.

Birkitt, James N. *Carving Out a Kingdom: A History of Carmel Baptist Church and Persecuted Baptists of Caroline County, Virginia*. Glen Allen, VA: n.p., 1998.

Bonomi, Patricia U. *Under the Cope of Heaven: Religion, Society, and Politics in Colonial America*. New York: Oxford University Press, 1986.

Boorstin, Daniel J. *The Americans: The National Experience*. New York: Random House, 2002.

Bowen, Catherine Drinker. *Miracle at Philadelphia: The Story of the Constitutional Convention May to September, 1787*. 3rd ed. Boston: Little, Brown, 1986.

Boyd, Gregory A. *The Myth of a Christian Nation: How the Quest for Political Power is Destroying the Church*. Grand Rapids: Zondervan, 2005.

Brands, H. W. *Woodrow Wilson*. The American Presidents 5. New York: Henry Holt, 2003.

Brauer, Jerald C., editor. *Religion and the American Revolution*. Philadelphia: Fortress, 1976.

Brown, Harold O. J. *The Protest of a Troubled Protestant*. Grand Rapids: Zondervan, 1969.

———. *The Reconstruction of the Republic*. Milford, MI: Mott Media, 1981.

Brown, Ruth Murray. *For A "Christian America:" A History of the Religious Right*. Amherst, NY: Prometheus, 2002.

Browne, M. Neil, and Stuart M. Keeley. *Asking the Right Questions: A Guide to Critical Thinking*. 7th ed. Upper Saddle River, NJ: Prentice Hall, 2004.

Buckingham, Thomas. "Moses and Aaron." In *The New England Soul: Preaching and Religious Culture in Colonial New England*, by Harry S. Stout, 171. New York: Oxford University Press, 1986.

Budziszewski, J., David L. Weeks, John Bolt, William Edgar, and Ashley Woodiwiss. *Evangelicals in the Public Square: Four Formative Voices on Political Thought and Action*. Grand Rapids: Baker Academic, 2006.

Butler, Jon. *Awash in a Sea of Faith: Christianizing the American People*. Studies in Cultural History. Cambridge: Harvard University Press, 1990.

Cherry, Conrad, editor. *God's New Israel: Religious Interpretations of American Destiny*. Rev. ed. Chapel Hill: The University of North Carolina Press, 1998.

Clark, David K. *To Know and Love God: Method for Theology*. Foundations for Evangelical Theology. Wheaton, IL: Crossway, 2003.

Clark, Gordon H. *Historiography: Secular and Religious*. 2nd ed. Jefferson, MD: Trinity Foundation, 1994.

Cogan, Neil H., David Lindsay Adams, and Theresa Lynn Harvey, editors. *The Complete Bill of Rights: The Drafts, Debates, Sources, and Origins*. New York: Oxford University Press, 1997.

Colbourn, Trevor. *The Lamp of Experience: Whig History and the Intellectual Origins of the American Revolution*. 2nd ed. Indianapolis: Liberty Fund, 1998.

Copleston, Frederick, S. J. *A History of Philosophy*. Vol. 5, *Modern Philosophy: The British Philosophers from Hobbes to Hume*. New York: Image, 1994.

Cotton, John. "An Exposition upon the 13th Chapter of the Revelation." In *The Puritans: A Sourcebook of Their Writings: Two Volumes Bound as One*, edited by Perry Miller and Thomas H. Johnson, 212–14. Mineola, NY: Dover, 2001. Originally published by American Book Co., 1938.

———. "God's Promise to His Plantation." Quoted in *The Annals of America*, vol. 1, *1493–1754: Discovering a New World*, edited by Mortimer J. Adler, 107. Chicago: Encyclopaedia Britannica, 1968.

Cousins, Norman, editor. *"In God We Trust": The Religious Beliefs and Ideas of the American Founding Fathers*. New York: Harper and Brothers, 1958.

Cromartie, Michael, editor. *Disciples and Democracy: Religious Conservatives and the Future of American Politics*. Grand Rapids: Eerdmans, 1994.

———, editor. *No Longer Exiles: The Religious New Right in American Politics*. Washington, DC: Ethics and Public Policy Center, 1993.

Curry, Thomas J. *The First Freedoms: Church and State in America to the Passage of the First Amendment*. New York: Oxford University Press, 1986.

Davie, Emily, editor. *Profile of America: An Autobiography of the U. S. A.* New York: Thomas Y. Crowell, 1954.

Davies, A. Mervyn. *Foundation of American Freedom*. Nashville: Abingdon, 1955.

Dawson, Joseph M. "The Meaning of Separation of Church and State in the First Amendment." *Journal of Church and State* 50 (2008) 677–81.

Dean, Eric. "The Insoluble Problem: Civil Religion or Christian Nation." *Encounter* 44 (1983) 353–67.

Delbanco, Andrew. *The Puritan Ordeal*. Cambridge: Harvard University Press, 1989.

DeMar, Gary. *America's Christian Heritage*. Nashville: Broadman & Holman, 2003.

———. *America's Christian History: The Untold Story*. Atlanta: American Vision, 1993.

———. *God and Government*. 3 vols. Brentwood, TN: Wolgemuth and Hyatt, 1989.

Dreisbach, Daniel. *Thomas Jefferson and the Wall of Separation Between Church and State.* New York: New York University Press, 2003.

Drinnon, Richard. *Facing West: The Metaphysics of Indian-Hating and Empire Building.* 3rd ed. Norman: University of Oklahoma Press, 1997.

Durant, Will and Ariel. *The Story of Civilization.* Vol. 9, *The Age of Voltaire.* New York: Simon and Schuster, 1965.

Eck, Diana L. *A New Religious America: How a "Christian Country" Has Now Become the World's Most Religiously Diverse Nation.* San Francisco: HarperSanFrancisco, 2001.

———. "Prospects for Pluralism: Voice and Vision in the Study of Religion." *Journal of the American Academy of Religion* 75 (2007) 743–76.

Eidsmoe, John. *Christianity and the Constitution: The Faith of Our Founding Fathers.* Grand Rapids: Baker, 1987.

———. "Operation Josiah: Rediscovering the Biblical Roots." In *The Christian and American Law: Christianity's Impact on America's Founding Documents and Future Direction,* edited by H. Wayne House, 83–106. Grand Rapids: Kregel, 1998.

Ellis, Joseph J. *American Creation: Triumphs and Tragedies at the Founding of the Republic.* New York: Knopf, 2007.

Ericson, Edward L. *American Freedom and the Radical Right.* New York: Frederick Ungar, 1982.

Estep, William R. *Revolution Within the Revolution: The First Amendment in Historical Context: 1612–1789.* Grand Rapids: Eerdmans, 1990.

Evans, M. Stanton. *The Theme is Freedom: Religion, Politics, and the American Tradition.* Washington, DC: Regnery, 2007.

Fackre, Gabriel, editor. *Judgment Day at the White House: A Critical Declaration Exploring Moral Issues and the Political Use and Abuse of Religion.* Grand Rapids: Eerdmans, 1999.

———. *The Religious Right and Christian Faith.* Grand Rapids: Eerdmans, 1982.

Falwell, Jerry. *Listen, America!* New York: Doubleday, 1980.

Freehling, William W. *The Road to Disunion: Secessionists at Bay, 1776–1854.* New York: Oxford University Press, 1990.

Gaines, James R. *For Liberty and Glory: Washington, Lafayette, and Their Revolutions.* New York: Norton, 2007.

Gaustad, Edwin S. *Faith of the Founders: Religion and the New Nation 1776–1826.* 2nd ed. Waco, TX: Baylor University Press, 2004.

———. *Roger Williams.* New York: Oxford University Press, 2005.

———. *Sworn on the Altar of God: A Religious Biography of Thomas Jefferson.* Grand Rapids: Eerdmans, 1996.

———, editor. *Religious Issues in American History.* New York: Harper and Row, 1968.

Gaustad, Edwin S., and Leigh E. Schmidt. *The Religious History of America.* rev. ed. New York: HarperSanFrancisco, 2002.

Gelernter, David. *Americanism: The Fourth Great Western Religion.* New York: Doubleday, 2007.

Goldberg, Michelle. *Kingdom Coming: The Rise of Christian Nationalism.* New York: Norton, 2006.

Griffin, David Ray, John B. Cobb Jr., Richard A. Falk, and Catherine Keller. *The American Empire and the Commonwealth of God: A Political, Economic, Religious Statement.* Louisville, KY: Westminster John Knox, 2006.

Hadden, Jeffrey K. and Anson Shupe, editors. *Prophetic Religions and Politics: Religion and the Political Order.* New York: Paragon House, 1986.
Hall, David D., editor. *Puritans in the New World: A Critical Anthology.* Princeton: Princeton University Press, 2004.
Hall, David W. *The Genevan Reformation and the American Founding.* Lanham, MD: Lexington, 2003.
Hamburger, Philip. *Separation of Church and State.* Cambridge: Harvard University Press, 2002.
Hamilton, Alexander, James Madison, and John Jay. *The Federalist.* The Great Books of the Western World 43. Chicago: Encyclopedia Britannica, 1952.
Hamlyn, D. W. *A History of Western Philosophy.* New York: Penguin, 1987.
Handy, Robert T. "American Messianic Consciousness: The Concept of the Chosen People and Manifest Destiny." *Review and Expositor* 73 (1976) 47–58.
———. *A Christian America: Protestant Hopes and Historical Realities.* New York: Oxford University Press, 1971.
———. *The Protestant Quest for a Christian America, 1830–1930.* Historical Series (American Church) 5. Philadelphia: Fortress, 1967.
Harrell, David Edwin. *Pat Robertson: A Personal, Religious, and Political Portrait.* San Francisco: Harper and Row, 1987.
Hart, Benjamin. *Faith and Freedom: The Christian Roots of American Liberty.* San Bernardino, CA: Here's Life, 1988.
Hartley, L. P. *The Go-Between.* Penguin Passnotes. New York: Penguin, 1987.
Hatch, Nathan O. *The Democratization of American Christianity.* New Haven: Yale University Press, 1989.
———. *The Sacred Cause of Liberty: Republican Thought and the Millennium in Revolutionary New England.* New Haven: Yale University Press, 1977.
Hatch, Nathan O., and Mark Noll, editors. *The Bible in America: Essays in Cultural History.* New York: Oxford University Press, 1982.
Heimert, Alan. *Religion and the American Mind: From the Great Awakening to the Revolution.* Eugene, OR: Wipf and Stock, 2006. First published 1966 by Harvard University Press.
Herberg, Will. *Protestant—Catholic—Jew: An Essay in American Religious Sociology.* New York: Doubleday, 1955.
Holmes, David L. *The Faiths of the Founding Fathers.* New York: Oxford University Press, 2006.
Hordern, William E. *A Layman's Guide to Protestant Theology.* London: Macmillan, 1969.
House, H. Wayne, editor. *The Christian and American Law: Christianity's Impact on America's Founding Documents and Future Direction.* Grand Rapids: Kregel, 1998.
Howse, Brannon. *One Nation Under Man? The Worldview War Between Christians and the Secular Left.* Nashville: Broadman and Holman: 2005.
Hughes, Richard T. *Christian America and the Kingdom of God.* Chicago: University of Illinois Press, 2009.
———. *Myths America Lives By.* Chicago: University of Illinois Press, 2003.
———. "Recovering First Times: The Logic of Primitivism in American Life." In *Religion and the Life of the Nation: American Recoveries,* edited by Rowland A. Sherrill, 193–218. Chicago: University of Illinois Press, 1990.
Hughes, Richard T., and C. Leonard Allen. *Illusions of Innocence: Protestant Primitivism in America, 1630–1875.* Chicago: The University of Chicago Press, 1988.

Hume, David. *An Enquiry Concerning Human Understanding.* The Great Books of the Western World 35. Chicago: Encyclopedia Britannica, 1952.
Hunter, James Davison. *American Evangelicalism: Conservative Religion and the Quandary of Modernity.* New Brunswick, NJ: Rutgers University Press, 1983.
———. *Evangelicalism: The Coming Generation.* Chicago: The University of Chicago Press, 1987.
Hutson, James. *Church and State in America: The First Two Centuries.* Cambridge Essential Histories. New York: Cambridge University Press, 2008.
———. *Forgotten Features of the Founding: The Recovery of Religious Themes in the Early American Republic.* American Republic. New York: Lexington, 2003.
———, editor. *The Founders on Religion: A Book of Quotations.* Princeton: Princeton University Press, 2005.
———, editor. *Religion and the New Republic: Faith in the Founding of America.* Lanham, MD: Rowman and Littlefield, 2000.
Jefferson, Thomas. Thomas Jefferson to James Madison, 20 December 1787. In *The Origins of the American Constitution: A Documentary History*, edited by Michael Kammen, 90–93. New York: Penguin, 1986.
Johnson, Paul. "The Almost-Chosen People: Why America is Different." In *Unsecular America*, edited by Richard John Neuhaus, 1–13. Encounter Series 2. Grand Rapids: Eerdmans, 1986.
Kammen, Michael, editor. *The Origins of the American Constitution: A Documentary History.* New York: Penguin, 1986.
Keillor, Stephen J. *God's Judgments: Interpreting History and the Christian Faith.* Downers Grove, IL: InterVarsity, 2007.
———. *This Rebellious House: American History & the Truth of Christianity.* Downers Grove, IL: InterVarsity, 1996.
Kelly, George Armstrong. *Politics and Religious Consciousness in America.* London: Transaction, 1984.
Kennedy, D. James, and Jerry Newcombe. *What If Jesus Had Never Been Born? The Positive Impact of Christianity in History.* Nashville: Thomas Nelson, 1994.
Kidd, Thomas S. *The Great Awakening: The Roots of Evangelical Christianity in Colonial America.* New Haven: Yale University Press, 2007.
———. *The Protestant Interest: New England after Protestantism.* New Haven: Yale University Press, 2004.
Kluger, Richard. *Seizing Destiny: How America Grew From Sea to Shining Sea.* New York: Knopf, 2007.
Kosmin, Barry A. and Seymour P. Lachman. *One Nation Under God: Religion in Contemporary American Society.* New York: Harmony, 1993.
Kramnick, Isaac, and R. Laurence Moore. *The Godless Constitution: A Moral Defense of the Secular State.* 2nd ed. New York: Norton, 2006.
Kuklick, Bruce. *Churchmen and Philosophers: From Jonathan Edwards to John Dewey.* New Haven: Yale University Press, 1985.
LaHaye, Tim. *Faith of Our Founding Fathers: A Comprehensive Study of America's Christian Foundations.* Green Forest, AR: Master Books, 1990.
Lambert, Frank. *The Founding Fathers and the Place of Religion in America.* Princeton: Princeton University Press, 2003.
Land, Richard. *The Divided States of America: What Liberals AND Conservatives are Missing in the God-and-Country Shouting Match!* Nashville: Thomas Nelson, 2007.

———. *Imagine! A God-Blessed America: How it Could Happen and What It Would Look Like.* Nashville: Broadman and Holman, 2005.

———. *Real Homeland Security: The America God Will Bless.* Nashville: Broadman and Holman, 2004.

Land, Richard D., and Lee Holloway, editors. *Christians in the Public Square: Faith in Action?* Nashville: ERLC, 1996.

Lawrence, Bruce B. *Defenders of God: The Fundamentalist Revolt Against the Modern Age.* San Francisco: Harper and Row, 1989.

Levy, Leonard W. *The Establishment Clause: Religion and the First Amendment.* 2nd ed. Chapel Hill: The University of North Carolina Press, 1994.

———. *Original Intent and the Framers' Constitution.* Chicago: Ivan R. Dee, 1988.

———. *Origins of the Bill of Rights.* New Haven: Yale University Press, 1999.

Lillback, Peter A. "Pluralism, Postmodernity, and Religious Liberty: The Abiding Necessity of Free Speech and Religious Conviction in the Public Square." *Journal of Ecumenical Studies* 44 (2009) 26–56.

Lillback, Peter A., and Jerry Newcombe. *George Washington's Sacred Fire.* Bryn Mawr, PA: Providence Forum, 2006.

Little, Lewis Peyton. *Imprisoned Preachers and Religious Liberty in Virginia.* Lynchburg, VA: J. P. Bell, 1938.

Locke, John. *Concerning Civil Government, Second Essay.* The Great Books of the Western World, no. 35, edited by Robert Maynard Hutchins. Chicago: Encyclopedia Britannica, 1952.

———. *An Essay Concerning Human Understanding.* The Great Books of the Western World, no. 35, edited by Robert Maynard Hutchins. Chicago: Encyclopedia Britannica, 1952.

———. *A Letter Concerning Toleration.* Translated by William Popple. The Great Books of the Western World, no. 35, edited by Robert Maynard Hutchins. Chicago: Encyclopedia Britannica, 1952.

Ludden, Jennifer. "1965 Immigration Law Changed Face of America." *NPR.* May 9, 2006. No pages. Online: http://www.npr.org/templates/story/story.php?storyId=53913.

Lutz, Donald S. *The Origins of American Constitutionalism.* Baton Rouge: Louisiana State University Press, 1988.

Madison, James. James Madison to William Bradford, January 24, 1774. In *James Madison on Religious Liberty*, edited by Robert S. Alley, 47–48. Amherst, NY: Prometheus, 1985.

Magill, Frank N., editor. *Masterpieces of World Philosophy.* New York: HarperCollins, 1990.

Maier, Pauline. *American Scripture: Making the Declaration of Independence.* New York: Vintage, 1997.

———. *From Resistance to Revolution: Colonial Radicals and the Development of American Opposition to Britain, 1765–1776.* New York: Norton, 1991.

Marsden, George M. *Fundamentalism and American Culture.* 2nd ed. New York: Oxford University Press, 2006.

———. *Religion and American Culture.* New York: Harcourt Brace Jovanovich, 1990.

———. *Understanding Fundamentalism and Evangelicalism.* Grand Rapids: Eerdmans, 1991.

———, editor. *Evangelicalism and Modern America.* Grand Rapids: Eerdmans, 1984.

Marshall, Paul. *God and the Constitution: Christianity and American Politics.* New York: Rowman and Littlefield, 2002.

Marshall, Peter, and David Manuel. *The Light and the Glory*. Grand Rapids: Baker, 1977.
Marty, Martin E. *Church-State Separation in America: The Tradition Nobody Knows*. Washington, DC: People for the American Way, 1982.
———. *A Nation of Behavers*. Chicago: The University of Chicago Press, 1976.
———. *Religion and Republic: The American Circumstance*. Boston: Beacon, 1987.
———. *Righteous Empire: The Protestant Experience in America*. New York: Dial, 1970.
———. *The Pro & Con Book of Religious America: A Bicentennial Argument*. Waco, TX: Word, 1975.
———. "The Religious Foundations for Law." *Emory Law Journal* 54 (2005) 291–324.
———. "Will Success Spoil Evangelicalism? Changes That Come With Prosperity." *Christian Century* 117, no. 21 (2000) 757.
Martin, William. *With God on Our Side: The Rise of the Religious Right in America*. New York: Broadway, 1996.
Massie, Robert K. *Dreadnought: Britain, Germany and the Coming of the Great War*. New York: Random House, 1991.
Massachusetts Body of Liberties.
Maxfield, John A. "Divine Providence, History, and Progress in Saint Augustine's *City of God*." *Concordia Theological Quarterly* 66 (2002) 339–60.
May, Henry F. *The Enlightenment in America*. New York: Oxford University Press, 1976.
Mayhew, Jonathan. "A Discourse Concerning Unlimited Submission." In *The Puritans: A Sourcebook of Their Writings: Two Volumes Bound as One*, edited by Perry Miller and Thomas H. Johnson, 277. Mineola, NY: Dover, 2001. Originally published by American Book Co., 1938.
McDonald, Forrest. *Novus Ordo Seclorum: The Intellectual Origins of the Constitution*. Lawrence: University Press of Kansas, 1985.
McDowell, Stephen. *America, a Christian Nation? Examining the Evidence of the Christian Foundation of America*. Charlottesville, VA: Providence Foundation, 2004.
McDowell, Stephen, and Mark Beliles. *The American Dream: Jamestown and the Planting of the American Christian Republic*. Charlottesville, VA: Providence Foundation, 2007.
McInerny, D. Q. *Being Logical: A Guide to Good Thinking*. New York: Random House, 2005.
McKenna, George. *The Puritan Origins of American Patriotism*. New Haven: Yale University Press, 2007.
McLoughlin, William G., and Robert N. Bellah, editors. *Religion in America*. Boston: Beacon, 1968.
Meacham, Jon. *American Gospel: God, the Founding Fathers, and the Making of a Nation*. New York: Random House, 2006.
Mead, Sidney E. *History and Identity*. AAR Studies in Religion 19. Missoula, MT: Scholars, 1979.
———. *The Lively Experiment: The Shaping of Christianity in America*. New York: Harper and Row, 1963.
———. *The Nation with the Soul of a Church*. New York: Harper and Row, 1975.
Merk, Frederick. *Manifest Destiny and Mission in American History: A Reinterpretation*. Cambridge, MA: Harvard University Press, 1995. Originally published by Knopf, 1963.
Miller, Perry. *Errand into The Wilderness*. Cambridge, MA: Belknap, 1956.
———. *Nature's Nation*. Cambridge, MA: Belknap, 1967.
———. *The New England Mind: The Seventeenth Century*. 2nd ed. Cambridge, MA: Harvard University Press, 1954.

———. *Roger Williams: His Contribution to the American Tradition*. Makers of the American Tradition Series 2. New York: Bobbs-Merrill, 1953.
Miller, Perry, and Thomas H. Johnson. *The Puritans: A Sourcebook of Their Writings: Two Volumes Bound as One*. Mineola, NY: Dover, 2001. Originally published by American Book Co., 1938.
Miller, Robert. "Religious Conscience in Colonial New England." *Journal of Church and State* 50 (2008) 661–76.
Miller, William Lee. *The Business of May Next: James Madison and the Founding*. Charlottesville: University Press of Virginia, 1992.
Milton, John. *Areopagitica*. The Great Books of the Western World 32. Chicago: Encyclopedia Britannica, 1952.
Montgomery, John Warwick. *The Meaning of Independence: John Adams, George Washington, Thomas Jefferson*. Charlottesville: The University of Virginia Press, 1975.
———. *The Shape of the Past: An Introduction to Philosophical Historiography*. Minneapolis: Bethany House, 1975.
———. *The Shaping of America*. Minneapolis: Bethany House, 1981.
Morris, Benjamin F. *The Christian Life and Character of the Civil Institutions of the United States*. Cincinnati: Rickey & Carroll, 1864.
Morris, James. *Heaven's Command: An Imperial Progress*. New York: Harcourt Brace Jovanovich, 1973.
———. *Pax Britannica: The Climax of an Empire*. New York: Harcourt Brace Jovanovich, 1968.
Moyer III, William Andrew. "Battle for the City on the Hill: Evangelical Interpretations of American History 1960–1996." PhD diss., George Washington University, 1998.
Moynahan, Brian. *The Faith: A History of Christianity*. New York: Doubleday, 2002.
Neuhaus, Richard John, "Contract and Covenant: In Search of American Identity." *National Review* 59, no. 7 (2007) 39–41.
———. "From Providence to Privacy: Religion and the Redefinition of America." In *Unsecular America*. Grand Rapids: Eerdmans, 1986.
———. *The Naked Public Square: Religion and Democracy in America*. Grand Rapids: Eerdmans, 1984.
———, editor. *The Chosen People in an Almost Chosen Nation: Jews and Judaism in America*. Grand Rapids: Eerdmans, 2002.
Neuhaus, Richard John, and Michael Cromartie, editors. *Piety and Politics: Evangelicals and Fundamentalists Confront the World*. Lanham, MD: University Press, 1987.
Newton, Isaac. *Mathematical Principles of Natural Philosophy*. Translated by Andrew Motte. Revised by Florian Cajori. The Great Books of the Western World 34. Chicago: Encyclopedia Britannica, 1952.
Nichols, Stephen J. *Jesus Made in America: A Cultural History from the Puritans to the Passion of the Christ*. Downers Grove, IL: InterVarsity, 2008.
Niebuhr, Reinhold. *The Irony of American History*. New York: Scribner's, 1952.
Niebuhr, Reinhold, and Alan Heimert. *A Nation So Conceived: Reflections on the History of America from Its Early Visions to Its Present Power*. New York: Scribner's, 1963.
Noll, Mark A. *American Evangelical Christianity: An Introduction*. Malden, MA: Blackwell, 2001.
———. *America's God: From Jonathan Edwards to Abraham Lincoln*. New York: Oxford University Press, 2002.

———. "American History Through the Eyes of Faith." *Christian Century* 114, no. 17 (1997) 515–18.

———. *Christians in the American Revolution*. Washington, DC: Christian College Consortium, 1977.

———. "Evangelicals in the American Founding and Evangelical Political Mobilization Today." In *Religion and the New Republic: Faith in the Founding of America*, edited by James H. Hutson, 137–58. Lanham, MD: Rowman and Littlefield, 2000.

———. *A History of Christianity in the United States and Canada*. Grand Rapids: Eerdmans, 1992.

———. *The Old Religion in the New World: The History of North American Christianity*. Grand Rapids: Eerdmans, 2002.

———. *One Nation Under God? Christian Faith and Political Action in America*. San Francisco: Harper and Row, 1988.

———. *The Rise of Evangelicalism: The Age of Edwards, Whitefield and the Wesleys*. A History of Evangelicalism: People, Movements and Ideas in the English-Speaking World 1. Downers Grove, IL: InterVarsity, 2003.

———. *The Scandal of the Evangelical Mind*. Grand Rapids: Eerdmans, 1994.

———. *The Work We Have To Do: A History of Protestants in America*. Oxford: Oxford University Press, 2002.

———, editor. *Religion and American Politics from the Colonial Period to the 1980s*. Oxford: Oxford University Press, 1990.

Noll, Mark A., Nathan O. Hatch, and George M. Marsden. *The Search for a Christian America*. Exp. ed. Colorado Springs: Helmers and Howard, 1989.

Noll, Mark A., Nathan O. Hatch, George M. Marsden, David F. Wells, and John D. Woodbridge, editors. *Christianity in America: A Handbook*. Grand Rapids: Eerdmans, 1983.

Noonan, John T., Jr. *The Lustre of Our Country: The American Experience of Religious Freedom*. Berkeley: University of California Press, 1998.

Novak, Michael. "The Influence of Judaism and Christianity on the American Founding." In *Religion and the New Republic: Faith in the Founding of America*, edited by James H. Hutson, 159–86. Lanham, MD: Rowman and Littlefield, 2000.

———. "The Moral-Religious Basis of Democratic Capitalism." In *Christianity and Politics: Catholic and Protestant Perspectives*, edited by Carol Friedley Griffith, 54–61. Washington, DC: The Ethics and Public Policy Center, 1981.

———. *On Two Wings: Humble Faith and Common Sense at the American Founding*. San Francisco: Encounter, 2003.

———. "The Truth About Religious Freedom." *First Things* 161 (March 2006) 17–20.

Novak, Michael, and Jana Novak. *Washington's God: Religion, Liberty, and the Father of Our Country*. New York: Basic, 2006.

Paul, Pamela. "Religious Identity and Mobility." *American Demographics* 25, no. 2 (2003) 20–21.

Penn, William. "Preface to the Frame of Government of Pennsylvania." In *Church and State in American History: The Burden of Religious Pluralism*, 2nd ed., edited by John F. Wilson and Donald L. Drakeman, 17–19. Boston: Beacon, 1987.

Perry, John. "John Locke's America: The Character of Liberal Democracy and Jeffrey Stout's Debate with Christian Traditionalists." *Journal of the Society of Christian Ethics* 27 (2007) 227–52.

Perry, Ralph Barton. *Puritanism and Democracy*. New York: Vanguard, 1944.

Peterson, Kurt W. "American Idol: David Barton's Dream of a Christian Nation." *Christian Century* 123, no. 22 (2006) 20–23.

Pierard, Richard V. "Standing the Founding Fathers on Their Heads." *Christian Century* 100 (April 20, 1983) 368–72.

Polishook, Irwin H. *Roger Williams, John Cotton and Religious Freedom: A Controversy in New and Old England*. American Historical Sources Series: Research and Interpretation. Englewood Cliffs, NJ: Prentice-Hall, 1967.

Reeves, Thomas C. "Not So Christian America." *First Things* 66 (October 1, 1996) 16–21.

Robbins, Caroline. *The Eighteenth Century Commonwealthman: Studies in the Transmission, Development and Circumstance of English Liberal Thought from the Restoration of Charles II until the War with the Thirteen Colonies*. New York: Atheneum, 1968.

Robertson, Pat. *America's Dates With Destiny*. Nashville: Thomas Nelson, 1986.

Russell, Bertrand. *A History of Western Philosophy*. New York: Simon & Schuster. 1972.

Rutherford, Samuel. *Lex, Rex, or The Law and the Prince*. Harrisonburg, VA: Sprinkle, 1982.

Sandoz, Ellis, editor. *The Roots of Liberty: Magna Carta, Ancient Constitution, and the Anglo- American Tradition of Rule of Law*. Indianapolis: Liberty Fund, 1993.

Sanford, Charles B. *Thomas Jefferson and His Library: A Study of His Literary Interests and of the Religious Attitudes Revealed by Relevant Titles in His Library*. Hamden, CT: Archon, 1977.

Sassi, Jonathan D. *A Republic of Righteousness: The Public Christianity of the Post-Revolutionary New England Clergy*. Oxford: Oxford University Press, 2001.

Schaeffer, Francis. *The Complete Works of Francis A. Schaeffer*. Vol. 5, *A Christian View of the West*. 2nd ed. Westchester, IL: Crossway, 1982.

Schlossberg, Herbert. *Idols for Destruction: The Conflict of Christian Faith and American Culture*. Wheaton, IL: Crossway, 1990.

Segers, Mary C., and Ted G. Jelen. *A Wall of Separation? Debating the Public Role of Religion*. Lanham, MD: Rowman and Littlefield, 1998.

Shain, Barry Alan. *The Myth of American Individualism: The Protestant Origins of American Political Thought*. Princeton: Princeton University Press, 1996.

Sharlet, Jeff. "Through a Glass, Darkly: How the Christian Right is Reimagining U.S. History." *Harpers Magazine* 313, no. 1879 (December 2006) 33–43.

Sidney, Algernon. *Discourses Concerning Government*. Rev. ed. Edited by Thomas G. West. Indianapolis: Liberty Fund, 1996.

Silk, Mark. *Spiritual Politics: Religion and America Since World War II*. New York: Simon and Schuster: 1988.

Singer, C. Gregg. *A Theological Interpretation of American History*. 3rd ed. Greenville, SC: A Press, 1994.

Sittser, Gerald L. "Faithful Citizens: Being American and Christian." *Christian Century* 123, no. 4 (2006) 32–35.

Skillen, James W. "The Religion of the Founding Fathers." In *Christianity in America: A Handbook* , edited by Mark A. Noll, Nathan O. Hatch, George M. Marsden, David F. Wells, and John D. Woodbridge, 135–37. Grand Rapids: Eerdmans, 1983.

Smith, Anthony D. *Chosen Peoples: Sacred Sources of National Identity*. New York: Oxford University Press, 2003.

Smith, Christian. *Christian America? What Evangelicals Really Want*. Berkeley: University of California Press. 2000.

Smith, Page, editor. *Religious Origins of the American Revolution*. Missoula, MT: Scholars Press, 1976.

Spivey, Robert A., Edwin S. Gaustad, and Rodney F. Allen, editors. *Religious Issues in American Culture*. London: Addison-Wesley, 1972.

Stampp, Kenneth M. *America in 1857: A Nation on the Brink*. New York: Oxford University Press, 1990.

Stark, Rodney. *The Victory of Reason: How Christianity Led to Freedom, Capitalism, and Western Success*. New York: Random House, 2005.

Stephanson, Anders. *Manifest Destiny: American Expansion and the Empire of Right*. Edited by Eric Foner. New York: Farrar, Straus and Giroux, 1995.

Stout, Harry S. *The New England Soul: Preaching and Religious Culture in Colonial New England*. New York: Oxford University Press, 1988.

Swomley, John M. "One Nation, Under God." *Christian Social Action* 5 (May 1992) 12–15.

Tarnas, Richard. *The Passion of the Western Mind: Understanding the Ideas that Have Shaped Our World View*. New York: Ballantine, 1991.

Thiemann, Ronald F. *Religion in Public Life: A Dilemma for Democracy*. Washington, DC: Georgetown University Press, 1996.

Thomas, George. *The Christian Heritage in Politics*. London: Epworth, 1959.

Tinder, Glenn. *The Political Meaning of Christianity: The Prophetic Stance: An Interpretation*. San Francisco: HarperSanFrancisco, 1991.

Tocqueville, Alexis de. *Democracy in America*. Everyman's Library 179. New York: Knopf, 1994.

Tolson, Jay. "Divided, We Stand." *U. S. News & World Report* 139, no. 5 (August 8, 2005) 42–48.

Toulouse, Mark G. *God in Public: Four Ways American Christianity and Public Life Relate*. Foreword by Martin E. Marty. Louisville, KY: Westminster John Knox, 2006.

Trenchard, John, and Thomas Gordon. *Cato's Letters: Or, Essays on Liberty, Civil and Religious, And Other Important Subjects*. Edited by Ronald Hamowy. Indianapolis: Liberty Fund, 1995.

Van Doren, Charles. *A History of Knowledge, Past, Present, and Future: The Pivotal Events, People, and Achievements of World History*. New York: Ballantine, 1991.

Vaughan, Alden T., ed. *The Puritan Tradition in America: 1620–1730*. Columbia: University of South Carolina Press, 1972.

Veit, Helen E., Kenneth R. Bowling, and Charlene Bangs Bickford, editors. *Creating the Bill of Rights: The Documentary Record from the First Federal Congress*. Baltimore: Johns Hopkins University Press, 1991.

Voltaire. *Philosophical Dictionary*. Translated, with an introduction and glossary by Peter Gay. With a preface by Andre Maurois. New York: Harcourt, Brace and World, 1962.

———. "On the Lisbon Disaster, or An Examination of the Axiom 'All is Well.'" In *The Age of Voltaire: A History of Civilization in Western Europe from 1715 to 1756, with Special Emphasis on the Conflict between Religion and Philosophy*, by Will and Ariel Durant, 721–22. The Story of Civilization 9. New York: Simon and Schuster, 1965.

———. *Political Writings*. Translated and edited by David Williams. Cambridge Texts in the History of Political Thought. New York: Cambridge University Press, 1994.

———. *Treatise on Tolerance and Other Writings*. Translated by Brian Masters. Cambridge Texts in the History of Philosophy. New York: Cambridge University Press, 2000.

Wald, Kenneth D. *Religion and Politics in the United States*. 4th ed. Lanham, MD: Rowman and Littlefield, 2003.

Waldman, Steven. *Founding Faith: Providence, Politics, and the Birth of Religious Freedom in America*. New York: Random House, 2008.

WallBuilders: Our Goal. No pages. http://www.wallbuilders.com/ABTOverview.asp.
Wallis, Jim. *God's Politics: Why the Right Gets It Wrong and the Left Doesn't Get It*. San Francisco: HarperSanFrancisco, 2005.
Warner, R. Stephen. "Coming to America: Immigrants and the Faith They Bring." *Christian Century* 121, no. 4 (2004) 20–23.
Watson, Bradley C. S. "Creed and Culture in the American Founding." *The Intercollegiate Review* 41, no. 2 (2006) 32–39.
Way, H. Frank. "The Death of the Christian Nation: The Judiciary and Church-State Relations." *Journal of Church and State* 29 (1987) 509–29.
Weigley, Russell Frank. *A Great Civil War: A Military and Political History, 1861–1865*. Bloomington, IN: Indiana University Press, 2000.
Wells, Ronald A., editor. *History and the Christian Historian*. Grand Rapids: Eerdmans, 1998.
West, John G., Jr. *The Politics of Revelation and Reason: Religion and Civic Life in the New Nation*. Lawrence: University Press of Kansas, 1996.
Whitehead, John W. *The Second American Revolution*. Westchester, IL: Crossway, 1982.
Williams, Roger. "Letter to the Town of Providence." In *The Puritans: A Sourcebook of Their Writings: Two Volumes Bound as One*, edited by Perry Miller and Thomas H. Johnson, 224–25. Mineola, NY: Dover, 2001. Originally published by American Book Co., 1938.

———. "The Bloody Tenent yet More Bloody: by Mr. Cotton's endeavor to wash it white in the Blood of the Lambe." In *Roger Williams, John Cotton and Religious Freedom: A Controversy in New and Old England*, edited by Irwin H. Polishook, 66–67. American Historical Sources Series. Englewood Cliffs, NJ: Prentice-Hall, 1967.

Wills, Garry. *Reagan's America: Innocents At Home*. New York: Penguin, 2000.

———. *Under God: Religion and American Politics*. New York: Simon and Schuster, 1990.

Wilsey, John D. "A Critique of the Historiographical Construal of America as a Christian Nation." *Global Journal of Classical Theology* 8, no. 2 (September 2010). http://www.phc.edu/gj_journalindex.php.
Wilson, John F. *Religion and the American Nation: Historiography and History*. George H. Shriver Lecture Series in Religion in American History 1. Athens: The University of Georgia Press, 2003.
Wilson, John F., and Donald L. Drakeman, editors. *Church and State in American History: The Burden of Religious Pluralism*. 2nd ed. Boston: Beacon, 1987.
Winthrop, John. "A Little Speech on Liberty." In *Puritans in the New World: A Critical Anthology*, edited by David D. Hall, 178–80. Princeton: Princeton University Press, 2004.

———. "A Modell of Christian Charity." In *God's New Israel: Religious Interpretations of American Destiny*, rev. ed., edited by Conrad Cherry, 37–41. Chapel Hill: The University of North Carolina Press, 1998.

Wood, Gordon S. *The Creation of the American Republic: 1776–1787*. 2nd ed. Chapel Hill: University of North Carolina Press, 1998.

———. *The Radicalism of the American Revolution*. New York: Knopf, 1992.

Woodhouse, H. F. "Paraclete and Providence." *Expository Times* 115, no. 6 (2004) 189–91.
Woodward, Kenneth, and David Gates. "How the Bible Made America." *Newsweek* 27 (December 1982) 44.
Wuthnow, Robert. *The Restructuring of American Religion: Society and Faith Since World War II*. Studies in Church and State. Princeton: Princeton University Press, 1988.

www.ingramcontent.com/pod-product-compliance
Lightning Source LLC
Chambersburg PA
CBHW070254230426
43664CB00014B/2534